Java XML and JSON

Jeff Friesen

Apress®

Java XML and JSON

Jeff Friesen
Dauphin, Manitoba, Canada

ISBN-13 (pbk): 978-1-4842-1915-7   ISBN-13 (electronic): 978-1-4842-1916-4
DOI 10.1007/978-1-4842-1916-4

Library of Congress Control Number: 2016943840

Managing Director: Welmoed Spahr
Lead Editor: Steve Anglin
Technical Reviewer: Wallace Jackson
Editorial Board: Steve Anglin, Pramila Balan, Louise Corrigan, James T. DeWolf,
    Jonathan Gennick, Robert Hutchinson, Celestin Suresh John, James Markham,
    Susan McDermott, Matthew Moodie, Ben Renow-Clarke, Gwenan Spearing
Coordinating Editor: Mark Powers
Copy Editor: Mary Behr
Compositor: SPi Global
Indexer: SPi Global
Artist: SPi Global

Distributed to the book trade worldwide by Springer Science+Business Media New York, 233 Spring Street, 6th Floor, New York, NY 10013. Phone 1-800-SPRINGER, fax (201) 348-4505, e-mail orders-ny@springer-sbm.com, or visit www.springeronline.com. Apress Media, LLC is a California LLC and the sole member (owner) is Springer Science + Business Media Finance Inc (SSBM Finance Inc). SSBM Finance Inc is a Delaware corporation.

For information on translations, please e-mail rights@apress.com, or visit www.apress.com.

Apress and friends of ED books may be purchased in bulk for academic, corporate, or promotional use. eBook versions and licenses are also available for most titles. For more information, reference our Special Bulk Sales–eBook Licensing web page at www.apress.com/bulk-sales.

Any source code or other supplementary materials referenced by the author in this text is available to readers at www.apress.com/9781484219157. For detailed information about how to locate your book's source code, go to www.apress.com/source-code/. Readers can also access source code at SpringerLink in the Supplementary Material section for each chapter.

Printed on acid-free paper

To Dave, the late Father Lucian, Jane, and Rob.

Contents at a Glance

Contents

About the Author

Jeff Friesen is a freelance teacher and software developer with an emphasis on Java. In addition to authoring *Java I/O, NIO and NIO.2* (Apress) and *Java Threads and the Concurrency Utilities* (Apress), Jeff has written numerous articles on Java and other technologies (such as Android) for JavaWorld (JavaWorld.com), informIT (InformIT.com), Java.net, SitePoint (SitePoint.com), and other web sites. Jeff can be contacted via his web site at JavaJeff.ca. or via his LinkedIn (LinkedIn.com) profile (www.linkedin.com/in/javajeff).

About the Technical Reviewer

Wallace Jackson has been writing for leading multimedia publications about his work in new media content development since the advent of *Multimedia Producer Magazine* nearly two decades ago. He has authored a half-dozen Android book titles for Apress, including four titles in the popular Pro Android series. Wallace received his undergraduate degree in business economics from the University of California at Los Angeles and a graduate degree in MIS design and implementation from the University of Southern California. He is currently the CEO of Mind Taffy Design, a new media content production and digital campaign design and development agency.

Acknowledgments

Many people assisted me in the development of this book, and I thank them. I especially thank Steve Anglin for asking me to write it and Mark Powers for guiding me through the writing process.

Introduction

XML and (the more popular) JSON let you organize data in textual formats. This book introduces you to these technologies along with Java APIs for integrating them into your Java code. This book introduces you to XML and JSON as of Java 8 update 60.

Chapter 1 introduces XML, where you learn about basic language features (such as the XML declaration, elements and attributes, and namespaces). You also learn about well-formed XML documents and how to validate them via the Document Type Definition and XML Schema grammar languages.

Chapter 2 focuses on Java's SAX API for parsing XML documents. You learn how to obtain a SAX 2 parser; you then tour XMLReader methods along with handler and entity resolver interfaces. Finally, you explore a demonstration of this API and learn how to create a custom entity resolver.

Chapter 3 addresses Java's DOM API for parsing and creating XML documents. After discovering the various nodes that form a DOM document tree, you explore the DOM API, where you learn how to obtain a DOM parser/document builder and how to parse and create XML documents.

Chapter 4 places the spotlight on Java's StAX API for parsing and creating XML documents. You learn how to use StAX to parse XML documents with stream-based and event-based readers, and how to create XML documents with stream-based and event-based writers.

Moving on, Chapter 5 presents Java's XPath API for simplifying access to a DOM tree's nodes. You receive a primer on the XPath language, learning about location path expressions and general expressions. You also explore advanced features starting with namespace contexts.

Chapter 6 completes my coverage of XML by targeting Java's XSLT API. You learn about transformer factories and transformers, and much more.

Chapter 7 switches gears to JSON. You receive an introduction to JSON, take a tour of its syntax, explore a demonstration of JSON in a JavaScript context (because Java doesn't yet officially support JSON), and learn how to validate JSON objects in the context of JSON Schema.

You'll need to work with third-party libraries to parse and create JSON documents. Chapter 8 introduces you to the mJson library. After learning how to obtain and use mJson, you explore the Json class, which is the entry point for working with mJSon.

Google has released an even more powerful library for parsing and creating JSON documents. The Gson library is the focus of Chapter 9. In this chapter, you learn how to parse JSON objects through deserialization, how to create JSON objects through serialization, and much more.

Chapter 10 completes my coverage of JSON by presenting the JsonPath API for performing XPath-like operations on JSON documents.

Each chapter ends with assorted exercises that are designed to help you master the content. Along with long answers and true/false questions, you must also perform programming exercises. Appendix A provides the answers and solutions.

Thanks for purchasing this book. I hope you find it helpful in understanding XML and JSON in a Java context.

—Jeff Friesen
(April, 2016)

> **Note**   You can download this book's source code by pointing your web browser to www.apress.com/9781484219157 and clicking the Source Code tab followed by the Download Now link.

Chapter 1

Introducing XML

Applications commonly use XML documents to store and exchange data. XML defines rules for encoding documents in a format that is both human-readable and machine-readable. This chapter introduces XML, tours the XML language features, and discusses well-formed and valid documents.

What Is XML?

XML (eXtensible Markup Language) is a *metalanguage* (a language used to describe other languages) for defining *vocabularies* (custom markup languages), which is the key to XML's importance and popularity. XML-based vocabularies (such as XHTML) let you describe documents in a meaningful way.

XML vocabulary documents are like HTML (see http://en.wikipedia.org/wiki/HTML) documents in that they are text-based and consist of *markup* (encoded descriptions of a document's logical structure) and *content* (document text not interpreted as markup). Markup is evidenced via *tags* (angle bracket-delimited syntactic constructs) and each tag has a name. Furthermore, some tags have *attributes* (name-value pairs).

Electronic supplementary material The online version of this chapter (doi:10.1007/978-1-4842-1916-4_1) contains supplementary material, which is available to authorized users.

> **Note**   XML and HTML are descendants of *Standard Generalized Markup Language (SGML)*, which is the original metalanguage for creating vocabularies. XML is essentially a restricted form of SGML, while HTML is an *application* of SGML. The key difference between XML and HTML is that XML invites you to create your own vocabularies with its own tags and rules, whereas HTML gives you a single precreated vocabulary with its own fixed set of tags and rules. XHTML and other XML-based vocabularies are *XML applications*. XHTML was created to be a cleaner implementation of HTML.

If you haven't previously encountered XML, you might be surprised by its simplicity and how closely its vocabularies resemble HTML. You don't need to be a rocket scientist to learn how to create an XML document. To prove this to yourself, check out Listing 1-1.

Listing 1-1. XML-Based Recipe for a Grilled Cheese Sandwich

```
<recipe>
   <title>
      Grilled Cheese Sandwich
   </title>
   <ingredients>
      <ingredient qty="2">
         bread slice
      </ingredient>
      <ingredient>
         cheese slice
      </ingredient>
      <ingredient qty="2">
         margarine pat
      </ingredient>
   </ingredients>
   <instructions>
      Place frying pan on element and select medium heat. For each bread
slice, smear one pat of margarine on one side of bread slice. Place cheese
slice between bread slices with margarine-smeared sides away from the
cheese. Place sandwich in frying pan with one margarine-smeared side in
contact with pan. Fry for a couple of minutes and flip. Fry other side for a
minute and serve.
   </instructions>
</recipe>
```

Listing 1-1 presents an XML document that describes a recipe for making a grilled cheese sandwich. This document is reminiscent of an HTML document in that it consists of tags, attributes, and content. However, that's where the similarity ends. Instead of presenting HTML tags such as `<html>`, `<head>`, `<img>`, and `<p>`, this informal recipe language presents its own `<recipe>`, `<ingredients>`, and other tags.

> **Note**   Although Listing 1-1's `<title>` and `</title>` tags are also found in HTML, they differ from their HTML counterparts. Web browsers typically display the content between these tags in their title bars. In contrast, the content between Listing 1-1's `<title>` and `</title>` tags might be displayed as a recipe header, spoken aloud, or presented in some other way, depending on the application that parses this document.

Language Features Tour

XML provides several language features for use in defining custom markup languages: XML declaration, elements and attributes, character references and CDATA sections, namespaces, and comments and processing instructions. You will learn about these language features in this section.

XML Declaration

An XML document usually begins with the *XML declaration*, which is special markup telling an XML parser that the document is XML. The absence of the XML declaration in Listing 1-1 reveals that this special markup isn't mandatory. When the XML declaration is present, nothing can appear before it.

The XML declaration minimally looks like `<?xml version="1.0"?>` in which the nonoptional `version` attribute identifies the version of the XML specification to which the document conforms. The initial version of this specification (1.0) was introduced in 1998 and is widely implemented.

> **Note**   The World Wide Web Consortium (W3C), which maintains XML, released version 1.1 in 2004. This version mainly supports the use of line-ending characters used on EBCDIC platforms (see http://en.wikipedia.org/wiki/EBCDIC) and the use of scripts and characters that are absent from Unicode 3.2 (see http://en.wikipedia.org/wiki/Unicode). Unlike XML 1.0, XML 1.1 isn't widely implemented and should be used only by those needing its unique features.

XML supports Unicode, which means that XML documents consist entirely of characters taken from the Unicode character set. The document's characters are encoded into bytes for storage or transmission, and the encoding is specified via the XML declaration's optional encoding attribute. One common encoding is *UTF-8* (see http://en.wikipedia.org/wiki/UTF-8), which is a variable-length encoding of the Unicode character set. UTF-8 is a strict superset of ASCII (see http://en.wikipedia.org/wiki/ASCII), which means that pure ASCII text files are also UTF-8 documents.

> **Note**   In the absence of the XML declaration or when the XML declaration's encoding attribute isn't present, an XML parser typically looks for a special character sequence at the start of a document to determine the document's encoding. This character sequence is known as the *byte-order-mark (BOM)* and is created by an editor program (such as Microsoft Windows Notepad) when it saves the document according to UTF-8 or some other encoding. For example, the hexadecimal sequence EF BB BF signifies UTF-8 as the encoding. Similarly, FE FF signifies UTF-16 big endian (see https://en.wikipedia.org/wiki/UTF-16), FF FE signifies UTF-16 little endian, 00 00 FE FF signifies UTF-32 big endian (see https://en.wikipedia.org/wiki/UTF-32), and FF FE 00 00 signifies UTF-32 little endian. UTF-8 is assumed when no BOM is present.

If you'll never use characters apart from the ASCII character set, you can probably forget about the encoding attribute. However, when your native language isn't English or when you're called to create XML documents that include non-ASCII characters, you need to properly specify encoding. For example, when your document contains ASCII plus characters from a non-English Western European language (such as ç, the cedilla used in French, Portuguese, and other languages), you might want to choose ISO-8859-1 as the encoding attribute's value—the document will probably have a smaller size when encoded in this manner than when encoded with UTF-8. Listing 1-2 shows you the resulting XML declaration.

Listing 1-2. An Encoded Document Containing Non-ASCII Characters

```
<?xml version="1.0" encoding="ISO-8859-1"?>
<movie>
    <name>Le Fabuleux Destin d'Amélie Poulain</name>
    <language>français</language>
</movie>
```

The final attribute that can appear in the XML declaration is `standalone`. This optional attribute, which is only relevant with DTDs (discussed later), determines if there are external markup declarations that affect the information passed from an *XML processor* (a parser) to the application. Its value defaults to no, implying that there are, or may be, such declarations. A yes value indicates that there are no such declarations. For more information, check out "The standalone pseudo-attribute is only relevant if a DTD is used" article at (`www.xmlplease.com/xml/xmlquotations/standalone`).

Elements and Attributes

Following the XML declaration is a *hierarchical* (tree) structure of elements, where an *element* is a portion of the document delimited by a *start tag* (such as `<name>`) and an *end tag* (such as `</name>`), or is an *empty-element tag* (a standalone tag whose name ends with a forward slash (/), such as `<break/>`). Start tags and end tags surround content and possibly other markup whereas empty-element tags don't surround anything. Figure 1-1 reveals Listing 1-1's XML document tree structure.

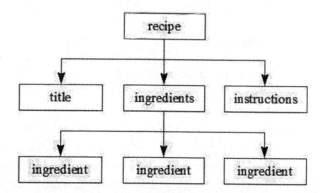

Figure 1-1. Listing 1-1's tree structure is rooted in the `recipe` element

As with the HTML document structure, the structure of an XML document is anchored in a *root element* (the topmost element). In HTML, the root element is `html` (the `<html>` and `</html>` tag pair). Unlike in HTML, you can choose the root element for your XML documents. Figure 1-1 shows the root element to be `recipe`.

Unlike the other elements, which have parent elements, `recipe` has no parent. Also, `recipe` and `ingredients` have child elements: `recipe`'s children are `title`, `ingredients`, and `instructions`; and `ingredients`' children are three instances of `ingredient`. The `title`, `instructions`, and `ingredient` elements don't have child elements.

Elements can contain child elements, content, or *mixed content* (a combination of child elements and content). Listing 1-2 reveals that the movie element contains name and language child elements, and also reveals that each of these child elements contains content (language contains français, for example). Listing 1-3 presents another example that demonstrates mixed content along with child elements and content.

Listing 1-3. An abstract Element Containing Mixed Content

```
<?xml version="1.0"?>
<article title="The Rebirth of JavaFX" lang="en">
   <abstract>
      JavaFX 2 marks a significant milestone in the history of JavaFX. Now
that Sun Microsystems has passed the torch to Oracle, we have seen the
demise of JavaFX Script and the emergence of Java APIs (such as <code-
inline>javafx.application.Application</code-inline>) for interacting with
this technology. This article introduces you to this new flavor of JavaFX,
where you learn about JavaFX 2 architecture and key APIs.
   </abstract>
   <body>
   </body>
</article>
```

This document's root element is article, which contains abstract and body child elements. The abstract element mixes content with a code-inline element, which contains content. In contrast, the body element is empty.

> **Note** As with Listings 1-1 and 1-2, Listing 1-3 also contains *whitespace* (invisible characters such as spaces, tabs, carriage returns, and line feeds). The XML specification permits whitespace to be added to a document. Whitespace appearing within content (such as spaces between words) is considered part of the content. In contrast, the parser typically ignores whitespace appearing between an end tag and the next start tag. Such whitespace isn't considered part of the content.

An XML element's start tag can contain one or more attributes. For example, Listing 1-1's <ingredient> tag has a qty (quantity) attribute and Listing 1-3's <article> tag has title and lang attributes. Attributes provide additional details about elements. For example, qty identifies the amount of an ingredient that can be added, title identifies an article's title, and lang identifies the language in which the article is written (en for English). Attributes can be optional. For example, when qty isn't specified, a default value of 1 is assumed.

> **Note**   Element and attribute names may contain any alphanumeric character from English or another language, and may also include the underscore (_), hyphen (-), period (.), and colon (:) punctuation characters. The colon should only be used with namespaces (discussed later in this chapter), and **names cannot contain whitespace**.

Character References and CDATA Sections

Certain characters cannot appear literally in the content that appears between a start tag and an end tag or within an attribute value. For example, you cannot place a literal < character between a start tag and an end tag because doing so would confuse an XML parser into thinking that it had encountered another tag.

One solution to this problem is to replace the literal character with a *character reference*, which is a code that represents the character. Character references are classified as numeric character references or character entity references:

- A *numeric character reference* refers to a character via its Unicode code point and adheres to the format &#*nnnn*; (not restricted to four positions) or &#x*hhhh*; (not restricted to four positions), where *nnnn* provides a decimal representation of the code point and *hhhh* provides a hexadecimal representation. For example, Σ and Σ represent the Greek capital letter sigma. Although XML mandates that the x in &#x*hhhh*; be lowercase, it's flexible in that the leading zero is optional in either format and in allowing you to specify an uppercase or lowercase letter for each *h*. As a result, Σ, Σ, and Σ are also valid representations of the Greek capital letter sigma.

- A *character entity reference* refers to a character via the name of an *entity* (aliased data) that specifies the desired character as its replacement text. Character entity references are predefined by XML and have the format &*name*;, in which *name* is the entity's name. XML predefines five character entity references: < (<), > (>), & (&), ' ('), and " (").

Consider <expression>6 < 4</expression>. You could replace the < with numeric reference <, yielding <expression>6 < 4</expression>, or better yet with <, yielding <expression>6 < 4</expression>. The second choice is clearer and easier to remember.

Suppose you want to embed an HTML or XML document within an element. To make the embedded document acceptable to an XML parser, you would need to replace each literal < (start of tag) and & (start of entity) character with its < and & predefined character entity reference, a tedious and possibly error-prone undertaking—you might forget to replace one of these characters. To save you from tedium and potential errors, XML provides an alternative in the form of a CDATA (character data) section.

A *CDATA section* is a section of literal HTML or XML markup and content surrounded by the `<![CDATA[` prefix and the `]]>` suffix. You don't need to specify predefined character entity references within a CDATA section, as demonstrated in Listing 1-4.

Listing 1-4. Embedding an XML Document in Another Document's CDATA Section

```
<?xml version="1.0"?>
<svg-examples>
   <example>
      The following Scalable Vector Graphics document describes a blue-
      filled and black-stroked rectangle.
      <![CDATA[<svg width="100%" height="100%" version="1.1"
         xmlns="http://www.w3.org/2000/svg">
         <rect width="300" height="100"
             style="fill:rgb(0,0,255);stroke-width:1; stroke:rgb(0,0,0)"/>
      </svg>]]>
   </example>
</svg-examples>
```

Listing 1-4 embeds a Scalable Vector Graphics (SVG; [see https://en.wikipedia.org/wiki/Scalable_Vector_Graphics) XML document within the example element of an SVG examples document. The SVG document is placed in a CDATA section, obviating the need to replace all < characters with < predefined character entity references.

Namespaces

It's common to create XML documents that combine features from different XML languages. Namespaces are used to prevent name conflicts when elements and other XML language features appear. Without namespaces, an XML parser couldn't distinguish between same-named elements or other language features that mean different things, such as two same-named title elements from two different languages.

> **Note**   Namespaces aren't part of XML 1.0. They arrived about a year after this specification was released. To ensure backward compatibility with XML 1.0, namespaces take advantage of colon characters, which are legal characters in XML names. Parsers that don't recognize namespaces return names that include colons.

A *namespace* is a Uniform Resource Identifier (URI)-based container that helps differentiate XML vocabularies by providing a unique context for its contained identifiers. The namespace URI is associated with a *namespace prefix* (an alias for the URI) by specifying, typically in an XML document's root element, either the xmlns attribute by itself (which signifies the default namespace) or the xmlns:*prefix* attribute (which signifies the namespace identified as *prefix*), and assigning the URI to this attribute.

> **Note**   A namespace's scope starts at the element where it's declared and applies to all of the element's content unless overridden by another namespace declaration with the same prefix name.

When *prefix* is specified, the prefix and a colon character are prepended to the name of each element tag that belongs to that namespace (see Listing 1-5).

Listing 1-5. Introducing a Pair of Namespaces

```
<?xml version="1.0"?>
<h:html xmlns:h="http://www.w3.org/1999/xhtml"
        xmlns:r="http://www.javajeff.ca/">
   <h:head>
      <h:title>
         Recipe
      </h:title>
   </h:head>
   <h:body>
   <r:recipe>
      <r:title>
         Grilled Cheese Sandwich
      </r:title>
      <r:ingredients>
         <h:ul>
         <h:li>
```

```
            <r:ingredient qty="2">
               bread slice
            </r:ingredient>
            </h:li>
            <h:li>
            <r:ingredient>
               cheese slice
            </r:ingredient>
            </h:li>
            <h:li>
            <r:ingredient qty="2">
               margarine pat
            </r:ingredient>
            </h:li>
            </h:ul>
         </r:ingredients>
         <h:p>
         <r:instructions>
            Place frying pan on element and select medium heat. For each
bread slice, smear one pat of margarine on one side of bread slice. Place
cheese slice between bread slices with margarine-smeared sides away from
the cheese. Place sandwich in frying pan with one margarine-smeared side in
contact with pan. Fry for a couple of minutes and flip. Fry other side for a
minute and serve.
         </r:instructions>
         </h:p>
      </r:recipe>
      </h:body>
</h:html>
```

Listing 1-5 describes a document that combines elements from XHTML (see http://en.wikipedia.org/wiki/XHTML) with elements from the recipe language. All element tags that associate with XHTML are prefixed with h: and all element tags that associate with the recipe language are prefixed with r:.

The h: prefix associates with the www.w3.org/1999/xhtml URI and the r: prefix associates with the www.javajeff.ca URI. XML doesn't mandate that URIs point to document files. It only requires that they be unique to guarantee unique namespaces.

This document's separation of the recipe data from the XHTML elements makes it possible to preserve this data's structure while also allowing an XHTML-compliant web browser (such as Mozilla Firefox) to present the recipe via a web page (see Figure 1-2).

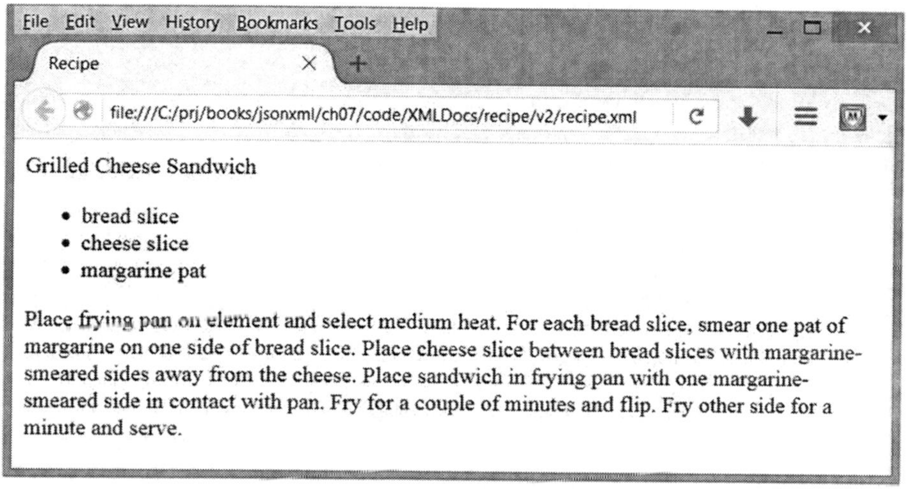

Figure 1-2. Mozilla Firefox presents the recipe data via XHTML tags

A tag's attributes don't need to be prefixed when those attributes belong to the element. For example, qty isn't prefixed in <r:ingredient qty="2">. However, a prefix is required for attributes belonging to other namespaces. For example, suppose you want to add an XHTML style attribute to the document's <r:title> tag to provide styling for the recipe title when displayed via an application. You can accomplish this task by inserting an XHTML attribute into the title tag, as follows:

```
<r:title h:style="font-family: sans-serif;">
```

The XHTML style attribute has been prefixed with h: because this attribute belongs to the XHTML language namespace and not to the recipe language namespace.

When multiple namespaces are involved, it can be convenient to specify one of these namespaces as the default namespace to reduce the tedium in entering namespace prefixes. Consider Listing 1-6.

Listing 1-6. Specifying a Default Namespace

```
<?xml version="1.0"?>
<html xmlns="http://www.w3.org/1999/xhtml"
      xmlns:r="http://www.javajeff.ca/">
   <head>
      <title>
         Recipe
      </title>
   </head>
```

```
<body>
<r:recipe>
   <r:title>
      Grilled Cheese Sandwich
   </r:title>
   <r:ingredients>
      <ul>
      <li>
      <r:ingredient qty="2">
         bread slice
      </r:ingredient>
      </li>
      <li>
      <r:ingredient>
         cheese slice
      </r:ingredient>
      </li>
      <li>
      <r:ingredient qty="2">
         margarine pat
      </r:ingredient>
      </li>
      </ul>
   </r:ingredients>
   <p>
   <r:instructions>
         Place frying pan on element and select medium heat. For each
bread slice, smear one pat of margarine on one side of bread slice. Place
cheese slice between bread slices with margarine-smeared sides away from
the cheese. Place sandwich in frying pan with one margarine-smeared side in
contact with pan. Fry for a couple of minutes and flip. Fry other side for a
minute and serve.
   </r:instructions>
   </p>
</r:recipe>
</body>
</html>
```

Listing 1-6 specifies a default namespace for the XHTML language. No XHTML
element tag needs to be prefixed with h:. However, recipe language element
tags must still be prefixed with the r: prefix.

Comments and Processing Instructions

XML documents can contain *comments*, which are character sequences beginning with `<!--` and ending with `-->`. For example, you might place `<!-- Todo -->` in Listing 1-3's body element to remind yourself that you need to finish coding this element.

Comments are used to clarify portions of a document. They can appear anywhere after the XML declaration except within tags, cannot be nested, cannot contain a double hyphen (`--`) because doing so might confuse an XML parser that the comment has been closed, shouldn't contain a hyphen (`-`) for the same reason, and are typically ignored during processing. Comments are not content.

XML also permits processing instructions to be present. A *processing instruction* is an instruction that's made available to the application parsing the document. The instruction begins with `<?` and ends with `?>`. The `<?` prefix is followed by a name known as the *target*. This name typically identifies the application to which the processing instruction is intended. The rest of the processing instruction contains text in a format appropriate to the application. The following are two examples of processing instructions:

- `<?xml-stylesheet href="modern.xsl" type="text/xml"?>` to associate an eXtensible Stylesheet Language (XSL) style sheet with an XML document (see `http://en.wikipedia.org/wiki/XSL`).

- `<?php /* PHP code */ ?>` to pass a PHP code fragment to the application (see `http://en.wikipedia.org/wiki/PHP`). Although the XML declaration looks like a processing instruction, this isn't the case.

> **Note**   The XML declaration isn't a processing instruction.

Well-Formed Documents

HTML is a sloppy language in which elements can be specified out of order, end tags can be omitted, and so on. The complexity of a web browser's page layout code is partly due to the need to handle these special cases. In contrast, XML is a much stricter language. To make XML documents easier to parse, XML mandates that XML documents follow certain rules:

- *All elements must either have start and end tags or consist of empty-element tags.* For example, unlike the HTML `<p>` tag that's often specified without a `</p>` counterpart, `</p>` must also be present from an XML document perspective.

- *Tags must be nested correctly.* For example, while you'll probably get away with specifying `<b><i>XML</b></i>` in HTML, an XML parser would report an error. In contrast, `<b><i>XML</i></b>` doesn't result in an error, because the nested tag pairs mirror each other.

- *All attribute values must be quoted.* Either single quotes (') or double quotes (") are permissible (although double quotes are the more commonly specified quotes). It's an error to omit these quotes.

- *Empty elements must be properly formatted.* For example, HTML's `<br>` tag would have to be specified as `<br/>` in XML. You can specify a space between the tag's name and the / character although the space is optional.

- *Be careful with case.* XML is a **case-sensitive** language in which tags differing in case (such as `<author>` and `<Author>`) are considered different. It's an error to mix start and end tags of different cases, for example, `<author>` with `</Author>`.

XML parsers that are aware of namespaces enforce two additional rules:

- Each element and attribute name must not include more than one colon character.

- No entity names, processing instruction targets, or notation names (discussed later) can contain colons.

An XML document that conforms to these rules is *well formed*. The document has a logical and clean appearance and is much easier to process. XML parsers will only parse well-formed XML documents.

Valid Documents

It's not always enough for an XML document to be well formed; in many cases the document must also be valid. A *valid* document adheres to constraints. For example, a constraint could be placed upon Listing 1-1's recipe document to ensure that the `ingredients` element always precedes the `instructions` element; perhaps an application must first process `ingredients`.

> **Note**   XML document validation is similar to a compiler analyzing source code to make sure that the code makes sense in a machine context. For example, each of `int`, `count`, `=`, `1`, and `;` are valid Java character sequences but `1 count ; int = ` isn't a valid Java construct (whereas `int count = 1;` is a valid Java construct).

Some XML parsers perform validation, whereas other parsers don't because validating parsers are harder to write. A parser that performs validation compares an XML document to a *grammar document*. Any deviation from the grammar document is reported as an error to the application—the XML document isn't valid. The application may choose to fix the error or reject the XML document. Unlike well-formedness errors, validity errors aren't necessarily fatal and the parser can continue to parse the XML document.

> **Note**   Validating XML parsers often don't validate by default because validation can be time-consuming. They must be instructed to perform validation.

Grammar documents are written in a special language. Two commonly used grammar languages are Document Type Definition and XML Schema.

Document Type Definition

Document Type Definition (DTD) is the oldest grammar language for specifying an XML document's *grammar*. DTD grammar documents (known as DTDs) are written in accordance to a strict syntax that states what elements may be present and in what parts of a document, and also what is contained within elements (child elements, content, or mixed content) and what attributes may be specified. For example, a DTD may specify that a `recipe` element must have an `ingredients` element followed by an `instructions` element.

Listing 1-7 presents a DTD for the recipe language that was used to construct Listing 1-1's document.

Listing 1-7. The Recipe Language's DTD

```
<!ELEMENT recipe (title, ingredients, instructions)>
<!ELEMENT title (#PCDATA)>
<!ELEMENT ingredients (ingredient+)>
<!ELEMENT ingredient (#PCDATA)>
<!ELEMENT instructions (#PCDATA)>
<!ATTLIST ingredient qty CDATA "1">
```

This DTD first declares the recipe language's elements. Element declarations take the form <!ELEMENT *name content-specifier*>, where *name* is any legal XML name (it cannot contain whitespace, for example), and *content-specifier* identifies what can appear within the element.

The first element declaration states that exactly one recipe element can appear in the XML document—this declaration doesn't imply that recipe is the root element. Furthermore, this element must include exactly one each of the title, ingredients, and instructions child elements, and in that order. Child elements must be specified as a comma-separated list. Furthermore, a list is always surrounded by parentheses.

The second element declaration states that the title element contains *parsed character data* (nonmarkup text). The third element declaration states that at least one ingredient element must appear in ingredients. The + character is an example of a regular expression that means one or more. Other expressions that may be used are * (zero or more) and ? (once or not at all). The fourth and fifth element declarations are similar to the second by stating that ingredient and instructions elements contain parsed character data.

> **Note**   Element declarations support three other content specifiers. You can specify <!ELEMENT *name* ANY> to allow any type of element content or <!ELEMENT *name* EMPTY> to disallow any element content. To state that an element contains mixed content, you would specify #PCDATA and a list of element names, separated by vertical bars (|). For example, <!ELEMENT ingredient (#PCDATA | measure | note)*> states that the ingredient element can contain a mix of parsed character data, zero or more measure elements, and zero or more note elements. It doesn't specify the order in which the parsed character data and these elements occur. However, #PCDATA must be the first item specified in the list. When a regular expression is used in this context, it must appear to the right of the closing parenthesis.

Listing 1-7's DTD lastly declares the recipe language's attributes, of which there is only one: qty. Attribute declarations take the form <!ATTLIST *ename aname type default-value*>, where *ename* is the name of the element to which the attribute belongs, *aname* is the name of the attribute, *type* is the attribute's type, and *default-value* is the attribute's default value.

The attribute declaration identifies qty as an attribute of ingredient. It also states that qty's type is CDATA (any string of characters not including the ampersand, less than or greater than signs, or double quotes may appear; these characters may be represented via &, <, >, or ", respectively), and that qty is optional, assuming default value 1 when absent.

MORE ABOUT ATTRIBUTES

DTD lets you specify additional attribute types: ID (create a unique identifier for an attribute that identifies an element), IDREF (an attribute's value is an element located elsewhere in the document), IDREFS (the value consists of multiple IDREFs), ENTITY (you can use external binary data or unparsed entities), ENTITIES (the value consists of multiple entities), NMTOKEN (the value is restricted to any valid XML name), NMTOKENS (the value is composed of multiple XML names), NOTATION (the value is already specified via a DTD notation declaration), and enumerated (a list of possible values to choose from; values are separated with vertical bars).

Instead of specifying a default value verbatim, you can specify #REQUIRED to mean that the attribute must always be present with some value (<!ATTLIST *ename aname type* #REQUIRED>), #IMPLIED to mean that the attribute is optional and no default value is provided (<!ATTLIST *ename aname type* #IMPLIED>), or #FIXED to mean that the attribute is optional and must always take on the DTD-assigned default value when used (<!ATTLIST *ename aname type* #FIXED "value">).

You can specify a list of attributes in one ATTLIST declaration. For example, <!ATTLIST *ename aname1 type1 default-value1 aname2 type2 default-value2*> declares two attributes identified as *aname1* and *aname2*.

A DTD-based validating XML parser requires that a document include a *document type declaration* identifying the DTD that specifies the document's grammar before it will validate the document.

> **Note**   Document Type Definition and document type declaration are two different things. The DTD acronym identifies a Document Type Definition and never identifies a document type declaration.

A document type declaration appears immediately after the XML declaration and is specified in one of the following ways:

- ▓ `<!DOCTYPE` *root-element-name* `SYSTEM` *uri*`>` references an external but private DTD via *uri*. The referenced DTD isn't available for public scrutiny. For example, I might store my recipe language's DTD file (`recipe.dtd`) in a private dtds directory on my `www.javajeff.ca` web site, and use `<!DOCTYPE recipe SYSTEM "http://www.javajeff.ca/dtds/recipe.dtd">` to identify this DTD's location via *system identifier* `http://www.javajeff.ca/dtds/recipe.dtd`.

- ▓ `<!DOCTYPE` *root-element-name* `PUBLIC` *fpi uri*`>` references an external but public DTD via *fpi*, a *formal public identifier* (see `http://en.wikipedia.org/wiki/Formal_Public_Identifier`), and *uri*. If a validating XML parser cannot locate the DTD via public identifier *fpi*, it can use system identifier *uri* to locate the DTD. For example, `<!DOCTYPE html PUBLIC "-//W3C//DTD XHTML 1.0 Transitional//EN" "http://www.w3.org/TR/xhtml1/DTD/xhtml1-transitional.dtd">` references the XHTML 1.0 DTD first via public identifier `-//W3C//DTD XHTML 1.0 Transitional//EN` and second via system identifier `http://www.w3.org/TR/xhtml1/DTD/xhtml1-transitional.dtd`.

- ▓ `<!DOCTYPE` *root-element* `[` *dtd* `]>` references an internal DTD, one that is embedded within the XML document. The internal DTD must appear between square brackets.

Listing 1-8 presents Listing 1-1 (minus the child elements between the `<recipe>` and `</recipe>` tags) with an internal DTD.

Listing 1-8. The Recipe Document with an Internal DTD

```
<?xml version="1.0"?>
<!DOCTYPE recipe [
   <!ELEMENT recipe (title, ingredients, instructions)>
   <!ELEMENT title (#PCDATA)>
   <!ELEMENT ingredients (ingredient+)>
   <!ELEMENT ingredient (#PCDATA)>
   <!ELEMENT instructions (#PCDATA)>
   <!ATTLIST ingredient qty CDATA "1">
]>
<recipe>
   <!-- Child elements removed for brevity. -->
</recipe>
```

> **Note**   A document can have internal and external DTDs; for example,
> `<!DOCTYPE recipe SYSTEM "http://www.javajeff.ca/dtds/recipe.dtd" [ <!ELEMENT ...>]>`. The internal DTD is referred to as the *internal DTD subset* and the external DTD is referred to as the *external DTD subset*. Neither subset can override the element declarations of the other subset.

You can also declare notations and general and parameter entities within DTDs. A *notation* is an arbitrary piece of data that typically describes the format of unparsed binary data, and typically has the form `<!NOTATION name SYSTEM uri>`, where *name* identifies the notation and *uri* identifies some kind of plug-in that can process the data on behalf of the application that's parsing the XML document. For example, `<!NOTATION image SYSTEM "psp.exe">` declares a notation named image and identifies Windows executable psp.exe as a plug-in for processing images.

It's also common to use notations to specify binary data types via media types (see `https://en.wikipedia.org/wiki/Media_type`). For example, `<!NOTATION image SYSTEM "image/jpeg">` declares an image notation that identifies the image/jpeg media type for Joint Photographic Experts Group images.

General entities are entities referenced from inside an XML document via *general entity references*, syntactic constructs of the form &name;. Examples include the predefined lt, gt, amp, apos, and quot character entities, whose <, >, &, ', and " character entity references are aliases for characters <, >, &, ', and ", respectively.

General entities are classified as internal or external. An *internal general entity* is a general entity whose value is stored in the DTD, and has the form `<!ENTITY name value>`, where *name* identifies the entity and *value* specifies its value. For example, `<!ENTITY copyright "Copyright &copy; 2016 Jeff Friesen. All rights reserved.">` declares an internal general entity named copyright. The value of this entity may include another declared entity, such as © (the HTML entity for the copyright symbol), and can be referenced from anywhere in an XML document by specifying &copyright;.

An *external general entity* is a general entity whose value is stored outside the DTD. The value might be textual data (such as an XML document) or it might be binary data (such as a JPEG image). External general entities are classified as external parsed general entities and external unparsed general entities.

An *external parsed general entity* references an external file that stores the entity's textual data, which is subject to being inserted into a document and parsed by a validating parser when a general entity reference is specified in the document, and which has the form `<!ENTITY` *name* `SYSTEM` *uri*`>`, where *name* identifies the entity and *uri* identifies the external file. For example, `<!ENTITY chapter-header SYSTEM "http://www.javajeff.ca/entities/ chapheader.xml">` identifies `chapheader.xml` as storing the XML content to be inserted into an XML document wherever `&chapter-header;` appears in the document. The alternative `<!ENTITY` *name* `PUBLIC` *fpi uri*`>` form can be specified.

Caution   Because the contents of an external file may be parsed, this content must be well formed.

An *external unparsed general entity* references an external file that stores the entity's binary data and has the form `<!ENTITY` *name* `SYSTEM` *uri* `NDATA` *nname*`>`, where *name* identifies the entity, *uri* locates the external file, and `NDATA` identifies the notation declaration named *nname*. The notation typically identifies a plug-in for processing the binary data or the Internet media type of this data. For example, `<!ENTITY photo SYSTEM "photo.jpg" NDATA image>` associates name photo with external binary file `photo.png` and notation image. The alternative `<!ENTITY` *name* `PUBLIC` *fpi uri* `NDATA` *name*`>` form can be specified.

Note   XML doesn't allow references to external general entities to appear in attribute values. For example, you cannot specify `&chapter-header;` in an attribute's value.

Parameter entities are entities referenced from inside a DTD via *parameter entity references*, syntactic constructs of the form %*name*;. They're useful for eliminating repetitive content from element declarations. For example, you're creating a DTD for a large company, and this DTD contains three element declarations: `<!ELEMENT salesperson (firstname, lastname)>`, `<!ELEMENT lawyer (firstname, lastname)>`, and `<!ELEMENT accountant (firstname, lastname)>`. Each element contains repeated child element content. If you need to add another child element (such as `middleinitial`), you need to make sure that all of the elements are updated; otherwise, you risk a malformed DTD. Parameter entities can help you solve this problem.

Parameter entities are classified as internal or external. An *internal parameter entity* is a parameter entity whose value is stored in the DTD and has the form `<!ENTITY % name value>`, where *name* identifies the entity and *value* specifies its value. For example, `<!ENTITY % person-name "firstname, lastname">` declares a parameter entity named `person-name` with value `firstname, lastname`. Once declared, this entity can be referenced in the three previous element declarations, as follows: `<!ELEMENT salesperson (%person-name;)>`, `<!ELEMENT lawyer (%person-name;)>`, and `<!ELEMENT accountant (%person-name;)>`. Instead of adding `middleinitial` to each of salesperson, lawyer, and accountant, as was done previously, you would now add this child element to `person-name`, as in `<!ENTITY % person-name "firstname, middleinitial, lastname">`, and this change would be applied to these element declarations.

An *external parameter entity* is a parameter entity whose value is stored outside the DTD. It has the form `<!ENTITY % name SYSTEM uri>`, where name identifies the entity and uri locates the external file. For example, `<!ENTITY % person-name SYSTEM "http://www.javajeff.ca/entities/names.dtd">` identifies `names.dtd` as storing the `firstname, lastname` text to be inserted into a DTD wherever `%person-name;` appears in the DTD. The alternative `<!ENTITY % name PUBLIC fpi uri>` form can be specified.

> **Note** This discussion sums up the basics of DTD. One additional topic that wasn't covered (for brevity) is *conditional inclusion*, which lets you specify those portions of a DTD to make available to parsers and is typically used with parameter entity references.

XML Schema

XML Schema is a grammar language for declaring the structure, content, and *semantics* (meaning) of an XML document. This language's grammar documents are known as *schemas* that are themselves XML documents. Schemas must conform to the XML Schema DTD (see www.w3.org/2001/XMLSchema.dtd).

XML Schema was introduced by the W3C to overcome limitations with DTD, such as DTD's lack of support for namespaces. Also, XML Schema provides an object-oriented approach to declaring an XML document's grammar. This grammar language provides a much larger set of primitive types than DTD's CDATA and PCDATA types. For example, integer, floating-point, various date and time, and string types are part of XML Schema.

> **Note**   XML Schema predefines 19 primitive types, which are expressed via the following identifiers: anyURI, base64Binary, boolean, date, dateTime, decimal, double, duration, float, hexBinary, gDay, gMonth, gMonthDay, gYear, gYearMonth, NOTATION, QName, string, and time.

XML Schema provides *restriction* (reducing the set of permitted values through constraints), *list* (allowing a sequence of values), and *union* (allowing a choice of values from several types) derivation methods for creating new *simple types* from these primitive types. For example, XML Schema derives 13 integer types from decimal through restriction; these types are expressed via the following identifiers: byte, int, integer, long, negativeInteger, nonNegativeInteger, nonPositiveInteger, positiveInteger, short, unsignedByte, unsignedInt, unsignedLong, and unsignedShort. It also provides support for creating *complex types* from simple types.

A good way to become familiar with XML Schema is to follow through an example, such as creating a schema for Listing 1-1's recipe language document. The first step in creating this recipe language schema is to identify all of its elements and attributes. The elements are recipe, title, ingredients, instructions, and ingredient; qty is the solitary attribute.

The next step is to classify the elements according to XML Schema's *content model*, which specifies the types of child elements and text *nodes* (see http://en.wikipedia.org/wiki/Node_(computer_science)) that can be included in an element. An element is considered to be *empty* when the element has no child elements or text nodes, *simple* when only text nodes are accepted, *complex* when only child elements are accepted, and *mixed* when child elements and text nodes are accepted. None of Listing 1-1's elements have empty or mixed content models. However, the title, ingredient, and instructions elements have simple content models; and the recipe and ingredients elements have complex content models.

For elements that have a simple content model, we can distinguish between elements having attributes and elements not having attributes. XML Schema classifies elements having a simple content model and no attributes as simple types. Furthermore, it classifies elements having a simple content model and attributes, or elements from other content models as complex types. Furthermore, XML Schema classifies attributes as simple types because they only contain text values—attributes don't have child elements. Listing 1-1's title and instructions elements and its qty attribute are simple types. Its recipe, ingredients, and ingredient elements are complex types.

At this point, you can begin to declare the schema. The following code fragment presents the introductory schema element:

```
<xs:schema xmlns:xs="http://www.w3.org/2001/XMLSchema">
```

The schema element introduces the grammar. It also assigns the commonly used xs namespace prefix to the standard XML Schema namespace; xs: is subsequently prepended to XML Schema element names.

Next, you use the element element to declare the title and instructions simple type elements, as follows:

```
<xs:element name="title" type="xs:string"/>
<xs:element name="instructions" type="xs:string"/>
```

XML Schema requires that each element have a name and (unlike DTD) be associated with a type, which identifies the kind of data stored in the element. For example, the first element declaration identifies title as the name via its name attribute and string as the type via its type attribute (string or character data appears between the <title> and </title> tags). The xs: prefix in xs:string is required because string is a predefined W3C type.

Continuing, you now use the attribute element to declare the qty simple type attribute, as follows:

```
<xs:attribute name="qty" type="xs:unsignedInt" default="1"/>
```

This attribute element declares an attribute named qty. I chose unsignedInt as this attribute's type because quantities are nonnegative values. Furthermore, I specified 1 as the default value for when qty isn't specified—attribute elements default to declaring optional attributes.

> **Note**   The order of element and attribute declarations isn't significant within a schema.

Now that you've declared the simple types, you can start to declare the complex types. To begin, declare recipe as follows:

```
<xs:element name="recipe">
    <xs:complexType>
        <xs:sequence>
            <xs:element ref="title"/>
            <xs:element ref="ingredients"/>
            <xs:element ref="instructions"/>
        </xs:sequence>
    </xs:complexType>
</xs:element>
```

This declaration states that recipe is a complex type (via the complexType element) consisting of a sequence (via the sequence element) of one title element followed by one ingredients element followed by one instructions element. Each of these elements is declared by a different element that's referred to by its element's ref attribute.

The next complex type to declare is ingredients. The following code fragment provides its declaration:

```
<xs:element name="ingredients">
   <xs:complexType>
      <xs:sequence>
         <xs:element ref="ingredient" maxOccurs="unbounded"/>
      </xs:sequence>
   </xs:complexType>
</xs:element>
```

This declaration states that ingredients is a complex type consisting of a sequence of one or more ingredient elements. The "or more" is specified by including element's maxOccurs attribute and setting this attribute's value to unbounded.

> **Note**   The maxOccurs attribute identifies the maximum number of times that an element can occur. A similar minOccurs attribute identifies the minimum number of times that an element can occur. Each attribute can be assigned 0 or a positive integer. Furthermore, you can specify unbounded for maxOccurs, which means that there's no upper limit on occurrences of the element. Each attribute defaults to a value of 1, which means that an element can appear only one time when neither attribute is present.

The final complex type to declare is ingredient. Although ingredient can contain only text nodes, which implies that it should be a simple type, it's the presence of the qty attribute that makes it complex. Check out the following declaration:

```
<xs:element name="ingredient">
   <xs:complexType>
      <xs:simpleContent>
         <xs:extension base="xs:string">
            <xs:attribute ref="qty"/>
         </xs:extension>
      </xs:simpleContent>
   </xs:complexType>
</xs:element>
```

The element named ingredient is a complex type (because of its optional qty attribute). The simpleContent element indicates that ingredient can only contain simple content (text nodes), and the extension element indicates that ingredient is a new type that extends the predefined string type (specified via the base attribute), implying that ingredient inherits all of string's attributes and structure. Furthermore, ingredient is given an additional qty attribute.

Listing 1-9 combines the previous examples into a complete schema.

Listing 1-9. The Recipe Document's Schema

```
<?xml version="1.0"?>
<xs:schema xmlns:xs="http://www.w3.org/2001/XMLSchema">
<xs:element name="title" type="xs:string"/>
<xs:element name="instructions" type="xs:string"/>
<xs:attribute name="qty" type="xs:unsignedInt" default="1"/>
<xs:element name="recipe">
    <xs:complexType>
        <xs:sequence>
            <xs:element ref="title"/>
            <xs:element ref="ingredients"/>
            <xs:element ref="instructions"/>
        </xs:sequence>
    </xs:complexType>
</xs:element>
<xs:element name="ingredients">
    <xs:complexType>
        <xs:sequence>
            <xs:element ref="ingredient" maxOccurs="unbounded"/>
        </xs:sequence>
    </xs:complexType>
</xs:element>
<xs:element name="ingredient">
    <xs:complexType>
        <xs:simpleContent>
            <xs:extension base="xs:string">
                <xs:attribute ref="qty"/>
            </xs:extension>
        </xs:simpleContent>
    </xs:complexType>
</xs:element>
```

After creating the schema, you can reference it from a recipe document. Accomplish this task by specifying xmlns:xsi and xsi:schemaLocation attributes on the document's root element start tag (<recipe>), as follows:

```
<recipe xmlns="http://www.javajeff.ca/"
        xmlns:xsi="http://www.w3.org/2001/XMLSchema-instance"
        xsi:schemaLocation="http://www.javajeff.ca/schemas recipe.xsd">
```

The xmlns attribute identifies http://www.javajeff.ca/ as the document's default namespace. Unprefixed elements and their unprefixed attributes belong to this namespace.

The xmlns:xsi attribute associates the conventional xsi (XML Schema Instance) prefix with the standard http://www.w3.org/2001/XMLSchema-instance namespace. The only item in the document that's prefixed with xsi: is schemaLocation.

The schemaLocation attribute is used to locate the schema. This attribute's value can be multiple pairs of space-separated values, but is specified as a single pair of such values in this example. The first value (http://www.javajeff.ca/schemas) identifies the target namespace for the schema, and the second value (recipe.xsd) identifies the location of the schema within this namespace.

> **Note**   Schema files that conform to XML Schema's grammar are commonly assigned the .xsd file extension.

If an XML document declares a namespace (xmlns default or xmlns:prefix), that namespace must be made available to the schema so that a validating parser can resolve all references to elements and other schema components for that namespace. You also need to mention which namespace the schema describes, and you do so by including the targetNamespace attribute on the schema element. For example, suppose your recipe document declares a default XML namespace, as follows:

```
<?xml version="1.0"?>
<recipe xmlns="http://www.javajeff.ca/">
```

At minimum, you would need to modify Listing 1-9's schema element to include targetNameSpace and the recipe document's default namespace as targetNameSpace's value, as follows:

```
<xs:schema targetNamespace="http://www.javajeff.ca/"
           xmlns:xs="http://www.w3.org/2001/XMLSchema">
```

EXERCISES

The following exercises are designed to test your understanding of Chapter 1's content.

1. Define XML.

2. True or false: XML and HTML are descendents of SGML.

3. What language features does XML provide for use in defining custom markup languages?

4. What is the XML declaration?

5. Identify the XML declaration's three attributes. Which attribute is nonoptional?

6. True or false: An element always consists of a start tag followed by content followed by an end tag.

7. Following the XML declaration, an XML document is anchored in what kind of element?

8. What is mixed content?

9. What is a character reference? Identify the two kinds of character references.

10. What is a CDATA section? Why would you use it?

11. Define namespace.

12. What is a namespace prefix?

13. True or false: A tag's attributes don't need to be prefixed when those attributes belong to the element.

14. What is a comment? Where can it appear in an XML document?

15. Define processing instruction.

16. Identify the rules that an XML document must follow to be considered well formed.

17. What does it mean for an XML document to be valid?

18. A parser that performs validation compares an XML document to a grammar document. Identify the two common grammar languages.

19. What is the general syntax for declaring an element in a DTD?

20. Which grammar language lets you create complex types from simple types?

21.   Create a books.xml document file with a books root element. The
       books element must contain one or more book elements, where a
       book element must contain one title element, one or more author
       elements, and one publisher element (and in that order). Also,
       the book element's <book> tag must contain isbn and pubyear
       attributes. Record Advanced C++/James Coplien/Addison
       Wesley/0201548550/1992 in the first book element, Beginning
       Groovy and Grails/Christopher M. Judd/Joseph Faisal
       Nusairat/James Shingler/Apress/9781430210450/2008 in the
       second book element, and Effective Java/Joshua Bloch/Addison
       Wesley/0201310058/2001 in the third book element.

22.   Modify books.xml to include an internal DTD that satisfies the
       previous exercise's requirements.

Summary

Applications often use XML documents to store and exchange data.
XML defines rules for encoding documents in a format that is both
human-readable and machine-readable. It's a metalanguage for defining
vocabularies, which is the key to XML's importance and popularity.

XML provides several language features for use in defining custom markup
languages. These features include the XML declaration, elements and
attributes, character references and CDATA sections, namespaces, and
comments and processing instructions.

HTML is a sloppy language where elements can be specified out of order,
end tags can be omitted, and so on. In contrast, XML documents are well
formed in that they conform to specific rules, which make them easier to
process. XML parsers only parse well-formed XML documents.

In many cases, an XML document must also be valid. A valid document
adheres to constraints as described by a grammar document. Grammar
documents are written in a grammar language, such as the commonly used
Document Type Definition and XML Schema.

Chapter 2 introduces Java's SAX API for parsing XML documents.

Parsing XML Documents with SAX

Java provides several APIs for parsing XML documents. The most basic of these APIs is SAX, which is the focus of this chapter.

What Is SAX?

Simple API for XML (SAX) is an event-based Java API for parsing an XML document sequentially from start to finish. When a SAX-oriented parser encounters an item from the document's *infoset* (an abstract data model describing an XML document's information; see `http://en.wikipedia.org/wiki/XML_Information_Set`), it makes this item available to an application as an *event* by calling one of the methods in one of the application's *handlers* (objects whose methods are called by the parser to make event information available), which the application has previously registered with the parser. The application can then *consume* this event by processing the infoset item in some manner.

A SAX parser is more memory efficient than a DOM parser (see Chapter 3) in that it doesn't require the entire document to fit into memory. This benefit becomes a drawback for using XPath (see Chapter 5) and XSLT (see Chapter 6), which require that the entire document be stored in memory.

© Jeff Friesen 2016
J. Friesen, *Java XML and JSON*, DOI 10.1007/978-1-4842-1916-4_2

> **Note**   According to its official web site (www.saxproject.org), SAX originated as an XML-parsing API for Java. However, SAX isn't exclusive to Java. Microsoft also supports SAX for its .NET framework (see http://saxdotnet.sourceforge.net).

Exploring the SAX API

SAX exists in two major versions. Java implements SAX 1 through the javax.xml.parsers package's abstract SAXParser and SAXParserFactory classes, and implements SAX 2 through the org.xml.sax package's XMLReader interface and through the org.xml.sax.helpers package's XMLReaderFactory class. The org.xml.sax, org.xml.sax.ext, and org.xml.sax.helpers packages provide various types that augment both Java implementations.

> **Note**   I explore only the SAX 2 implementation because SAX 2 makes available additional infoset items about an XML document (such as comments and CDATA section notifications).

Obtaining a SAX 2 Parser

Classes that implement the XMLReader interface describe SAX 2-based parsers. Instances of these classes are obtained by calling the XMLReaderFactory class's createXMLReader() class methods. For example, the following code fragment invokes this class's XMLReader createXMLReader() class method to create and return an XMLReader object:

```
XMLReader xmlr = XMLReaderFactory.createXMLReader();
```

The method call returns an instance of an XMLReader-implementing class and assigns its reference to xmlr.

> **Note** Behind the scenes, `createXMLReader()` attempts to create an
> XMLReader object from system defaults according to a lookup procedure that first
> examines the `org.xml.sax.driver` system property to see if it has a value. If so,
> this property's value is used as the name of the class that implements XMLReader.
> Furthermore, an attempt to instantiate this class and return the instance is
> made. An instance of the `org.xml.sax.SAXException` class is thrown when
> `createXMLReader()` cannot obtain an appropriate class or instantiate the class.

Touring XMLReader Methods

The returned XMLReader object makes available several methods for configuring
the parser and parsing a document's content. These methods are as follows:

- `ContentHandler getContentHandler()` returns the
  current content handler, which is an instance of a class
  that implements the `org.xml.sax.ContentHandler`
  interface, or null when none has been registered.

- `DTDHandler getDTDHandler()` returns the current DTD
  handler, which is an instance of a class that implements
  the `org.xml.sax.DTDHandler` interface, or null when
  none has been registered.

- `EntityResolver getEntityResolver()` returns the
  current entity resolver, which is an instance of a class
  that implements the `org.xml.sax.EntityResolver`
  interface, or null when none has been registered.

- `ErrorHandler getErrorHandler()` returns the current
  error handler, which is an instance of a class that
  implements the `org.xml.sax.ErrorHandler` interface,
  or null when none has been registered.

- `boolean getFeature(String name)` returns the Boolean
  value that corresponds to the feature identified by name,
  which must be a fully-qualified URI. This method throws
  `org.xml.sax.SAXNotRecognizedException` when the name
  isn't recognized as a feature, and throws `org.xml.sax.`
  `SAXNotSupportedException` when the name is recognized
  but the associated value cannot be determined when
  `getFeature()` is called. SAXNotRecognizedException
  and SAXNotSupportedException are subclasses of
  SAXException.

- `Object getProperty(String name)` returns the `java.lang.Object` instance that corresponds to the property identified by name, which must be a fully-qualified URI. This method throws `SAXNotRecognizedException` when the name isn't recognized as a property, and throws `SAXNotSupportedException` when the name is recognized but the associated value cannot be determined when `getProperty()` is called.

- `void parse(InputSource input)` parses an XML document and doesn't return until the document has been parsed. The `input` parameter stores a reference to an `org.xml.sax.InputSource` object, which describes the document's source (such as a `java.io.InputStream` object, or even a `java.lang.String`-based system identifier URI). This method throws `java.io.IOException` when the source cannot be read and `SAXException` when parsing fails, probably due to a well-formedness violation.

- `void parse(String systemId)` parses an XML document by executing `parse(new InputSource(systemId));`.

- `void setContentHandler(ContentHandler handler)` registers the content handler identified by handler with the parser. The `ContentHandler` interface provides 11 callback methods that are called to report various parsing events (such as the start and end of an element).

- `void setDTDHandler(DTDHandler handler)` registers the DTD handler identified by handler with the parser. The `DTDHandler` interface provides a pair of callback methods for reporting on notations and external unparsed entities.

- `void setEntityResolver(EntityResolver resolver)` registers the entity resolver identified by resolver with the parser. The `EntityResolver` interface provides a single callback method for resolving entities.

- void setErrorHandler(ErrorHandler handler) registers the error handler identified by handler with the parser. The ErrorHandler interface provides three callback methods that report *fatal errors* (problems that prevent further parsing, such as well-formedness violations), *recoverable errors* (problems that don't prevent further parsing, such as validation failures), and *warnings* (nonerrors that need to be addressed, such as prefixing an element name with the W3C-reserved xml prefix).

- void setFeature(String name, boolean value) assigns value to the feature identified by name, which must be a fully-qualified URI. This method throws SAXNotRecognizedException when the name isn't recognized as a feature, and throws SAXNotSupportedException when the name is recognized but the associated value cannot be set when setFeature() is called.

- void setProperty(String name, Object value) assigns value to the property identified by name, which must be a fully-qualified URI. This method throws SAXNotRecognizedException when the name isn't recognized as a property, and throws SAXNotSupportedException when the name is recognized but the associated value cannot be set when setProperty() is called.

When a handler isn't installed, all events pertaining to that handler are silently ignored. Not installing an error handler can be problematic because normal processing might not continue and the application wouldn't be aware that anything had gone wrong. When an entity resolver isn't installed, the parser performs its own default resolution. I'll have more to say about entity resolution later in this chapter.

> **Note**   You typically install a new content handler, DTD handler, entity resolver, or error handler before a document is parsed, but you can also do so while parsing the document. The parser starts using the handler when the next event occurs.

Setting Features and Properties

After obtaining an XMLReader object, you can configure that object by setting its features and properties. A *feature* is a name-value pair that describes a parser mode, such as validation. In contrast, a *property* is a name-value pair that describes some other aspect of the parser interface, such as a lexical handler that augments the content handler by providing callback methods for reporting on comments, CDATA delimiters, and a few other syntactic constructs.

Features and properties have names, which must be absolute URIs beginning with the http:// prefix. A feature's value is always a Boolean true/false value. In contrast, a property's value is an arbitrary object. The following code fragment demonstrates setting a feature and a property:

```
xmlr.setFeature("http://xml.org/sax/features/validation", true);
xmlr.setProperty("http://xml.org/sax/properties/lexical-handler", ↵
            new LexicalHandler() { /* ... */ });
```

The setFeature() call enables the validation feature so that the parser will perform validation. Feature names are prefixed with http://xml.org/sax/features/.

> **Note**   Parsers must support the namespaces and namespace-prefixes features. namespaces decides whether URIs and local names are passed to ContentHandler's startElement() and endElement() methods. It defaults to true—these names are passed. The parser can pass empty strings when false. namespace-prefixes decides whether a namespace declaration's xmlns and xmlns:prefix attributes are included in the org.xml.sax.Attributes list passed to startElement(), and also decides whether qualified names are passed as the method's third argument—a *qualified name* is a prefix plus a local name. It defaults to false, meaning that xmlns and xmlns:prefix aren't included, and meaning that parsers don't have to pass qualified names. No properties are mandatory. The JDK documentation's org.xml.sax package page lists standard SAX 2 features and properties.

The setProperty() call assigns an instance of a class that implements the org.xml.sax.ext.LexicalHandler interface to the lexical-handler property so that interface methods can be called to report on comments, CDATA sections, and so on. Property names are prefixed with http://xml.org/sax/properties/.

> **Note**   Unlike `ContentHandler`, `DTDHandler`, `EntityResolver`, and `ErrorHandler`, `LexicalHandler` is an extension (it's not part of the core SAX API), which is why `XMLReader` doesn't declare a void `setLexicalHandler(LexicalHandler handler)` method. If you want to install a lexical handler, you must use `XMLReader`'s `setProperty()` method to install the handler as the value of the `http://xml.org/sax/properties/lexical-handler` property.

Features and properties can be read-only or read-write. (In some rare cases, a feature or property might be write-only.) When setting or reading a feature or property, `SAXNotSupportedException` or `SAXNotRecognizedException` might be thrown. For example, if you try to modify a read-only feature/property, an instance of the `SAXNotSupportedException` class is thrown. Also, this exception could be thrown if you call `setFeature()` or `setProperty()` during parsing. Trying to set the validation feature for a parser that doesn't perform validation is a scenario where an instance of the `SAXNotRecognizedException` class is thrown.

Touring the Handler and Resolver Interfaces

The interface-based handlers installed by `setContentHandler()`, `setDTDHandler()`, and `setErrorHandler()`; the entity resolver installed by `setEntityResolver()`; and the handler described by the `lexical-handler` property provide various callback methods. You need to understand these methods before you can codify them to respond effectively to parsing events.

Touring ContentHandler

`ContentHandler` declares the following content-oriented informational callback methods:

- void `characters(char[] ch, int start, int length)` reports an element's character data via the ch array. The arguments that are passed to `start` and `length` identify the portion of the array that's relevant to this method call. Characters are passed via a `char[]` array instead of via a `String` object as a performance optimization. Parsers commonly store a large amount of the document in an array and repeatedly pass a reference to this array along with updated `start` and `length` values to `characters()`.

- ▪ void endDocument() reports that the end of the document has been reached. An application might use this method to close an output file or perform some other cleanup.

- ▪ void endElement(String uri, String localName, String qName) reports that the end of an element has been reached. uri identifies the element's namespace URI, or is empty when there is no namespace URI or namespace processing hasn't been enabled. localName identifies the element's local name, which is the name without a prefix (the html in html or h:html, for example). qName references the qualified name, for example, h:html or html when there is no prefix. endElement() is invoked when an end tag is detected, or immediately following startElement() when an empty-element tag is detected.

- ▪ void endPrefixMapping(String prefix) reports that the end of a namespace prefix mapping (xmlns:h, for example) has been reached, and prefix reports this prefix (h, for example).

- ▪ void ignorableWhitespace(char[] ch, int start, int length) reports *ignorable whitespace* (whitespace located between tags where the DTD doesn't allow mixed content). This whitespace is often used to indent tags. The parameters serve the same purpose as those in the characters() method.

- ▪ void processingInstruction(String target, String data) reports a processing instruction, in which target identifies the application to which the instruction is directed and data provides the instruction's data (the null reference when there is no data).

- ▪ void setDocumentLocator(Locator locator) reports an org.xml.sax.Locator object (an instance of a class implementing the Locator interface) whose int getColumnNumber(), int getLineNumber(), String getPublicId(), and String getSystemId() methods can be called to obtain location information at the end position of any document-related event, even when the parser isn't reporting an error. This method is called before startDocument() and is a good place to save the Locator object so that it can be accessed from other callback methods.

- void skippedEntity(String name) reports all skipped entities. Validating parsers resolve all general entity references, but nonvalidating parsers have the option of skipping them because nonvalidating parsers don't read DTDs where these entities are declared. If the nonvalidating parser doesn't read a DTD, it will not know if an entity is properly declared. Instead of attempting to read the DTD and report the entity's replacement text, the nonvalidating parser calls skippedEntity() with the entity's name.

- void startDocument() reports that the start of the document has been reached. An application might use this method to create an output file or perform some other initialization.

- void startElement(String uri, String localName, String qName, Attributes attributes) reports that the start of an element has been reached. uri identifies the element's namespace URI or is empty when there is no namespace URI or namespace processing hasn't been enabled. localName identifies the element's local name, qName references its qualified name, and attributes references a list of the element's attributes—this list is empty when there are no attributes. startElement() is invoked when a start tag or an empty-element tag is detected.

- void startPrefixMapping(String prefix, String uri) reports that the start of a namespace prefix mapping (xmlns:h="http://www.w3.org/1999/xhtml", for example) has been reached, in which prefix reports this prefix (such as h) and uri reports the URI to which the prefix is mapped (http://www.w3.org/1999/xhtml, for example).

Each method, except for setDocumentLocator(), is declared to throw SAXException, which an overriding callback method might choose to throw when it detects a problem.

Touring DTDHandler

DTDHandler declares the following DTD-oriented informational callback methods:

- void notationDecl(String name, String publicId, String systemId) reports a notation declaration, in which name provides this declaration's name attribute value, publicId provides this declaration's public attribute value (the null reference when this value isn't available), and systemId provides this declaration's system attribute value.

- void unparsedEntityDecl(String name, String publicId, String systemId, String notationName) reports an external unparsed entity declaration, in which name provides the value of this declaration's name attribute, publicId provides the value of the public attribute (the null reference when this value isn't available), systemId provides the value of the system attribute, and notationName provides the NDATA name.

Each method is declared to throw SAXException, which an overriding callback method might choose to throw when it detects a problem.

Touring ErrorHandler

ErrorHandler declares the following error-oriented informational callback methods:

- void error(SAXParseException exception) reports that a recoverable parser error (typically the document isn't valid) has occurred; the details are specified via the argument passed to exception. This method is typically overridden to report the error via a command window or to log it to a file or a database.

- void fatalError(SAXParseException exception) reports that an unrecoverable parser error (the document isn't well formed) has occurred; the details are specified via the argument passed to exception. This method is typically overridden so that the application can log the error before it stops processing the document (because the document is no longer reliable).

- void warning(SAXParseException e) reports that a
  nonserious error (such as an element name beginning
  with the reserved xml character sequence) has occurred;
  the details are specified via the argument passed
  to exception. This method is typically overridden to
  report the warning via a console or to log it to a file or a
  database.

Each method is declared to throw SAXException, which an overriding
callback method might choose to throw when it detects a problem.

Touring EntityResolver

EntityResolver declares the following callback method:

- InputSource resolveEntity(String publicId, String
  systemId) is called to let the application resolve an
  external entity (such as an external DTD subset) by
  returning a custom InputSource object that's based
  on a different URI. This method is declared to throw
  SAXException when it detects a SAX-oriented problem,
  and is also declared to throw IOException when it
  encounters an I/O error, possibly in response to creating
  an InputStream object or a java.io.Reader object for
  the InputSource being created.

Touring LexicalHandler

LexicalHandler declares the following additional content-oriented
informational callback methods:

- void comment(char[] ch, int start, int length)
  reports a comment via the ch array. The arguments that
  are passed to start and length identify that portion of
  the array that's relevant to this method call.

- void endCDATA() reports the end of a CDATA section.

- void endDTD() reports the end of a DTD.

- void endEntity(String name) reports the end of the
  entity identified by name.

- void startCDATA() reports the start of a CDATA section.

- void startDTD(String name, String publicId, String systemId) reports the start of the DTD identified by name. publicId specifies the declared public identifier for the external DTD subset or is the null reference when none was declared. Similarly, systemId specifies the declared system identifier for the external DTD subset or is the null reference when none was declared.

- void startEntity(String name) reports the start of the entity identified by name.

Each method is declared to throw SAXException, which an overriding callback method might choose to throw when it detects a problem.

Because it can be tedious to implement all of the methods in each interface, the SAX API conveniently provides the org.xml.sax.helpers. DefaultHandler adapter class to relieve you of this tedium. DefaultHandler implements ContentHandler, DTDHandler, EntityResolver, and ErrorHandler. SAX also provides org.xml.sax.ext.DefaultHandler2, which subclasses DefaultHandler, and which also implements LexicalHandler.

Demonstrating the SAX API

Listing 2-1 presents the source code to SAXDemo, an application that demonstrates the SAX API. The application consists of a SAXDemo entry-point class and a Handler subclass of DefaultHandler2.

Listing 2-1. SAXDemo

```
import java.io.FileReader;
import java.io.IOException;

import org.xml.sax.InputSource;
import org.xml.sax.SAXException;
import org.xml.sax.XMLReader;

import org.xml.sax.helpers.XMLReaderFactory;

public class SAXDemo
{
    public static void main(String[] args)
    {
        if (args.length < 1 || args.length > 2)
        {
            System.err.println("usage: java SAXDemo xmlfile [v]");
            return;
        }
```

```
    try
    {
        XMLReader xmlr = XMLReaderFactory.createXMLReader();
        if (args.length == 2 && args[1].equals("v"))
            xmlr.setFeature("http://xml.org/sax/features/validation", true);
        xmlr.setFeature("http://xml.org/sax/features/namespace-prefixes", true);
        Handler handler = new Handler();
        xmlr.setContentHandler(handler);
        xmlr.setDTDHandler(handler);
        xmlr.setEntityResolver(handler);
        xmlr.setErrorHandler(handler);
        xmlr.setProperty("http://xml.org/sax/properties/lexical-handler",
                         handler);
        xmlr.parse(new InputSource(new FileReader(args[0])));
    }
    catch (IOException ioe)
    {
        System.err.println("IOE: " + ioe);
    }
    catch (SAXException saxe)
    {
        System.err.println("SAXE: " + saxe);
    }
    }
}
```

SAXDemo's main() method first verifies that one or two command-line arguments (the name of an XML document optionally followed by lowercase letter v, which tells SAXDemo to create a validating parser) have been specified. It then creates an XMLReader object; conditionally enables the validation feature and enables the namespace-prefixes feature; instantiates the companion Handler class; installs this Handler object as the parser's content handler, DTD handler, entity resolver, and error handler; installs this Handler object as the value of the lexical-handler property; creates an input source to read the document from a file; and parses the document.

The Handler class's source code is presented in Listing 2-2.

Listing 2-2. The Handler Class

```
import org.xml.sax.Attributes;
import org.xml.sax.InputSource;
import org.xml.sax.Locator;
import org.xml.sax.SAXParseException;

import org.xml.sax.ext.DefaultHandler2;
```

```java
public class Handler extends DefaultHandler2
{
   private Locator locator;

   @Override
   public void characters(char[] ch, int start, int length)
   {
      System.out.print("characters() [");
      for (int i = start; i < start + length; i++)
         System.out.print(ch[i]);
      System.out.println("]");
   }

   @Override
   public void comment(char[] ch, int start, int length)
   {
      System.out.print("characters() [");
      for (int i = start; i < start + length; i++)
         System.out.print(ch[i]);
      System.out.println("]");
   }

   @Override
   public void endCDATA()
   {
      System.out.println("endCDATA()");
   }

   @Override
   public void endDocument()
   {
      System.out.println("endDocument()");
   }

   @Override
   public void endDTD()
   {
      System.out.println("endDTD()");
   }

   @Override
   public void endElement(String uri, String localName, String qName)
   {
      System.out.print("endElement() ");
      System.out.print("uri=[" + uri + "], ");
      System.out.print("localName=[" + localName + "], ");
      System.out.println("qName=[" + qName + "]");
   }
```

```java
@Override
public void endEntity(String name)
{
   System.out.print("endEntity() ");
   System.out.println("name=[" + name + "]");
}

@Override
public void endPrefixMapping(String prefix)
{
   System.out.print("endPrefixMapping() ");
   System.out.println("prefix=[" + prefix + "]");
}

@Override
public void error(SAXParseException saxpe)
{
   System.out.println("error() " + saxpe);
}

@Override
public void fatalError(SAXParseException saxpe)
{
   System.out.println("fatalError() " + saxpe);
}

@Override
public void ignorableWhitespace(char[] ch, int start, int length)
{
   System.out.print("ignorableWhitespace() [");
   for (int i = start; i < start + length; i++)
      System.out.print(ch[i]);
   System.out.println("]");
}

@Override
public void notationDecl(String name, String publicId, String systemId)
{
   System.out.print("notationDecl() ");
   System.out.print("name=[" + name + "]");
   System.out.print("publicId=[" + publicId + "]");
   System.out.println("systemId=[" + systemId + "]");
}

@Override
public void processingInstruction(String target, String data)
{
   System.out.print("processingInstruction() [");
   System.out.println("target=[" + target + "]");
   System.out.println("data=[" + data + "]");
}
```

```java
@Override
public InputSource resolveEntity(String publicId, String systemId)
{
    System.out.print("resolveEntity() ");
    System.out.print("publicId=[" + publicId + "]");
    System.out.println("systemId=[" + systemId + "]");
    // Do not perform a remapping.
    InputSource is = new InputSource();
    is.setPublicId(publicId);
    is.setSystemId(systemId);
    return is;
}

@Override
public void setDocumentLocator(Locator locator)
{
    System.out.print("setDocumentLocator() ");
    System.out.println("locator=[" + locator + "]");
    this.locator = locator;
}

@Override
public void skippedEntity(String name)
{
    System.out.print("skippedEntity() ");
    System.out.println("name=[" + name + "]");
}

@Override
public void startCDATA()
{
    System.out.println("startCDATA()");
}

@Override
public void startDocument()
{
    System.out.println("startDocument()");
}

@Override
public void startDTD(String name, String publicId, String systemId)
{
    System.out.print("startDTD() ");
    System.out.print("name=[" + name + "]");
    System.out.print("publicId=[" + publicId + "]");
    System.out.println("systemId=[" + systemId + "]");
}
```

```java
@Override
public void startElement(String uri, String localName, String qName,
                         Attributes attributes)
{
   System.out.print("startElement() ");
   System.out.print("uri=[" + uri + "], ");
   System.out.print("localName=[" + localName + "], ");
   System.out.println("qName=[" + qName + "]");
   for (int i = 0; i < attributes.getLength(); i++)
      System.out.println("  Attribute: " + attributes.getLocalName(i) +
                         ", " + attributes.getValue(i));
   System.out.println("Column number=[" + locator.getColumnNumber() +
                      "]");
   System.out.println("Line number=[" + locator.getLineNumber() + "]");
}

@Override
public void startEntity(String name)
{
   System.out.print("startEntity() ");
   System.out.println("name=[" + name + "]");
}

@Override
public void startPrefixMapping(String prefix, String uri)
{
   System.out.print("startPrefixMapping() ");
   System.out.print("prefix=[" + prefix + "]");
   System.out.println("uri=[" + uri + "]");
}

@Override
public void unparsedEntityDecl(String name, String publicId,
                               String systemId, String notationName)
{
   System.out.print("unparsedEntityDecl() ");
   System.out.print("name=[" + name + "]");
   System.out.print("publicId=[" + publicId + "]");
   System.out.print("systemId=[" + systemId + "]");
   System.out.println("notationName=[" + notationName + "]");
}

@Override
public void warning(SAXParseException saxpe)
{
   System.out.println("warning() " + saxpe);
}
}
```

The Handler subclass is pretty straightforward; it outputs every possible piece of information about an XML document, subject to feature and property settings. You'll find this class handy for exploring the order in which events occur along with various features and properties.

Assuming that files based on Listings 2-1 and 2-2 are located in the same directory, compile them as follows:

```
javac SAXDemo.java
```

Execute the following command to parse Listing 1-4's svg-examples.xml document:

```
java SAXDemo svg-examples.xml
```

SAXDemo responds by presenting the following output (the hashcode may be different):

```
setDocumentLocator() locator=[com.sun.org.apache.xerces.internal.parsers.Abs
tractSAXParser$LocatorProxy@6d06d69c]
startDocument()
startElement() uri=[], localName=[svg-examples], qName=[svg-examples]
Column number=[15]
Line number=[2]
characters() [
    ]
startElement() uri=[], localName=[example], qName=[example]
Column number=[13]
Line number=[3]
characters() [
        The following Scalable Vector Graphics document describes a ]
characters() [
        blue-filled and black-stroked rectangle.
        ]
startCDATA()
characters() [<svg width="100%" height="100%" version="1.1"
            xmlns="http://www.w3.org/2000/svg">
        <rect width="300" height="100"
                style="fill:rgb(0,0,255);stroke-width:1; stroke:rgb(0,0,0)"/>
        </svg>]
endCDATA()
characters() [
    ]
endElement() uri=[], localName=[example], qName=[example]
characters() [
]
endElement() uri=[], localName=[svg-examples], qName=[svg-examples]
endDocument()
```

The first output line proves that setDocumentLocator() is called first. It also identifies the Locator object whose getColumnNumber() and getLineNumber() methods are called to output the parser location when startElement() is called—these methods return column and line numbers starting at 1.

Perhaps you're curious about the three instances of the following output:

```
characters() [
  ]
```

The instance of this output that follows the endCDATA() output is reporting a carriage return/line feed combination that wasn't included in the preceding characters() method call, which was passed the contents of the CDATA section minus these line terminator characters. In contrast, the instances of this output that follow the startElement() call for svg-examples and follow the endElement() call for example are somewhat curious. There's no content between <svg-examples> and <example>, and between </example> and </svg-examples>, or is there?

You can satisfy this curiosity by modifying svg-examples.xml to include an internal DTD. Place the following DTD (which indicates that an svg-examples element contains one or more example elements, and that an example element contains parsed character data) between the XML declaration and the <svg-examples> start tag:

```
<!DOCTYPE svg-examples [
<!ELEMENT svg-examples (example+)>
<!ELEMENT example (#PCDATA)>
]>
```

Continuing, execute the following command:

```
java SAXDemo svg-examples.xml
```

This time, you should see the following output (although the hashcode will probably differ):

```
setDocumentLocator() locator=[com.sun.org.apache.xerces.internal.parsers.Abs
tractSAXParser$LocatorProxy@6d06d69c]
startDocument()
startDTD() name=[svg-examples]publicId=[null]systemId=[null]
endDTD()
startElement() uri=[], localName=[svg-examples], qName=[svg-examples]
Column number=[15]
Line number=[6]
ignorableWhitespace() [
  ]
```

```
startElement() uri=[], localName=[example], qName=[example]
Column number=[13]
Line number=[7]
characters() [
      The following Scalable Vector Graphics document describes a
      blue-filled and black-stroked rectangle.]
characters() [
      ]
startCDATA()
characters() [<svg width="100%" height="100%" version="1.1"
          xmlns="http://www.w3.org/2000/svg">
        <rect width="300" height="100"
              style="fill:rgb(0,0,255);stroke-width:1; stroke:rgb(0,0,0)"/>
      </svg>]
endCDATA()
characters() [
    ]
endElement() uri=[], localName=[example], qName=[example]
ignorableWhitespace() [
]
endElement() uri=[], localName=[svg-examples], qName=[svg-examples]
endDocument()
```

This output reveals that the ignorableWhitespace() method was called after startElement() for svg-examples and after endElement() for example. The former two calls to characters() that produced the strange output were reporting ignorable whitespace.

Recall that I previously defined *ignorable whitespace* as whitespace located between tags where the DTD doesn't allow mixed content. For example, the DTD indicates that svg-examples shall contain only example elements, not example elements and parsed character data. However, the line terminator following the <svg-examples> tag and the leading whitespace before <example> are parsed character data. The parser now reports these characters by calling ignorableWhitespace().

This time, there are only two occurrences of the following output:

```
characters() [
    ]
```

The first occurrence reports the line terminator separately from the example element's text (before the CDATA section); it didn't do so previously, which proves that characters() is called with either all or part of an element's content. Once again, the second occurrence reports the line terminator that follows the CDATA section.

Let's validate svg-examples.xml without the previously presented internal DTD. You do so by executing the following command—don't forget to include the v command-line argument or the document won't validate:

```
java SAXDemo svg-examples.xml v
```

Among its output are a couple of error()-prefixed lines that are similar to those shown below:

```
error() org.xml.sax.SAXParseException; lineNumber: 2; columnNumber: 14;
Document is invalid: no grammar found.
error() org.xml.sax.SAXParseException; lineNumber: 2; columnNumber: 14;
Document root element "svg-examples", must match DOCTYPE root "null".
```

These lines reveal that a DTD grammar hasn't been found. Furthermore, the parser reports a mismatch between svg-examples (it considers the first encountered element to be the root element) and null (it considers null to be the name of the root element in the absence of a DTD). Neither violation is considered to be fatal, which is why error() is called instead of fatalError().

Add the internal DTD to svg-examples.xml and re-execute java SAXDemo svg-examples.xml v. This time, you should see no error()-prefixed lines in the output.

> **Tip**   SAX 2 validation defaults to validating against a DTD. To validate against an XML Schema-based schema instead, add the schemaLanguage property with the http://www.w3.org/2001/XMLSchema value to the XMLReader object. Accomplish this task for SAXDemo by specifying xmlr.setProperty("http://java.sun.com/xml/jaxp/properties/schemaLanguage", "http://www.w3.org/2001/XMLSchema"); before xmlr.parse(new InputSource(new FileReader(args[0])));.

Creating a Custom Entity Resolver

While exploring XML in Chapter 1, I introduced you to the concept of *entities*, which are aliased data. I then discussed general entities and parameter entities in terms of their internal and external variants.

Unlike internal entities, whose values are specified in a DTD, the values of external entities are specified outside of a DTD and are identified via public and/or system identifiers. The system identifier is a URI whereas the public identifier is a formal public identifier.

An XML parser reads an external entity (including the external DTD subset) via an InputSource object that's connected to the appropriate system identifier. In many cases, you pass a system identifier or InputSource object to the parser and let it discover where to find other entities that are referenced from the current document entity.

However, for performance or other reasons, you might want the parser to read the external entity's value from a different system identifier, such as a local DTD copy's system identifier. You can accomplish this task by creating an *entity resolver* that uses the public identifier to choose a different system identifier. Upon encountering an external entity, the parser calls the custom entity resolver to obtain this identifier.

Consider Listing 2-3's formal specification of Listing 1-1's grilled cheese sandwich recipe.

Listing 2-3. XML-Based Recipe for a Grilled Cheese Sandwich Specified in Recipe Markup Language

```
<?xml version="1.0" encoding="UTF-8"?>
<!DOCTYPE recipeml PUBLIC "-//FormatData//DTD RecipeML 0.5//EN"

"http://www.formatdata.com/recipeml/recipeml.dtd">
<recipeml version="0.5">
   <recipe>
      <head>
         <title>Grilled Cheese Sandwich</title>
      </head>
      <ingredients>
         <ing>
            <amt><qty>2</qty><unit>slice</unit></amt>
            <item>bread</item>
         </ing>
         <ing>
            <amt><qty>1</qty><unit>slice</unit></amt>
            <item>cheese</item>
         </ing>
         <ing>
            <amt><qty>2</qty><unit>pat</unit></amt>
            <item>margarine</item>
         </ing>
      </ingredients>
      <directions>
         <step>Place frying pan on element and select medium heat.</step>
         <step>For each bread slice, smear one pat of margarine on one side
         of bread slice.</step>
         <step>Place cheese slice between bread slices with margarine-
         smeared sides away from the cheese.</step>
         <step>Place sandwich in frying pan with one margarine-smeared size
         in contact with pan.</step>
```

```
        <step>Fry for a couple of minutes and flip.</step>
        <step>Fry other side for a minute and serve.</step>
      </directions>
    </recipe>
</recipeml>
```

Listing 2-3 specifies the grilled cheese sandwich recipe in *Recipe Markup Language (RecipeML)*, an XML-based language for marking up recipes. (A company named FormatData released this format in 2000; see www.formatdata.com.)

The document type declaration reports -//FormatData//DTD RecipeML 0.5// EN as the formal public identifier and http://www.formatdata.com/recipeml/ recipeml.dtd as the system identifier. Instead of keeping the default mapping, let's map this formal public identifier to recipeml.dtd, a system identifier for a local copy of this DTD file.

To create a custom entity resolver to perform this mapping, you declare a class that implements the EntityResolver interface in terms of its InputSource resolveEntity(String publicId, String systemId) method. You then use the passed publicId value as a key into a map that points to the desired systemId value, and then use this value to create and return a custom InputSource. Listing 2-4 presents the resulting class.

Listing 2-4. LocalRecipeML

```java
import java.util.HashMap;
import java.util.Map;

import org.xml.sax.EntityResolver;
import org.xml.sax.InputSource;
import org.xml.sax.SAXException;

public class LocalRecipeML implements EntityResolver
{
    private Map<String, String> mappings = new HashMap<>();

    LocalRecipeML()
    {
        mappings.put("-//FormatData//DTD RecipeML 0.5//EN", "recipeml.dtd");
    }

    @Override
    public InputSource resolveEntity(String publicId, String systemId)
    {
        if (mappings.containsKey(publicId))
        {
            System.out.println("obtaining cached recipeml.dtd");
            systemId = mappings.get(publicId);
```

```
        InputSource localSource = new InputSource(systemId);
        return localSource;
    }
    return null;
}
}
```

Listing 2-4 declares LocalRecipeML. This class's constructor stores the formal public identifier for the RecipeML DTD and the system identifier for a local copy of this DTD's document in a map.

> **Note** Although it's unnecessary to use a map in this example (an if
> (publicId.equals("-//FormatData//DTD RecipeML 0.5//EN"))
> return new InputSource("recipeml.dtd") else return null;
> statement would suffice), I've chosen to use a map in case I want to expand the
> number of mappings in the future. In another scenario, you would probably find
> a map to be very convenient. For example, it's easier to use a map than to use
> a series of if statements in a custom entity resolver that maps XHTML's strict,
> transitional, and frameset formal public identifiers, and also maps its various
> entity sets to local copies of these document files.

The overriding resolveEntity() method uses publicId's argument to locate the corresponding system identifier in the map—the systemId parameter value is ignored because it never refers to the local copy of recipeml.dtd. When the mapping is found, an InputSource object is created and returned. If the mapping couldn't be found, null would be returned.

To install this custom entity resolver in SAXDemo, specify xmlr.setEntityResolver(new LocalRecipeML()); before the parse() method call. After recompiling the source code, execute the following command:

```
java SAXDemo gcs.xml
```

Here, gcs.xml stores Listing 2-3's text. In the resulting output, you should observe the message "obtaining cached recipeml.dtd" before the call to startEntity().

> **Tip** The SAX API includes an `org.xml.sax.ext.EntityResolver2` interface that provides improved support for resolving entities. If you prefer to implement `EntityResolver2` instead of `EntityResolver`, replace the `setEntityResolver()` call to install the entity resolver with a `setFeature()` call whose feature name is `use-entity-resolver2` (don't forget the `http://xml.org/sax/features/` prefix).

EXERCISES

The following exercises are designed to test your understanding of Chapter 2's content.

1. Define SAX.

2. How do you obtain a SAX 2-based parser?

3. What is the purpose of the `XMLReader` interface?

4. How do you tell a SAX parser to perform validation?

5. Identify the four kinds of SAX-oriented exceptions that can be thrown when working with SAX.

6. What interface does a handler class implement to respond to content-oriented events?

7. Identify the three other core interfaces that a handler class is likely to implement.

8. Define ignorable whitespace.

9. True or false: `void error(SAXParseException exception)` is called for all kinds of errors.

10. What is the purpose of the `DefaultHandler` class?

11. What is an entity? What is an entity resolver?

12. *Apache Tomcat* is an open-source web server developed by the Apache Software Foundation. Tomcat stores usernames, passwords, and roles (for authentication purposes) in its `tomcat-users.xml` configuration file. Create a `DumpUserInfo` application that uses SAX to parse the `user` elements in the following `tomcat-users.xml` file

and, for each user element, dump its username, password, and roles attribute values to standard output in a *key = value* format:

```
<?xml version='1.0' encoding='utf-8'?>

<tomcat-users>
  <role rolename="dbadmin"/>
  <role rolename="manager"/>
  <user username="JohnD" password="password1"
roles="dbadmin,manager"/>
    <user username="JillD" password="password2" roles="manager"/>
</tomcat-users>
```

13. Create a SAXSearch application that searches Exercise 1-21's books.xml file for those book elements whose publisher child elements contain text that equals the application's single command-line publisher name argument. Once there is a match, output the title element's text followed by the book element's isbn attribute value. For example, java SAXSearch Apress should output title = Beginning Groovy and Grails, isbn = 9781430210450, whereas java SAXSearch "Addison Wesley" should output title = Advanced C++, isbn = 0201548550 followed by title = Effective Java, isbn = 0201310058 on separate lines. Nothing should output when the command-line publisher name argument doesn't match a publisher element's text.

14. Use Listing 2-1's SAXDemo application to validate Exercise 1-22's books.xml content against its DTD. Execute java SAXDemo books.xml -v to perform the validation.

Summary

SAX is an event-based Java API for parsing an XML document sequentially from start to finish. When a SAX-oriented parser encounters an item from the document's infoset, it makes this item available to an application as an event by calling one of the methods in one of the application's handlers, which the application has previously registered with the parser. The application can then consume this event by processing the infoset item in some manner.

SAX exists in two major versions. Java implements SAX 1 through the javax.xml.parsers package's abstract SAXParser and SAXParserFactory classes, and implements SAX 2 through the org.xml.sax package's XMLReader interface and through the org.xml.sax.helpers package's XMLReaderFactory class. The org.xml.sax, org.xml.sax.ext, and org. xml.sax.helpers packages provide various types that augment both Java implementations.

XMLReader makes available several methods for configuring the parser and parsing a document's content. Some of these methods get and set the content handler, DTD handler, entity resolver, and error handler, which are described by the ContentHandler, DTDHandler, EntityResolver, and ErrorHandler interfaces. After learning about XMLReader's methods and these interfaces, you learned about the nonstandard LexicalHandler interface and how to create a custom entity resolver.

Chapter 3 introduces Java's DOM API for parsing/creating XML documents.

Chapter **3**

Parsing and Creating XML Documents with DOM

SAX can parse XML documents but cannot create them. In contrast, DOM can parse and create XML documents. This chapter introduces you to DOM.

What Is DOM?

Document Object Model (DOM) is a Java API for parsing an XML document into an in-memory tree of nodes, and for creating an XML document from a node tree. After a DOM parser creates a tree, an application uses the DOM API to navigate over and extract infoset items from the tree's nodes.

DOM has two big advantages over SAX:

- DOM permits random access to a document's infoset items, whereas SAX only permits serial access.

- DOM also lets you create XML documents, whereas you can only parse documents with SAX.

However, SAX is advantageous over DOM in that it can parse documents of arbitrary sizes, whereas the size of documents parsed or created by DOM is limited by the amount of available memory for storing the document's node-based tree structure.

© Jeff Friesen 2016
J. Friesen, *Java XML and JSON*, DOI 10.1007/978-1-4842-1916-4_3

> **Note** DOM originated as an object model for the Netscape Navigator 3 and Microsoft Internet Explorer 3 web browsers. Collectively, these implementations are known as DOM Level 0. Because each vendor's DOM implementation was only slightly compatible with the other, the W3C subsequently took charge of DOM's development to promote standardization and has so far released DOM Levels 1, 2, and 3 (with Level 4 under development). Java 8 supports all three DOM levels through its DOM API.

A Tree of Nodes

DOM views an XML document as a tree that is composed of several kinds of nodes. This tree has a single *root node* and all nodes, except for the root, have a *parent node*. Also, each node has a list of *child nodes*. When this list is empty, the child node is known as a *leaf node*.

> **Note** DOM permits nodes to exist that are not part of the tree structure. For example, an element node's attribute nodes are not regarded as child nodes of the element node. Also, nodes can be created but not inserted into the tree; they can also be removed from the tree.

Each node has a *node name*, which is the complete name for nodes that have names (such as an element's or an attribute's prefixed name), and *#node-type* for unnamed nodes, where *node-type* is one of cdata-section, comment, document, document-fragment, or text. Nodes also have *local names* (names without prefixes), prefixes, and namespace URIs (although these attributes may be null for certain kinds of nodes, such as comments). Finally, nodes have string values, which happen to be the content of text nodes, comment nodes, and similar text-oriented nodes; normalized values for attributes; and null for everything else.

DOM classifies nodes into 12 types, of which seven types can be considered part of a DOM tree. All of these types are described below:

- *Attribute node*: One of an element's attributes. It has a name, a local name, a prefix, a namespace URI, and a normalized string value. The value is *normalized* by resolving any entity references and by converting sequences of whitespace to a single whitespace character. An attribute node has children, which are the text and any entity reference nodes that form its value. Attribute nodes are not regarded as children of their associated element nodes.

- *CDATA section node*: The contents of a CDATA section. Its name is #cdata-section and its value is the CDATA section's text.

- *Comment node*: A document comment. Its name is #comment and its value is the comment text. A comment node has a parent, which is the node that contains the comment.

- *Document node*: The root of a DOM tree. Its name is #document. It always has a single element child node, and it also has a document type child node when the document has a document type declaration. Furthermore, it can have additional child nodes describing comments or processing instructions that appear before or after the root element's start tag. There can be only one document node in the tree.

- *Document fragment node*: An alternative root node. Its name is #document-fragment and it contains anything that an element node can contain (such as other element nodes and even comment nodes). A parser never creates this kind of a node. However, an application can create a document fragment node when it extracts part of a DOM tree to be moved somewhere else. Document fragment nodes let you work with subtrees.

- *Document type node*: A document type declaration. Its name is the name specified by the document type declaration for the root element. Also, it has a (possibly null) public identifier, a required system identifier, an internal DTD subset (which is possibly null), a parent (the document node that contains the document type node), and lists of DTD-declared notations and general entities. Its value is always set to null.

- *Element node*: A document's element. It has a name, a local name, a (possibly null) prefix, and a namespace URI, which is null when the element doesn't belong to any namespace. An element node contains children, including text nodes, and even comment and processing instruction nodes.

- *Entity node*: The parsed and unparsed entities that are declared in a document's DTD. When a parser reads a DTD, it attaches a map of entity nodes (indexed by entity name) to the document type node. An entity node has a name and a system identifier, and can also have a public identifier if one appears in the DTD. Finally, when the parser reads the entity, the entity node is given a list of read-only child nodes that contain the entity's replacement text.

- *Entity reference node*: A reference to a DTD-declared entity. Each entity reference node has a name and is included in the tree when the parser doesn't replace entity references with their values. The parser never includes entity reference nodes for character references (such as & or Σ) because they're replaced by their respective characters and included in a text node.

- *Notation node*: A DTD-declared notation. A parser that reads the DTD attaches a map of notation nodes (indexed by notation name) to the document type node. Each notation node has a name and a public identifier or a system identifier, whichever identifier was used to declare the notation in the DTD. Notation nodes don't have children.

- *Processing instruction node*: A processing instruction that appears in the document. It has a name (the instruction's target), a string value (the instruction's data), and a parent (its containing node).

- *Text node*: Document content. Its name is #text and it represents a portion of an element's content when an intervening node (such as a comment) must be created. Characters such as < and & that are represented in the document via character references are replaced by the literal characters they represent. When these nodes are written to a document, these characters must be escaped.

Although these node types store considerable information about an XML document, there are limitations, such as not exposing whitespace outside of the root element. Also, most DTD or schema information, such as element types (<!ELEMENT...>) and attribute types (<xs:attribute...>), cannot be accessed through the DOM.

DOM Level 3 addresses some of the DOM's various limitations. For example, although DOM doesn't provide a node type for the XML declaration, DOM Level 3 makes it possible to access the XML declaration's version, encoding, and standalone attribute values via attributes of the document node.

> **Note** Nonroot nodes never exist in isolation. For example, it's never the case for an element node to not belong to a document or to a document fragment. Even when such nodes are disconnected from the main tree, they remain aware of the document or document fragment to which they belong.

Exploring the DOM API

Java implements DOM through the javax.xml.parsers package's abstract DocumentBuilder and DocumentBuilderFactory classes and the nonabstract FactoryConfigurationError and ParserConfigurationException classes. The org.w3c.dom, org.w3c.dom.bootstrap, org.w3c.dom.events, org.w3c.dom.ls, and org.w3c.dom.views packages provide various types that augment this implementation.

Obtaining a DOM Parser/Document Builder

A DOM parser is also known as a *document builder* because of its dual role in parsing and creating XML documents. You obtain a DOM parser/ document builder by first instantiating DocumentBuilderFactory, by calling one of its newInstance() class methods. For example, the following code fragment invokes DocumentBuilderFactory's DocumentBuilderFactory newInstance() class method:

```
DocumentBuilderFactory dbf = DocumentBuilderFactory.newInstance();
```

Behind the scenes, newInstance() follows an ordered lookup procedure to identify the DocumentBuilderFactory implementation class to load. This procedure first examines the javax.xml.parsers.DocumentBuilderFactory system property and lastly chooses the Java platform's default DocumentBuilderFactory implementation class when no other class is found.

If an implementation class isn't available (perhaps the class identified by the `javax.xml.parsers.DocumentBuilderFactory` system property doesn't exist) or cannot be instantiated, `newInstance()` throws an instance of the `FactoryConfigurationError` class. Otherwise, it instantiates the class and returns its instance.

After obtaining a `DocumentBuilderFactory` instance, you can call various configuration methods to configure the factory. For example, you could call `DocumentBuilderFactory`'s void `setNamespaceAware(boolean awareness)` method with a `true` argument to tell the factory that any returned document builder must provide support for XML namespaces. You can also call void `setValidating(boolean validating)` with `true` as the argument to validate documents against their DTDs, or call void `setSchema(Schema schema)` to validate documents against the `javax.xml.validation.Schema` instance identified by `schema`.

VALIDATION API

Schema is a member of Java's Validation API, which decouples document parsing from validation, making it easier for applications to take advantage of specialized validation libraries that support additional schema languages (such as Relax NG—see `http://en.wikipedia.org/wiki/RELAX_NG`), and making it easier to specify the location of a schema.

The Validation API is associated with the `javax.xml.validation` package, which also includes `SchemaFactory`, `SchemaFactoryLoader`, `TypeInfoProvider`, `Validator`, and `ValidatorHandler`. Schema is the central class and represents an immutable in-memory representation of a grammar.

DOM supports the Validation API via `DocumentBuilderFactory`'s void `setSchema(Schema schema)` and Schema `getSchema()` methods. Similarly, SAX 1.0 supports Validation via `javax.xml.parsers.SAXParserFactory`'s void `setSchema(Schema schema)` and Schema `getSchema()` methods. SAX 2.0 and StAX (see Chapter 4) don't support the Validation API.

The following code fragment demonstrates the Validation API in a DOM context:

```
// Parse an XML document into a DOM tree.
DocumentBuilder parser =
    DocumentBuilderFactory.newInstance().newDocumentBuilder();
Document document = parser.parse(new File("instance.xml"));
// Create a SchemaFactory capable of understanding W3C XML Schema (WXS).
    SchemaFactory factory =
SchemaFactory.newInstance(XMLConstants.W3C_XML_SCHEMA_NS_URI);
// Load a WXS schema, represented by a Schema instance.
Source schemaFile = new StreamSource(new File("mySchema.xsd"));
```

```
Schema schema = factory.newSchema(schemaFile);
// Create a Validator instance, which is used to validate an XML document.
Validator validator = schema.newValidator();
// Validate the DOM tree.
try
{
    validator.validate(new DOMSource(document));
}
catch (SAXException saxe)
{
    // XML document is invalid!
}
```

This example refers to XSLT types such as Source. I explore XSLT in Chapter 6.

After the factory has been configured, call its DocumentBuilder newDocumentBuilder() method to return a document builder that supports the configuration, as demonstrated here:

```
DocumentBuilder db = dbf.newDocumentBuilder();
```

If a document builder cannot be returned (perhaps the factory cannot create a document builder that supports XML namespaces), this method throws a ParserConfigurationException instance.

Parsing and Creating XML Documents

Assuming that you've successfully obtained a document builder, what happens next depends on whether you want to parse or create an XML document.

DocumentBuilder provides several overloaded parse() methods for parsing an XML document into a node tree. These methods differ in how they obtain the document. For example, Document parse(String uri) parses the document that's identified by its string-based URI argument.

> **Note**   Each parse() method throws java.lang.IllegalArgumentException when null is passed as the method's first argument, java.io.IOException when an input/output error occurs, and org.xml.sax.SAXException when the document cannot be parsed. This last exception type indicates that DocumentBuilder's parse() methods rely on SAX to take care of the actual parsing work. Because they are more involved in building the node tree, DOM parsers are commonly referred to as *document builders*.

`DocumentBuilder` also declares the abstract `Document newDocument()` method for creating a document tree.

The returned `org.w3c.dom.Document` object provides access to a parsed document through methods such as `DocumentType getDoctype()`, which makes the document type declaration available through the `org.w3c.dom.DocumentType` interface. Conceptually, `Document` is the root of the document's node tree. It also declares various "create" and other methods for creating a node tree. For example, `Element createElement(String tagName)` creates an element named `tagName`, returning a new `org.w3c.dom.Element` object with the specified name but with its local name, prefix, and namespace URI set to null.

> **Note** Apart from `DocumentBuilder`, `DocumentBuilderFactory`, and a few other classes, DOM is based on interfaces, of which `Document` and `DocumentType` are examples. Behind the scenes, DOM methods (such as the `parse()` methods) return objects whose classes implement these interfaces.

`Document` and all other `org.w3c.dom` interfaces that describe different kinds of nodes are subinterfaces of the `org.w3c.dom.Node` interface. As such, they inherit `Node`'s constants and methods.

`Node` declares 12 constants that represent the various kinds of nodes; `ATTRIBUTE_NODE` and `ELEMENT_NODE` are examples. To identify the kind of node represented by a given `Node` object, call `Node`'s short `getNodeType()` method and compare the returned value to one of these constants.

> **Note** The rationale for using `getNodeType()` and these constants, instead of using `instanceof` and a class name, is that DOM (the object model, not the Java DOM API) was designed to be language independent, and languages such as AppleScript don't have the equivalent of `instanceof`.

`Node` declares several methods for getting and setting common node properties. These methods include `String getNodeName()`, `String getLocalName()`, `String getNamespaceURI()`, `String getPrefix()`, `void setPrefix(String prefix)`, `String getNodeValue()`, and `void setNodeValue(String nodeValue)`, which let you get and (for some properties) set a node's name (such as #text), local name, namespace URI, prefix, and normalized string value.

> **Note** Various Node methods (such as `setPrefix()` and `getNodeValue()`)
> throw an instance of the `org.w3c.dom.DOMException` class when
> something goes wrong. For example, `setPrefix()` throws this exception
> when the `prefix` argument contains an illegal character, the node is read-
> only, or the argument is malformed. Similarly, `getNodeValue()` throws
> `DOMException` when `getNodeValue()` would return more characters than
> can fit into a `DOMString` (a W3C type) variable on the implementation platform.
> `DOMException` declares a series of constants (such as `DOMSTRING_SIZE_ERR`)
> that classify the reason for the exception.

Node declares several methods for navigating the node tree. Three of its
navigation methods are described here:

- boolean `hasChildNodes()` returns true when a node has
  child nodes.

- Node `getFirstChild()` returns the node's first child.

- Node `getLastChild()` returns the node's last child.

For nodes with multiple children, you'll find the `NodeList getChildNodes()`
method to be handy. This method returns an `org.w3c.dom.NodeList` instance
whose int `getLength()` method returns the number of nodes in the list,
and whose `Node item(int index)` method returns the node at the indexth
position in the list (or null when index's value isn't valid—it's less than zero
or greater than or equal to `getLength()`'s value).

Node declares four methods for modifying the tree by inserting, removing,
replacing, and appending child nodes:

- Node `insertBefore (Node newChild, Node refChild)`
  inserts newChild before the existing node specified by
  refChild and returns newChild.

- Node `removeChild (Node oldChild)` removes the child
  node identified by oldChild from the tree and returns
  oldChild.

- Node `replaceChild (Node newChild, Node oldChild)`
  replaces oldChild with newChild and returns oldChild.

- Node `appendChild (Node newChild)` adds newChild to
  the end of the current node's child nodes and returns
  newChild.

Finally, Node declares several utility methods, including Node cloneNode(boolean deep) (create and return a duplicate of the current node, recursively cloning its subtree when true is passed to deep), and void normalize() (descend the tree from the given node and merge all adjacent text nodes, deleting those text nodes that are empty).

> **Tip**   To obtain an element node's attributes, first call Node's NamedNodeMap getAttributes() method. This method returns an org.w3c.dom. NamedNodeMap implementation when the node represents an element; otherwise, it returns null. As well as declaring methods for accessing these nodes by name (such as Node getNamedItem (String name)), NamedNodeMap declares int getLength() and Node item(int index) methods for returning all attribute nodes by index. You then obtain the Node's name by calling a method such as getNodeName().

As well as inheriting Node's constants and methods, Document declares its own methods. For example, you can call Document's String getXmlEncoding(), boolean getXmlStandalone(), and String getXmlVersion() methods to return the XML declaration's encoding, standalone, and version attribute values, respectively.

Document declares three methods for locating one or more elements:

- Element getElementById(String elementId) returns the element that has an id attribute (as in <img id=...>) matching the value specified by elementId.

- NodeList getElementsByTagName(String tagname) returns a nodelist of a document's elements (in document order) matching the specified tagName.

- NodeList getElementsByTagNameNS(String namespaceURI,String localName) is equivalent to the second method except in adding to the nodelist only those elements matching localName and namespaceURI values. Pass "*" to namespaceURI to match all namespaces; pass "*" to localName to match all local names.

The returned element node and each element node in the list implement the Element interface. This interface declares methods to return nodelists of descendent elements in the tree, attributes associated with the element, and more. For example, String getAttribute(String name) returns the value of the attribute identified by name, whereas Attr getAttributeNode(String name) returns an attribute node by name. The returned node is an implementation of the org.w3c.dom.Attr interface.

Demonstrating the DOM API

You now have enough information to explore applications for parsing and creating XML documents. Listing 3-1 presents the source code to a DOM-based parsing application.

Listing 3-1. DOMDemo (Version 1)

```java
import java.io.IOException;

import javax.xml.parsers.DocumentRuilder;
import javax.xml.parsers.DocumentBuilderFactory;
import javax.xml.parsers.FactoryConfigurationError;
import javax.xml.parsers.ParserConfigurationException;

import org.w3c.dom.Attr;
import org.w3c.dom.Document;
import org.w3c.dom.Element;
import org.w3c.dom.NamedNodeMap;
import org.w3c.dom.Node;
import org.w3c.dom.NodeList;
import org.xml.sax.SAXException;

public class DOMDemo
{
    public static void main(String[] args)
    {
        if (args.length != 1)
        {
            System.err.println("usage: java DOMDemo xmlfile");
            return;
        }
        try
        {
            DocumentBuilderFactory dbf = DocumentBuilderFactory.newInstance();
            dbf.setNamespaceAware(true);
            DocumentBuilder db = dbf.newDocumentBuilder();
            Document doc = db.parse(args[0]);
            System.out.printf("Version = %s%n", doc.getXmlVersion());
            System.out.printf("Encoding = %s%n", doc.getXmlEncoding());
            System.out.printf("Standalone = %b%n%n", doc.getXmlStandalone());
            if (doc.hasChildNodes())
            {
                NodeList nl = doc.getChildNodes();
                for (int i = 0; i < nl.getLength(); i++)
```

```java
      {
          Node node = nl.item(i);
          if (node.getNodeType() == Node.ELEMENT_NODE)
              dump((Element) node);
      }
   }
}
catch (IOException ioe)
{
   System.err.println("IOE: " + ioe);
}
catch (SAXException saxe)
{
   System.err.println("SAXE: " + saxe);
}
catch (FactoryConfigurationError fce)
{
   System.err.println("FCE: " + fce);
}
catch (ParserConfigurationException pce)
{
   System.err.println("PCE: " + pce);
}
}

static void dump(Element e)
{
   System.out.printf("Element: %s, %s, %s, %s%n", e.getNodeName(),
                     e.getLocalName(), e.getPrefix(),
                     e.getNamespaceURI());
   NamedNodeMap nnm = e.getAttributes();
   if (nnm != null)
      for (int i = 0; i < nnm.getLength(); i++)
      {
         Node node = nnm.item(i);
         Attr attr = e.getAttributeNode(node.getNodeName());
         System.out.printf("  Attribute %s = %s%n", attr.getName(),
                           attr.getValue());
      }
   NodeList nl = e.getChildNodes();
   for (int i = 0; i < nl.getLength(); i++)
   {
      Node node = nl.item(i);
      if (node instanceof Element)
         dump((Element) node);
   }
}
}
```

DOMDemo's `main()` method first verifies that one command-line argument (the name of an XML document) has been specified. It then creates a document builder factory, informs the factory that it wants a namespace-aware document builder, and has the factory return this document builder.

Continuing, `main()` parses the document into a node tree; outputs the XML declaration's version number, encoding, and standalone attribute values; and recursively dumps all element nodes (starting with the root node) and their attribute values.

Notice the use of getNodeType() in one part of this listing and `instanceof` in another part. The getNodeType() method call isn't necessary (it's only present for demonstration) because `instanceof` can be used instead. However, the cast from `Node` type to `Element` type in the dump() method calls is necessary.

Compile Listing 3-1 as follows:

```
javac DOMDemo.java
```

Run the resulting application to dump Listing 1-3's article XML content, as follows:

```
java DOMDemo article.xml
```

You should observe the following output:

```
Version = 1.0
Encoding = null
Standalone = false

Element: article, article, null, null
  Attribute lang = en
  Attribute title = The Rebirth of JavaFX
Element: abstract, abstract, null, null
Element: code-inline, code-inline, null, null
Element: body, body, null, null
```

Each `Element`-prefixed line presents the node name, followed by the local name, followed by the namespace prefix, followed by the namespace URI. The node and local names are identical because namespaces aren't being used. For the same reason, the namespace prefix and namespace URI are null.

Continuing, execute the following command to dump Listing 1-5's recipe content:

```
java DOMDemo recipe.xml
```

This time, you observe the following output, which includes namespace information:

```
Version = 1.0
Encoding = null
Standalone = false

Element: h:html, html, h, http://www.w3.org/1999/xhtml
   Attribute xmlns:h = http://www.w3.org/1999/xhtml
   Attribute xmlns:r = http://www.javajeff.ca/
Element: h:head, head, h, http://www.w3.org/1999/xhtml
Element: h:title, title, h, http://www.w3.org/1999/xhtml
Element: h:body, body, h, http://www.w3.org/1999/xhtml
Element: r:recipe, recipe, r, http://www.javajeff.ca/
Element: r:title, title, r, http://www.javajeff.ca/
Element: r:ingredients, ingredients, r, http://www.javajeff.ca/
Element: h:ul, ul, h, http://www.w3.org/1999/xhtml
Element: h:li, li, h, http://www.w3.org/1999/xhtml
Element: r:ingredient, ingredient, r, http://www.javajeff.ca/
   Attribute qty = 2
Element: h:li, li, h, http://www.w3.org/1999/xhtml
Element: r:ingredient, ingredient, r, http://www.javajeff.ca/
Element: h:li, li, h, http://www.w3.org/1999/xhtml
Element: r:ingredient, ingredient, r, http://www.javajeff.ca/
   Attribute qty = 2
Element: h:p, p, h, http://www.w3.org/1999/xhtml
Element: r:instructions, instructions, r, http://www.javajeff.ca/
```

Listing 3-2 presents another version of the DOMDemo application that briefly demonstrates the creation of a document tree.

Listing 3-2. DOMDemo (Version 2)

```java
import javax.xml.parsers.DocumentBuilder;
import javax.xml.parsers.DocumentBuilderFactory;
import javax.xml.parsers.FactoryConfigurationError;
import javax.xml.parsers.ParserConfigurationException;

import org.w3c.dom.Document;
import org.w3c.dom.Element;
import org.w3c.dom.Node;
import org.w3c.dom.NodeList;
import org.w3c.dom.Text;
```

```java
public class DOMDemo
{
   public static void main(String[] args)
   {
      try
      {
         DocumentBuilderFactory dbf = DocumentBuilderFactory.newInstance();
         DocumentBuilder db = dbf.newDocumentBuilder();
         Document doc = db.newDocument();
         // Create the root element.
         Element root = doc.createElement("movie");
         doc.appendChild(root);
         // Create name child element and add it to the root.
         Element name = doc.createElement("name");
         root.appendChild(name);
         // Add a text element to the name element.
         Text text = doc.createTextNode("Le Fabuleux Destin d'Amélie " + ↵
         "Poulain"); name.appendChild(text);
         // Create language child element and add it to the root.
         Element language = doc.createElement("language");
         root.appendChild(language);
         // Add a text element to the language element.
         text = doc.createTextNode("français");
         language.appendChild(text);
         System.out.printf("Version = %s%n", doc.getXmlVersion());
         System.out.printf("Encoding = %s%n", doc.getXmlEncoding());
         System.out.printf("Standalone = %b%n%n", doc.getXmlStandalone());
         NodeList nl = doc.getChildNodes();
         for (int i = 0; i < nl.getLength(); i++)
         {
            Node node = nl.item(i);
            if (node.getNodeType() == Node.ELEMENT_NODE)
               dump((Element) node);
         }
      }
      catch (FactoryConfigurationError fce)
      {
         System.err.println("FCE: " + fce);
      }
      catch (ParserConfigurationException pce)
      {
         System.err.println("PCE: " + pce);
      }
   }
```

```java
static void dump(Element e)
{
    System.out.printf("Element: %s, %s, %s, %s%n", e.getNodeName(),
e.getLocalName(), e.getPrefix(),  e.getNamespaceURI());
    NodeList nl = e.getChildNodes();
    for (int i = 0; i < nl.getLength(); i++)
    {
        Node node = nl.item(i);
        if (node instanceof Element)
            dump((Element) node);
        else
        if (node instanceof Text)
            System.out.printf("Text: %s%n", ((Text) node).getWholeText());
    }
  }
}
```

DOMDemo creates Listing 1-2's movie document. It uses Document's
createElement() method to create the root movie element and movie's
name and language child elements. It also uses Document's Text
createTextNode(String data) method to create text nodes that are
attached to the name and language nodes. Notice the calls to Node's
appendChild() method, to append child nodes (such as name) to parent
nodes (such as movie) .

After creating this tree, DOMDemo outputs the tree's element nodes and other
information. This output is as follows:

```
Version = 1.0
Encoding = null
Standalone = false

Element: movie, null, null, null
Element: name, null, null, null
Text: Le Fabuleux Destin d'Amélie Poulain
Element: language, null, null, null
Text: français
```

There's one problem with the output: the XML declaration's encoding
attribute hasn't been set to ISO-8859-1. You cannot accomplish this task via
the DOM API. Instead, you need to use the XSLT API. While exploring XSLT
in Chapter 6, you'll learn how to set the encoding attribute, and you'll also
learn how to output this tree to an XML document file.

EXERCISES

The following exercises are designed to test your understanding of Chapter 3's content.

1. Define DOM.

2. True or false: Java 8 supports DOM Levels 1 and 2 only.

3. Identify the 12 types of DOM nodes.

4. How do you obtain a document builder?

5. How do you use a document builder to parse an XML document?

6. True or false: Document and all other org.w3c.dom interfaces that describe different kinds of nodes are subinterfaces of the Node interface.

7. How do you use a document builder to create a new XML document?

8. How would you determine If a node has children?

9. True or false: When creating a new XML document, you can use the DOM API to specify the XML declaration's encoding attribute.

10. Exercise 2-12 asked you to create a DumpUserInfo application that uses SAX to parse the user elements in an example tomcat-users. xml file and, for each user element, dump its username, password, and roles attribute values to standard output in a *key = value* format. Recreate this application to use DOM.

11. Create a DOMSearch application that's the equivalent of Exercise 2-13's SAXSearch application.

12. Create a DOMValidate application based on Listing 3-1's DOMDemo source code (plus one new line that enables validation) to validate Exercise 1-22's books.xml content against its DTD. Execute java DOMValidate books.xml to perform the validation. You should observe no errors. However, if you attempt to validate books.xml without the DTD, you should observe errors.

Summary

Document Object Model (DOM) is a Java API for parsing an XML document into an in-memory tree of nodes, and for creating an XML document from a node tree. After a DOM parser creates a tree, an application uses the DOM API to navigate over and extract infoset items from the tree's nodes.

DOM views an XML document as a tree that's composed of several kinds of nodes: attribute, CDATA section, comment, document, document fragment, document type, element, entity, entity reference, notation, processing instruction, and text.

A DOM parser is also known as a document builder because of its dual role in parsing and creating XML documents. You obtain a document builder by first instantiating `DocumentBuilderFactory`. You then invoke the factory's `newDocumentBuilder()` method to return the document builder.

Call one of the document builder's `parse()` methods to parse an XML document into a node tree. Call the various document builder methods that are prefixed with "`create`" (along with a few additional methods) to create an XML document.

Chapter 4 introduces the StAX API for parsing/creating XML documents.

Parsing and Creating XML Documents with StAX

Java also includes the StAX API for parsing and creating XML documents. This chapter introduces you to StAX.

What Is StAX?

Streaming API for XML (StAX) is a Java API for parsing an XML document sequentially from start to finish, and also for creating XML documents. StAX was introduced by Java 6 as an alternative to SAX and DOM, and is located midway between these "polar opposites."

STAX VS. SAX AND DOM

Because Java already supports SAX and DOM for document parsing and DOM for document creation, you might be wondering why another XML API is needed. The following points justify StAX's presence in core Java:

- StAX (like SAX) can be used to parse documents of arbitrary sizes. In contrast, the maximum size of documents parsed by DOM is limited by the available memory, which makes DOM unsuitable for mobile devices with limited amounts of memory.

- StAX (like DOM) can be used to create documents. In contrast to DOM, which can create documents whose maximum size is constrained by available memory, StAX can create documents of arbitrary sizes. SAX cannot be used to create documents.

© Jeff Friesen 2016
J. Friesen, *Java XML and JSON*, DOI 10.1007/978-1-4842-1916-4_4

- StAX (like SAX) makes infoset items available to applications almost immediately. In contrast, these items are not made available by DOM until after it finishes building the tree of nodes.

- StAX (like DOM) adopts the *pull model*, in which the application tells the parser when it's ready to receive the next infoset item. This model is based on the iterator design pattern (see `http://sourcemaking.com/design_patterns/iterator`), which results in an application that's easier to write and debug. In contrast, SAX adopts the *push model*, in which the parser passes infoset items via events to the application, whether or not the application is ready to receive them. This model is based on the observer design pattern (see `http://sourcemaking.com/design_patterns/observer`), which results in an application that's often harder to write and debug.

Summing up, StAX can parse or create documents of arbitrary sizes, makes infoset items available to applications almost immediately, and uses the pull model to put the application in charge. Neither SAX nor DOM offers all of these advantages.

Exploring StAX

Java implements StAX through types stored in the `javax.xml.stream`, `javax.xml.stream.events`, and `javax.xml.stream.util` packages. This section introduces you to various types from the first two packages while showing you how to use StAX to parse and create XML documents.

STREAM-BASED VS. EVENT-BASED READERS AND WRITERS

StAX parsers are known as *document readers*, and StAX document creators are known as *document writers*. StAX classifies document readers and document writers as stream-based or event-based.

A *stream-based reader* extracts the next infoset item from an input stream via a *cursor* (infoset item pointer). Similarly, a *stream-based writer* writes the next infoset item to an output stream at the cursor position. The cursor can point to only one item at a time, and always moves forward, typically by one infoset item.

Stream-based readers and writers are appropriate when writing code for memory-constrained environments such as Java ME because you can use them to create smaller and more efficient code. They also offer better performance for low-level libraries, where performance is important.

An *event-based reader* extracts the next infoset item from an input stream by obtaining an event. Similarly, an *event-based writer* writes the next infoset item to the stream by adding an event to the output stream. In contrast to stream-based readers and writers, event-based readers and writers have no concept of a cursor.

Event-based readers and writers are appropriate for creating XML processing *pipelines* (sequences of components that transform the previous component's input and pass the transformed output to the next component in the sequence), for modifying an event sequence, and more.

Parsing XML Documents

Document readers are obtained by calling the various "create" methods that are declared in the javax.xml.stream.XMLInputFactory class. These creational methods are organized into two categories: methods for creating stream-based readers and methods for creating event-based readers.

Before you can obtain a stream-based or an event-based reader, you need to obtain an instance of the factory by calling one of the newFactory() class methods, such as XMLInputFactory newFactory():

```
XMLInputFactory xmlif = XMLInputFactory.newFactory();
```

> **Note**   You can also call the XMLInputFactory newInstance() class method, but you might not want to do so because its same-named but parameterized companion method has been deprecated to maintain API consistency, and it's possible that newInstance() will be deprecated as well.

The newFactory() methods follow an ordered lookup procedure to locate the XMLInputFactory implementation class. This procedure first examines the javax.xml.stream.XMLInputFactory system property, and lastly chooses the name of the Java platform's default XMLInputFactory implementation class. If this procedure cannot find a classname, or if the class cannot be loaded (or instantiated), the method throws an instance of the javax.xml.stream. FactoryConfigurationError class.

After creating the factory, call XMLInputFactory's void setProperty(String name, Object value) method to set various features and properties as necessary. For example, you might execute xmlif.setProperty(XMLInputFactory.IS_VALIDATING, true); (true is passed as a java.lang.Boolean object via *autoboxing*—see http://docs. oracle.com/javase/tutorial/java/data/autoboxing.html) to request a

DTD-validating stream-based reader. However, the default StAX factory implementation throws java.lang.IllegalArgumentException because it doesn't support DTD validation. Similarly, you might execute xmlif.setProperty(XMLInputFactory.IS_NAMESPACE_AWARE, true); to request a namespace-aware event-based reader, which is supported.

Parsing Documents with Stream-Based Readers

A stream-based reader is created by calling one of XMLInputFactory's createXMLStreamReader() methods, such as XMLStreamReader createXMLStreamReader(Reader reader). These methods throw javax.xml.stream.XMLStreamException when the stream-based reader cannot be created.

The following code fragment creates a stream-based reader whose source is a file named recipe.xml:

```
Reader reader = new FileReader("recipe.xml");
XMLStreamReader xmlsr = xmlif.createXMLStreamReader(reader);
```

The low-level javax.xml.stream.XMLStreamReader interface offers the most efficient way to read XML data with StAX. This interface's boolean hasNext() method returns true when there is a next infoset item to obtain; otherwise, it returns false. The int next() method advances the cursor by one infoset item and returns an integer code that identifies this item's type.

Instead of comparing next()'s return value with an integer value, you would compare this value against a javax.xml.stream.XMLStreamConstants infoset constant, such as START_ELEMENT or DTD—XMLStreamReader extends the XMLStreamConstants interface.

> **Note**   You can also obtain the type of the infoset item that the cursor is pointing to by calling XMLStreamReader's int getEventType() method. Specifying "Event" in the name of this method is unfortunate because it confuses stream-based readers with event-based readers.

The following code fragment uses the hasNext() and next() methods to codify a parsing loop that detects the start and end of each element:

```
while (xmlsr.hasNext())
{
   switch (xmlsr.next())
   {
      case XMLStreamReader.START_ELEMENT: // Do something at element start.
      break;
      case XMLStreamReader.END_ELEMENT  : // Do something at element end.
   }
}
```

XMLStreamReader also declares various methods for extracting infoset information. For example, QName getName() returns the qualified name (as a javax.xml.namespace.QName instance) of the element at the cursor position when next() returns XMLStreamReader.START_ELEMENT or XMLStreamReader. END_ELEMENT.

> **Note** QName describes a qualified name as a combination of namespace URI, local part, and prefix components. After instantiating this immutable class (via a constructor such as QName(String namespaceURI, String localPart, String prefix)), you can return these components by calling QName's String getNamespaceURI(), String getLocalPart(), and String getPrefix() methods.

Listing 4-1 presents the source code to a StAXDemo application that reports an XML document's start and end elements via a stream-based reader.

Listing 4-1. StAXDemo (version 1)

```
import java.io.FileNotFoundException;
import java.io.FileReader;

import javax.xml.stream.FactoryConfigurationError;
import javax.xml.stream.XMLInputFactory;
import javax.xml.stream.XMLStreamException;
import javax.xml.stream.XMLStreamReader;

class StAXDemo
{
   public static void main(String[] args)
   {
      if (args.length != 1)
```

```java
    {
        System.err.println("usage: java StAXDemo xmlfile");
        return;
    }
    try
    {
        XMLInputFactory xmlif = XMLInputFactory.newFactory();
        XMLStreamReader xmlsr;
        xmlsr = xmlif.createXMLStreamReader(new FileReader(args[0]));
        while (xmlsr.hasNext())
        {
            switch (xmlsr.next())
            {
                case XMLStreamReader.START_ELEMENT:
                    System.out.println("START_ELEMENT");
                    System.out.println("  Qname = " + xmlsr.getName());
                    break;
                case XMLStreamReader.END_ELEMENT:
                    System.out.println("END_ELEMENT");
                    System.out.println("  Qname = " + xmlsr.getName());
            }
        }
    }
    catch (FactoryConfigurationError fce)
    {
        System.err.println("FCE: " + fce);
    }
    catch (FileNotFoundException fnfe)
    {
        System.err.println("FNFE: " + fnfe);
    }
    catch (XMLStreamException xmlse)
    {
        System.err.println("XMLSE: " + xmlse);
    }
    }
}
```

After verifying the number of command-line arguments, Listing 4-1's
main() method creates a factory, uses the factory to create a stream-based
reader that obtains its XML data from the file identified by the solitary
command-line argument, and enters a parsing loop. Whenever next()
returns XMLStreamReader.START_ELEMENT or XMLStreamReader.END_ELEMENT,
XMLStreamReader's getName() method is called to return the element's
qualified name.

Compile Listing 4-1 as follows:

```
javac StAXDemo.java
```

Run the resulting application to dump Listing 1-2's movie XML content, as follows:

```
java StAXDemo movie.xml
```

You should observe the following output:

```
START_ELEMENT
  Qname = movie
START_ELEMENT
  Qname = name
END_ELEMENT
  Qname = name
START_ELEMENT
  Qname = language
END_ELEMENT
  Qname = language
END_ELEMENT
  Qname = movie
```

> **Note** XMLStreamReader declares a void close() method that you will want to call to free any resources associated with this stream-based reader if your application is designed to run for an extended period of time. Calling this method doesn't close the underlying input source.

Parsing Documents with Event-Based Readers

An event-based reader is created by calling one of XMLInputFactory's createXMLEventReader() methods, such as XMLEventReader createXMLEventReader(Reader reader). These methods throw XMLStreamException when the event-based reader cannot be created.

The following code fragment creates an event-based reader whose source is a file named recipe.xml:

```
Reader reader = new FileReader("recipe.xml");
XMLEventReader xmler = xmlif.createXMLEventReader(reader);
```

The high-level javax.xml.stream.XMLEventReader interface offers a somewhat less efficient but more object-oriented way to read XML data with StAX. This interface's boolean hasNext() method returns true when there is an event to obtain; otherwise, it returns false. The XMLEvent nextEvent() method returns the next event as an object whose class implements a subinterface of the javax.xml.stream.events.XMLEvent interface.

> **Note**   XMLEvent is the base interface for handling markup events. It declares methods that apply to all subinterfaces; for example, Location getLocation() (return a javax.xml.stream.Location object whose int getCharacterOffset() and other methods return location information about the event) and int getEventType() (return the event type as an XMLStreamConstants infoset constant, such as START_ELEMENT and PROCESSING_INSTRUCTION—XMLEvent extends XMLStreamConstants). XMLEvent is subtyped by other javax.xml.stream.events interfaces that describe different kinds of events (such as Attribute) in terms of methods that return infoset item-specific information (such as Attribute's QName getName() and String getValue() methods).

The following code fragment uses the hasNext() and nextEvent() methods to codify a parsing loop that detects the start and end of an element:

```
while (xmler.hasNext())
{
   switch (xmler.nextEvent().getEventType())
   {
      case XMLEvent.START_ELEMENT: // Do something at element start.
                                   break;
      case XMLEvent.END_ELEMENT  : // Do something at element end.
   }
}
```

Listing 4-2 presents the source code to a StAXDemo application that reports an XML document's start and end elements via an event-based reader.

Listing 4-2. StAXDemo (version 2)

```
import java.io.FileNotFoundException;
import java.io.FileReader;

import javax.xml.stream.FactoryConfigurationError;
import javax.xml.stream.XMLEventReader;
import javax.xml.stream.XMLInputFactory;
import javax.xml.stream.XMLStreamException;
```

```java
import javax.xml.stream.events.EndElement;
import javax.xml.stream.events.StartElement;
import javax.xml.stream.events.XMLEvent;

class StAXDemo
{
   public static void main(String[] args)
   {
      if (args.length != 1)
      {
         System.err.println("usage: java StAXDemo xmlfile");
         return;
      }
      try
      {
         XMLInputFactory xmlif = XMLInputFactory.newFactory();
         XMLEventReader xmler;
         xmler = xmlif.createXMLEventReader(new FileReader(args[0]));
         while (xmler.hasNext())
         {
            XMLEvent xmle = xmler.nextEvent();
            switch (xmle.getEventType())
            {
               case XMLEvent.START_ELEMENT:
                  System.out.println("START_ELEMENT");
                  System.out.println("  Qname = " +
                                     ((StartElement) xmle).getName());
                  break;
               case XMLEvent.END_ELEMENT:
                  System.out.println("END_ELEMENT");
                  System.out.println("  Qname = " +
                                     ((EndElement) xmle).getName());
            }
         }
      }
      catch (FactoryConfigurationError fce)
      {
         System.err.println("FCE: " + fce);
      }
      catch (FileNotFoundException fnfe)
      {
         System.err.println("FNFE: " + fnfe);
      }
      catch (XMLStreamException xmlse)
      {
         System.err.println("XMLSE: " + xmlse);
      }
   }
}
```

After verifying the number of command-line arguments, Listing 4-2's `main()` method creates a factory, uses the factory to create an event-based reader that obtains its XML data from the file identified by the solitary command-line argument, and enters a parsing loop. Whenever `nextEvent()` returns `XMLEvent.START_ELEMENT` or `XMLEvent.END_ELEMENT`, `StartElement`'s or `EndElement`'s `getName()` method is called to return the element's qualified name.

After compiling Listing 4-2, run the resulting application to dump Listing 1-3's article XML content, as follows:

```
java StAXDemo article.xml
```

You should observe the following output:

```
START_ELEMENT
   Qname = article
START_ELEMENT
   Qname = abstract
START_ELEMENT
   Qname = code-inline
END_ELEMENT
   Qname = code-inline
END_ELEMENT
   Qname = abstract
START_ELEMENT
   Qname = body
END_ELEMENT
   Qname = body
END_ELEMENT
   Qname = article
```

> **Note**   You can also create a filtered event-based reader to accept or reject various events by calling one of `XMLInputFactory`'s `createFilteredReader()` methods, such as `XMLEventReader create FilteredReader(XMLEventReader reader, EventFilter filter)`. The `javax.xml.stream.EventFilter` interface declares a boolean `accept(XMLEvent event)` method that returns `true` when the specified event is part of the event sequence; otherwise, it returns `false`.

Creating XML Documents

Document writers are obtained by calling the various "create" methods that are declared in the javax.xml.stream.XMLOutputFactory class. These creational methods are organized into two categories: methods for creating stream-based writers and methods for creating event-based writers.

Before you can obtain a stream-based or an event-based writer, you need to obtain an instance of the factory by calling one of the newFactory() class methods, such as XMLOutputFactory newFactory()·

```
XMLOutputFactory xmlof = XMLOutputFactory.newFactory();
```

> **Note** You can also call the XMLOutputFactory newInstance() class method, but you might not want to do so because its same-named but parameterized companion method has been deprecated to maintain API consistency, and it's possible that newInstance() will be deprecated as well.

The newFactory() methods follow an ordered lookup procedure to locate the XMLOutputFactory implementation class. This procedure first examines the javax.xml.stream.XMLOutputFactory system property, and lastly chooses the name of the Java platform's default XMLOutputFactory implementation class. If this procedure cannot find a classname, or if the class cannot be loaded (or instantiated), the method throws an instance of the FactoryConfigurationError class.

After creating the factory, call XMLOutputFactory's void setProperty(String name, Object value) method to set various features and properties as necessary. The only property currently supported by all writers is XMLOutputFactory.IS_REPAIRING_NAMESPACES. When enabled (by passing true or a Boolean object, such as Boolean.TRUE, to value), the document writer takes care of all namespace bindings and declarations, with minimal help from the application. The output is always well formed with respect to namespaces. However, enabling this property adds some overhead to the job of writing the XML.

Creating Documents with Stream-Based Writers

A stream-based writer is created by calling one of XMLOutputFactory's createXMLStreamWriter() methods, such as XMLStreamWriter createXMLStreamWriter(Writer writer). These methods throw XMLStreamException when the stream-based writer cannot be created.

The following code fragment creates a stream-based writer whose destination is a file named `recipe.xml`:

```
Writer writer = new FileWriter("recipe.xml");
XMLStreamWriter xmlsw = xmlof.createXMLStreamWriter(writer);
```

The low-level XMLStreamWriter interface declares several methods for writing infoset items to the destination. The following list describes a few of these methods:

- void close() closes this stream-based writer and frees any associated resources. The underlying writer is not closed.

- void flush() writes any cached data to the underlying writer.

- void setPrefix(String prefix, String uri) identifies the namespace prefix to which the uri value is bound. This prefix is used by variants of the writeStartElement(), writeAttribute(), and writeEmptyElement() methods that take namespace arguments but not prefixes. Also, it remains valid until the writeEndElement() invocation that corresponds to the last writeStartElement() invocation. This method doesn't create any output.

- void writeAttribute(String localName, String value) writes the attribute identified by localName and having the specified value to the underlying writer. A namespace prefix isn't included. This method escapes the & , <, >, and " characters.

- void writeCharacters(String text) writes text's characters to the underlying writer. This method escapes the & , <, and > characters.

- void writeEndDocument() closes any start tags and writes corresponding end tags to the underlying writer.

- void endElement() writes an end tag to the underlying writer, relying on the internal state of the stream-based writer to determine the tag's prefix and local name.

- void writeNamespace(String prefix, String namespaceURI) writes a namespace to the underlying writer. This method must be called to ensure that the namespace specified by setPrefix() and duplicated in this method call is written; otherwise, the resulting document will not be well formed from a namespace perspective.

- void writeStartDocument() writes the XML declaration to the underlying writer.

- void writeStartElement(String namespaceURI, String localName) writes a start tag with the arguments passed to namespaceURI and localName to the underlying writer.

Listing 4-3 presents the source code to a StAXDemo application that creates a recipe.xml file with many of Listing 1-5's infoset items via a stream-based writer.

Listing 4-3. StAXDemo (version 3)

```java
import java.io.FileWriter;
import java.io.IOException;

import javax.xml.stream.FactoryConfigurationError;
import javax.xml.stream.XMLOutputFactory;
import javax.xml.stream.XMLStreamException;
import javax.xml.stream.XMLStreamWriter;

class StAXDemo
{
   public static void main(String[] args)
   {
      try
      {
         XMLOutputFactory xmlof = XMLOutputFactory.newFactory();
         XMLStreamWriter xmlsw;
         xmlsw = xmlof.createXMLStreamWriter(new FileWriter("recipe.xml"));
         xmlsw.writeStartDocument();
         xmlsw.setPrefix("h", "http://www.w3.org/1999/xhtml");
         xmlsw.writeStartElement("http://www.w3.org/1999/xhtml", "html");
         xmlsw.writeNamespace("h", "http://www.w3.org/1999/xhtml");
         xmlsw.writeNamespace("r", "http://www.javajeff.ca/");
         xmlsw.writeStartElement("http://www.w3.org/1999/xhtml", "head");
         xmlsw.writeStartElement("http://www.w3.org/1999/xhtml", "title");
         xmlsw.writeCharacters("Recipe");
         xmlsw.writeEndElement();
         xmlsw.writeEndElement();
         xmlsw.writeStartElement("http://www.w3.org/1999/xhtml", "body");
```

```java
        xmlsw.setPrefix("r", "http://www.javajeff.ca/");
        xmlsw.writeStartElement("http://www.javajeff.ca/", "recipe");
        xmlsw.writeStartElement("http://www.javajeff.ca/", "title");
        xmlsw.writeCharacters("Grilled Cheese Sandwich");
        xmlsw.writeEndElement();
        xmlsw.writeStartElement("http://www.javajeff.ca/",
                                "ingredients");
        xmlsw.setPrefix("h", "http://www.w3.org/1999/xhtml");
        xmlsw.writeStartElement("http://www.w3.org/1999/xhtml", "ul");
        xmlsw.writeStartElement("http://www.w3.org/1999/xhtml", "li");
        xmlsw.setPrefix("r", "http://www.javajeff.ca/");
        xmlsw.writeStartElement("http://www.javajeff.ca/", "ingredient");
        xmlsw.writeAttribute("qty", "2");
        xmlsw.writeCharacters("bread slice");
        xmlsw.writeEndElement();
        xmlsw.setPrefix("h", "http://www.w3.org/1999/xhtml");
        xmlsw.writeEndElement();
        xmlsw.writeEndElement();
        xmlsw.setPrefix("r", "http://www.javajeff.ca/");
        xmlsw.writeEndElement();
        xmlsw.writeEndDocument();
        xmlsw.flush();
        xmlsw.close();
    }
    catch (FactoryConfigurationError fce)
    {
        System.err.println("FCE: " + fce);
    }
    catch (IOException ioe)
    {
        System.err.println("IOE: " + ioe);
    }
    catch (XMLStreamException xmlse)
    {
        System.err.println("XMLSE: " + xmlse);
    }
  }
}
```

Although Listing 4-3 is fairly easy to follow, you might be somewhat confused by the duplication of namespace URIs in the setPrefix() and writeStartElement() method calls. For example, you might be wondering about the duplicate URIs in xmlsw.setPrefix("h", "http://www.w3.org/1999/xhtml"); and its xmlsw.writeStartElement("http://www.w3.org/1999/xhtml", "html"); successor.

The setPrefix() method call creates a mapping between a namespace prefix (the value) and a URI (the key) without generating any output. The writeStartElement() method call specifies the URI key, which this method uses to access the prefix value, which it then prepends (with a colon character) to the html start tag's name before writing this tag to the underlying writer.

Compile Listing 4-3 and run the resulting application. You should discover a recipe.xml file in the current directory.

Creating Documents with Event-Based Writers

An event-based writer is created by calling one of XMLOutputFactory's createXMLEventWriter() methods, such as XMLEventWriter createXMLEventWriter(Writer writer). These methods throw XMLStreamException when the event-based writer cannot be created.

The following code fragment creates an event-based writer whose destination is a file named recipe.xml:

```
Writer writer = new FileWriter("recipe.xml");
XMLEventWriter xmlew = xmlof.createXMLEventWriter(writer);
```

The high-level XMLEventWriter interface declares the void add(XMLEvent event) method for adding events that describe infoset items to the output stream implemented by the underlying writer. Each argument passed to event is an instance of a class that implements a subinterface of XMLEvent (such as Attribute and StartElement).

> **Tip** XMLEventWriter also declares a void add(XMLEventReader reader) method that you can use to chain an XMLEventReader instance to an XMLEventWriter instance.

To save you the trouble of implementing these interfaces, StAX provides javax.xml.stream.EventFactory. This utility class declares various factory methods for creating XMLEvent subinterface implementations. For example, Comment createComment(String text) returns an object whose class implements the javax.xml.stream.events.Comment subinterface of XMLEvent.

Because these factory methods are declared abstract, you must first obtain an instance of the EventFactory class. You can easily accomplish this task by invoking EventFactory's XMLEventFactory newFactory() class method, as follows:

```
XMLEventFactory xmlef = XMLEventFactory.newFactory();
```

You can then obtain an XMLEvent subinterface implementation, as follows:

```
XMLEvent comment = xmlef.createComment("ToDo");
```

Listing 4-4 presents the source code to a StAXDemo application that creates a recipe.xml file with many of Listing 1-5's infoset items via an event-based writer.

Listing 4-4. StAXDemo (version 4)

```java
import java.io.FileWriter;
import java.io.IOException;

import java.util.Iterator;

import javax.xml.stream.FactoryConfigurationError;
import javax.xml.stream.XMLEventFactory;
import javax.xml.stream.XMLEventWriter;
import javax.xml.stream.XMLOutputFactory;
import javax.xml.stream.XMLStreamException;

import javax.xml.stream.events.Attribute;
import javax.xml.stream.events.Namespace;
import javax.xml.stream.events.XMLEvent;

class StAXDemo
{
    public static void main(String[] args)
    {
        try
        {
            XMLOutputFactory xmlof = XMLOutputFactory.newFactory();
            XMLEventWriter xmlew;
            xmlew = xmlof.createXMLEventWriter(new FileWriter("recipe.xml"));
            final XMLEventFactory xmlef = XMLEventFactory.newFactory();
            XMLEvent event = xmlef.createStartDocument();
            xmlew.add(event);
            Iterator<Namespace> nsIter;
            nsIter = new Iterator<Namespace>()
```

```
{
    int index = 0;
    Namespace[] ns;
    {
        ns = new Namespace[2];
        ns[0] = xmlef.
                   createNamespace("h",
                                "http://www.w3.org/1999/xhtml");
        ns[1] = xmlef.
                   createNamespace("r",
                                "http://www.javajeff.ca/");
    }
    @Override
    public boolean hasNext()
    {
        return index != 2;
    }
    @Override
    public Namespace next()
    {
        return ns[index++];
    }
    @Override
    public void remove()
    {
        throw new UnsupportedOperationException();
    }
};
event = xmlef.createStartElement("h",
                                "http://www.w3.org/1999/xhtml",
                                "html", null, nsIter);
xmlew.add(event);
event = xmlef.createStartElement("h",
                                "http://www.w3.org/1999/xhtml",
                                "head");
xmlew.add(event);
event = xmlef.createStartElement("h",
                                "http://www.w3.org/1999/xhtml",
                                "title");
xmlew.add(event);
event = xmlef.createCharacters("Recipe");
xmlew.add(event);
event = xmlef.createEndElement("h",
                                "http://www.w3.org/1999/xhtml",
                                "title");
xmlew.add(event);
```

```
            event = xmlef.createEndElement("h",
                                    "http://www.w3.org/1999/xhtml",
                                    "head");
xmlew.add(event);
            event = xmlef.createStartElement("h",
                                        "http://www.w3.org/1999/xhtml",
                                        "body");
xmlew.add(event);
            event = xmlef.createStartElement("r",
                                        "http://www.javajeff.ca/",
                                        "recipe");
xmlew.add(event);
            event = xmlef.createStartElement("r",
                                        "http://www.javajeff.ca/",
                                        "title");
xmlew.add(event);
            event = xmlef.createCharacters("Grilled Cheese Sandwich");
xmlew.add(event);
            event = xmlef.createEndElement("r",
                                        "http://www.javajeff.ca/",
                                        "title");
xmlew.add(event);
            event = xmlef.createStartElement("r",
                                        "http://www.javajeff.ca/",
                                        "ingredients");
xmlew.add(event);
            event = xmlef.createStartElement("h",
                                        "http://www.w3.org/1999/xhtml",
                                        "ul");
xmlew.add(event);
            event = xmlef.createStartElement("h",
                                        "http://www.w3.org/1999/xhtml",
                                        "li");
xmlew.add(event);
Iterator<Attribute> attrIter;
attrIter = new Iterator<Attribute>()
{
    int index = 0;
    Attribute[] attrs;
    {
        attrs = new Attribute[1];
        attrs[0] = xmlef.createAttribute("qty", "2");
    }
    @Override
    public boolean hasNext()
    {
        return index != 1;
    }
```

```java
            @Override
            public Attribute next()
            {
                return attrs[index++];
            }
            @Override
            public void remove()
            {
                throw new UnsupportedOperationException();
            }
        };
        event = xmlef.createStartElement("r",
                                        "http://www.javajeff.ca/",
                                        "ingredient", attrIter, null);
        xmlew.add(event);
        event = xmlef.createCharacters("bread slice");
        xmlew.add(event);
        event = xmlef.createEndElement("r",
                                        "http://www.javajeff.ca/",
                                        "ingredient");
        xmlew.add(event);
        event = xmlef.createEndElement("h",
                                        "http://www.w3.org/1999/xhtml",
                                        "li");
        xmlew.add(event);
        event = xmlef.createEndElement("h",
                                        "http://www.w3.org/1999/xhtml",
                                        "ul");
        xmlew.add(event);
        event = xmlef.createEndElement("r",
                                        "http://www.javajeff.ca/",
                                        "ingredients");
        xmlew.add(event);
        event = xmlef.createEndElement("r",
                                        "http://www.javajeff.ca/",
                                        "recipe");
        xmlew.add(event);
        event = xmlef.createEndElement("h",
                                        "http://www.w3.org/1999/xhtml",
                                        "body");
        xmlew.add(event);
        event = xmlef.createEndElement("h",
                                        "http://www.w3.org/1999/xhtml",
                                        "html");
        xmlew.add(event);
        xmlew.flush();
        xmlew.close();
    }
```

```
      catch (FactoryConfigurationError fce)
      {
         System.err.println("FCE: " + fce);
      }
      catch (IOException ioe)
      {
         System.err.println("IOE: " + ioe);
      }
      catch (XMLStreamException xmlse)
      {
         System.err.println("XMLSE: " + xmlse);
      }
   }
}
```

Listing 4-4 should be fairly easy to follow; it's the event-based equivalent of Listing 4-3. Notice that this listing includes the creation of java.util.Iterator instances from anonymous classes that implement this interface. These iterators are created to pass namespaces or attributes to XMLEventFactory's StartElement createStartElement(String prefix, String namespaceUri, String localName, Iterator attributes, Iterator namespaces) method. (You can pass null to this parameter when an iterator isn't applicable; for example, when the start tag has no attributes.)

Compile Listing 4-4 and run the resulting application. You should discover a recipe.xml file in the current directory.

EXERCISES

The following exercises are designed to test your understanding of Chapter 4's content.

1. Define StAX.

2. What packages make up the StAX API?

3. True or false: A stream-based reader extracts the next infoset item from an input stream by obtaining an event.

4. How do you obtain a document reader? How do you obtain a document writer?

5. What does a document writer do when you call XMLOutputFactory's void setProperty(String name, Object value) method with XMLOutputFactory.IS_REPAIRING_NAMESPACES as the property name and true as the value?

6. Create a `ParseXMLDoc` application that uses a StAX stream-based
    reader to parse its single command-line argument, an XML document.
    After creating this reader, the application should verify that a
    `START_DOCUMENT` infoset item has been detected, and then enter a
    loop that reads the next item and uses a `switch` statement to output
    a message corresponding to the item that has been read: `ATTRIBUTE`,
    `CDATA`, `CHARACTERS`, `COMMENT`, `DTD`, `END_ELEMENT`,
    `ENTITY_DECLARATION`, `ENTITY_REFERENCE`, `NAMESPACE`,
    `NOTATION_DECLARATION`, `PROCESSING_INSTRUCTION`, `SPACE`,
    or `START_ELEMENT`. When `START_ELEMENT` is detected, output
    this element's name and local name, and output the local names
    and values of all attributes. The loop ends when the `END_DOCUMENT`
    infoset item has been detected. Explicitly close the stream reader
    followed by the file reader upon which it's based. Test this application
    with Exercise 1-21's `books.xml` file.

Summary

StAX is a Java API for parsing an XML document sequentially from start
to finish, and also for creating XML documents. Java implements StAX
through types stored in the `javax.xml.stream`, `javax.xml.stream.events`,
and `javax.xml.stream.util` packages.

StAX parsers are known as document readers, and StAX document creators
are known as document writers. StAX classifies document readers and
document writers as stream-based or event-based.

Document readers are obtained by calling the various "create" methods
that are declared in the `XMLInputFactory` class. Document writers are
obtained by calling the various "create" methods that are declared in the
`XMLOutputFactory` class.

Chapter 5 introduces Java's XPath API for simplifying DOM node access.

Selecting Nodes with XPath

Java includes an XPath API for simplifying access to a DOM tree's nodes. This chapter introduces you to XPath.

What Is XPath?

XPath is a nonXML declarative query language (defined by the W3C) for selecting an XML document's infoset items as one or more nodes. For example, you can use XPath to locate Listing 1-1's third `ingredient` element and return this element node.

As well as simplifying access to a DOM tree's nodes, XPath is commonly used in the context of XSLT (discussed in Chapter 6) where it's typically employed to select (via XPath expressions) those input document elements that are to be copied to an output document. Java 8 supports XPath 1.0, which is assigned package `javax.xml.xpath`.

XPath Language Primer

XPath regards an XML document as a tree of nodes that starts from a root node. This language recognizes seven kinds of nodes: element, attribute, text, namespace, processing instruction, comment, and document. It doesn't recognize CDATA sections, entity references, or document type declarations.

© Jeff Friesen 2016
J. Friesen, *Java XML and JSON*, DOI 10.1007/978-1-4842-1916-4_5

> **Note**   A DOM tree's root node (an `org.w3c.dom.Document` object) isn't the same as a document's root element. The DOM tree's root node contains the entire document, including the root element, any comments or processing instructions that appear before the root element's start tag, and any comments or processing instructions that appear after the root element's end tag.

Location Path Expressions

XPath provides location path expressions for selecting nodes. A *location path expression* locates nodes via a sequence of *steps* starting from the *context node* (the root node or some other document node that's the current node). The returned set of nodes, which is known as a *nodeset*, might be empty, or it might contain one or more nodes.

The simplest location path expression selects the document's root node and consists of a single forward slash character (/). The next simplest location path expression is the name of an element, which selects all child elements of the context node that have that name. For example, `ingredient` refers to all `ingredient` child elements of the context node in Listing 1-1's recipe document. This XPath expression returns a set of three `ingredient` nodes when the context node is `ingredients`. However, if `recipe` or `instructions` happened to be the context node, `ingredient` wouldn't return any nodes (`ingredient` is a child of `ingredients` only). When an expression starts with a forward slash (/), the expression represents an absolute path that starts from the root node. For example, expression `/movie` selects all `movie` child elements of the root node in Listing 1-2's movie document.

Attributes are also handled by location path expressions. To select an element's attribute, specify @ followed by the attribute's name. For example, `@qty` selects the `qty` attribute node of the context node.

In most cases, you'll work with root nodes, element nodes, and attribute nodes. However, you might also need to work with namespace nodes, text nodes, processing-instruction nodes, and comment nodes. Unlike namespace nodes, which are typically handled by XSLT, you'll more likely need to process comments, text, and processing instructions. XPath provides `comment()`, `text()`, and `processing-instruction()` functions for selecting comment, text, and processing-instruction nodes.

The `comment()` and `text()` functions don't require arguments because comment and text nodes don't have names. Each comment is a separate comment node, and each text node specifies the longest run of text not interrupted by a tag. The `processing-instruction()` function may be called with an argument that identifies the target of the processing instruction. If called with no argument, all of the context node's processing-instruction child nodes are selected.

XPath provides three wildcards for selecting unknown nodes:

- * matches any element node regardless of the node's type. It doesn't match attributes, text nodes, comments, or processing-instruction nodes. When you place a namespace prefix before the *, only elements belonging to that namespace are matched.

- node() is a function that matches all nodes.

- @* matches all attribute nodes.

> **Note**   XPath lets you perform multiple selections by using the vertical bar (|). For example, author/*|publisher/* selects the children of author and the children of publisher, and *|@* matches all elements and attributes, but doesn't match text, comment, or processing-instruction nodes.

XPath lets you combine steps into *compound paths* by using the / character to separate them. For paths beginning with /, the first path step is relative to the root node; otherwise, the first path step is relative to another context node. For example, /movie/name starts with the root node, selects all movie element children of the root node, and selects all name children of the selected movie nodes. If you want to return all text nodes of the selected name elements, you specify /movie/name/text().

Compound paths can include // to select nodes from all descendents of the context node (including the context node). When placed at the start of an expression, // selects nodes from the entire tree. For example, //ingredient selects all ingredient nodes in the tree.

As with file systems that let you identify the current directory with a single period (.) and its parent directory with a double period (..), you can specify a single period to represent the current node and a double period to represent the parent of the current node. (You would typically use a single period in XSLT to indicate that you want to access the value of the currently matched element.)

It might be necessary to narrow the selection of nodes returned by an XPath expression. For example, expression /recipe/ingredients/ingredient returns all ingredient nodes, but perhaps you only want to return the first ingredient node. You can narrow the selection by including predicates in the location path.

A *predicate* is a square bracket-delimited Boolean expression that's tested against each selected node. If the expression evaluates to true, that node is included in the set of nodes returned by the XPath expression; otherwise, the node isn't included in the set. For example, `/recipe/ingredients/ingredient[1]` selects the first ingredient element that's a child of the ingredients element.

Predicates can include predefined functions (such as `last()` and `position()`), operators (such as -, <, and =), and other items. Consider the following examples:

- `/recipe/ingredients/ingredient[last()]` selects the last ingredient element that's a child of the ingredients element.

- `/recipe/ingredients/ingredient[last() - 1]` selects the next-to-last ingredient element that's a child of the ingredients element.

- `/recipe/ingredients/ingredient[position() < 3]` selects the first two ingredient elements that are children of the ingredients element.

- `//ingredient[@qty]` selects all ingredient elements (no matter where they're located) that have qty attributes.

- `//ingredient[@qty='1']` or `//ingredient[@qty="1"]` selects all ingredient elements (no matter where they're located) that have qty attributes with value 1.

> **Note**   XPath predefines several functions for use with nodesets: `last()` returns a number identifying the last node, `position()` returns a number identifying a node's position, `count()` returns the number of nodes in its nodeset argument, `id()` selects elements by their unique IDs and returns a nodeset of these elements, `local-name()` returns the local part of the qualified name of the first node in its nodeset argument, `namespace-uri()` returns the namespace part of the qualified name of the first node in its nodeset argument, and `name()` returns the qualified name of the first node in its nodeset argument.

Although predicates are supposed to be Boolean expressions, the predicate might not evaluate to a Boolean value. For example, it could evaluate to a number or a string—XPath supports Boolean, number (IEEE 754 double precision floating-point values), and string expression types as well as a location path expression's nodeset type. If a predicate evaluates to a number, XPath converts that number to true when it equals the context node's position; otherwise, XPath converts that number to false. If a predicate evaluates to a string, XPath converts that string to true when the string isn't empty; otherwise, XPath converts that string to false. Finally, if a predicate evaluates to a nodeset, XPath converts that nodeset to true when the nodeset is nonempty; otherwise, XPath converts that nodeset to false.

> **Note**   The previously presented location path expression examples demonstrate XPath's abbreviated syntax. However, XPath also supports an unabbreviated syntax that's more descriptive of what's happening and is based on an *axis specifier*, which indicates the navigation direction within the XML document's tree representation. For example, where /movie/name selects all movie child elements of the root node followed by all name child elements of the movie elements using the abbreviated syntax, /child::movie/ child::name accomplishes the same task with the expanded syntax. Check out Wikipedia's "XPath" entry (http://en.wikipedia.org/wiki/ XPath_1.0) for more information.

General Expressions

Location path expressions (which return nodesets) are one kind of XPath expression. XPath also supports general expressions that evaluate to Boolean (such as predicates), number, or string type; for example, position() = 2, 6.8, and "Hello". General expressions are often used in XSLT.

XPath Boolean values can be compared via relational operators <, <=, >, >=, =, and != . Boolean expressions can be combined by using operators and and or. Also, XPath predefines the following functions:

- boolean() returns a Boolean value for a number, string, or nodeset.

- not() returns true when its Boolean argument is false and vice versa.

- true() returns true.

- false() returns false.

- lang() returns true or false depending on whether the language of the context node (as specified by xml:lang attributes) is the same as or is a sublanguage of the language specified by the argument string.

XPath numeric values can be manipulated via operators +, -, *, div, and mod (remainder); the forward slash cannot be used for division because it's used to separate location steps. All five operators behave like their Java language counterparts. XPath also predefines the following functions:

- number() converts its argument to a number.

- sum() returns the sum of the numeric values represented by the nodes in its nodeset argument.

- floor() returns the largest (closest to positive infinity) number that's not greater than its number argument and that's an integer.

- ceiling() returns the smallest (closest to negative infinity) number that's not less than its number argument and that's an integer.

- round() returns the number that's closest to the argument and that's an integer. When there are two such numbers, the one closest to positive infinity is returned.

XPath strings are ordered character sequences that are enclosed in single quotes or double quotes. A string literal cannot contain the same kind of quote that's also used to delimit the string. For example, a string that contains a single quote cannot be delimited with single quotes. XPath provides the = and != operators for comparing strings. XPath also predefines the following functions:

- string() converts its argument to a string.

- concat() returns a concatenation of its string arguments.

- starts-with() returns true when its first argument string starts with its second argument string (and otherwise returns false).

- contains() returns true when its first argument string contains its second argument string (and otherwise returns false).

- substring-before() returns the substring of its first argument string that precedes the first occurrence of its second argument string in its first argument string or the empty string when its first argument string doesn't contain its second argument string.

- substring-after() returns the substring of its first argument string that follows the first occurrence of its second argument string in its first argument string or the empty string when its first argument string doesn't contain its second argument string.

- `substring()` returns the substring of its first (string) argument starting at the position specified in its second (number) argument with length specified in its third (number) argument.

- `string-length()` returns the number of characters in its string argument (or the length of the context node when converted to a string in the absence of an argument).

- `normalize-space()` returns the argument string with whitespace normalized by stripping leading and trailing whitespace and replacing sequences of whitespace characters by a single space (or performing the same action on the context node when converted to a string in the absence of an argument).

- `translate()` returns its first argument string with occurrences of characters in its second argument string replaced by the character at the corresponding position in its third argument string.

XPath and DOM

Suppose you need someone in your home to purchase a bag of sugar. You would ask this person to "Please buy me some sugar." Alternatively, you could say the following: "Please open the front door. Walk down to the sidewalk. Turn left. Walk up the sidewalk for three blocks. Turn right. Walk up the sidewalk one block. Enter the store. Go to aisle 7. Walk two meters down the aisle. Pick up a bag of sugar. Walk to a checkout counter. Pay for the sugar. Retrace your steps home." Most people would expect to receive the shorter instruction, and would probably have you committed to an institution if you made a habit out of providing the longer set of instructions.

Traversing a DOM tree of nodes is similar to providing the longer sequence of instructions. In contrast, XPath lets you traverse this tree via a succinct instruction. To see this difference for yourself, consider a scenario where you have an XML-based contacts document that lists your various professional contacts. Listing 5-1 presents a trivial example of such a document.

Listing 5-1. XML-Based Contacts Database

```
<?xml version="1.0"?>
<contacts>
   <contact>
      <name>John Doe</name>
      <city>Chicago</city>
      <city>Denver</city>
   </contact>
```

```
    <contact>
        <name>Jane Doe</name>
        <city>New York</city>
    </contact>
    <contact>
        <name>Sandra Smith</name>
        <city>Denver</city>
        <city>Miami</city>
    </contact>
    <contact>
        <name>Bob Jones</name>
        <city>Chicago</city>
    </contact>
</contacts>
```

Listing 5-1 reveals a simple XML grammar consisting of a contacts root element that contains a sequence of contact elements. Each contact element contains one name element and one or more city elements (various contacts travel frequently and spend a lot of time in each city). To keep the example simple, I'm not providing a DTD or a schema.

Suppose you want to locate and output the names of all contacts that live at least part of each year in Chicago. Listing 5-2 presents the source code to a DOMSearch application that accomplishes this task with the DOM API.

Listing 5-2. Locating Chicago Contacts with the DOM API

```java
import java.io.IOException;

import java.util.ArrayList;
import java.util.List;

import javax.xml.parsers.DocumentBuilder;
import javax.xml.parsers.DocumentBuilderFactory;
import javax.xml.parsers.FactoryConfigurationError;
import javax.xml.parsers.ParserConfigurationException;

import org.w3c.dom.Document;
import org.w3c.dom.Element;
import org.w3c.dom.Node;
import org.w3c.dom.NodeList;

import org.xml.sax.SAXException;

public class DOMSearch
{
    public static void main(String[] args)
    {
```

```java
try
{
   DocumentBuilderFactory dbf = DocumentBuilderFactory.newInstance();
   DocumentBuilder db = dbf.newDocumentBuilder();
   Document doc = db.parse("contacts.xml");
   List<String> contactNames = new ArrayList<String>();
   NodeList contacts = doc.getElementsByTagName("contact");
   for (int i = 0; i < contacts.getLength(); i++)
   {
      Element contact = (Element) contacts.item(i);
      NodeList cities = contact.getElementsByTagName("city");
      boolean chicago = false;
      for (int j = 0; j < cities.getLength(); j++)
      {
         Element city = (Element) cities.item(j);
         NodeList children = city.getChildNodes();
         StringBuilder sb = new StringBuilder();
         for (int k = 0; k < children.getLength(); k++)
         {
            Node child = children.item(k);
            if (child.getNodeType() == Node.TEXT_NODE)
               sb.append(child.getNodeValue());
         }
         if (sb.toString().equals("Chicago"))
         {
            chicago = true;
            break;
         }
      }
      if (chicago)
      {
         NodeList names = contact.getElementsByTagName("name");
         contactNames.add(names.item(0).getFirstChild().
                        getNodeValue());
      }
   }
   for (String contactName: contactNames)
      System.out.println(contactName);
}
catch (IOException ioe)
{
   System.err.println("IOE: " + ioe);
}
catch (SAXException saxe)
{
   System.err.println("SAXE: " + saxe);
}
```

```
      catch (FactoryConfigurationError fce)
      {
         System.err.println("FCE: " + fce);
      }
      catch (ParserConfigurationException pce)
      {
         System.err.println("PCE: " + pce);
      }
   }
}
```

After parsing contacts.xml and building the DOM tree, main() uses Document's getElementsByTagName() method to return an org.w3c.dom.NodeList of contact element nodes. For each member of this list, main() extracts the contact element node, and uses this node with getElementsByTagName() to return a NodeList of the contact element node's city element nodes.

For each member of the cities list, main() extracts the city element node, and uses this node with getElementsByTagName() to return a NodeList of the city element node's child nodes. There's only a single child text node in this example, but the presence of a comment or processing instruction would increase the number of child nodes. For example, <city>Chicago<!--The windy city--></city> increases the number of child nodes to 2.

If the child's node type indicates that it's a text node, the child node's value (obtained via getNodeValue()) is stored in a string builder (Only one child node is stored in the string builder in this example.) If the builder's contents indicate that Chicago has been found, the chicago flag is set to true and execution leaves the cities loop.

If the chicago flag is set when the cities loop exits, the current contact element node's getElementsByTagName() method is called to return a NodeList of the contact element node's name element nodes (of which there should only be one, and which I could enforce through a DTD or schema). It's now a simple matter to extract the first item from this list, call getFirstChild() on this item to return the text node (I assume that only text appears between <name> and </name>), and call getNodeValue() on the text node to obtain its value, which is then added to the contactNames list.

Compile Listing 5-2 as follows:

```
javac DOMSearch.java
```

Run the resulting application as follows:

```
java DOMSearch
```

You should observe the following output:

```
John Doe
Bob Jones
```

Traversing the DOM's tree of nodes is a tedious exercise at best and is error-prone at worst. Fortunately, XPath can greatly simplify this situation.

Before writing the XPath equivalent of Listing 5-2, it helps to define a location path expression. For this example, that expression is //contact[city = "Chicago"]/name/text(), which uses a predicate to select all contact nodes that contain a Chicago city node, then select all child name nodes from these contact nodes, and finally select all child text nodes from these name nodes.

Listing 5-3 presents the source code to an XPathSearch application that uses this XPath expression and Java's XPath API, which consists of various types in the javax.xml.xpath package, to locate Chicago contacts.

Listing 5-3. Locating Chicago Contacts with the XPath API

```java
import java.io.IOException;

import javax.xml.parsers.DocumentBuilder;
import javax.xml.parsers.DocumentBuilderFactory;
import javax.xml.parsers.FactoryConfigurationError;
import javax.xml.parsers.ParserConfigurationException;

import javax.xml.xpath.XPath;
import javax.xml.xpath.XPathConstants;
import javax.xml.xpath.XPathException;
import javax.xml.xpath.XPathExpression;
import javax.xml.xpath.XPathFactory;

import org.w3c.dom.Document;
import org.w3c.dom.NodeList;

import org.xml.sax.SAXException;

public class XPathSearch
{
   public static void main(String[] args)
   {
      try
      {
         DocumentBuilderFactory dbf = DocumentBuilderFactory.newInstance();
         DocumentBuilder db = dbf.newDocumentBuilder();
         Document doc = db.parse("contacts.xml");
         XPathFactory xpf = XPathFactory.newInstance();
```

```
            XPath xp = xpf.newXPath();
            XPathExpression xpe;
            xpe = xp.compile("//contact[city = 'Chicago']/name/text()");
            Object result = xpe.evaluate(doc, XPathConstants.NODESET);
            NodeList nl = (NodeList) result;
            for (int i = 0; i < nl.getLength(); i++)
                System.out.println(nl.item(i).getNodeValue());
        }
        catch (IOException ioe)
        {
            System.err.println("IOE: " + ioe);
        }
        catch (SAXException saxe)
        {
            System.err.println("SAXE: " + saxe);
        }
        catch (FactoryConfigurationError fce)
        {
            System.err.println("FCE: " + fce);
        }
        catch (ParserConfigurationException pce)
        {
            System.err.println("PCE: " + pce);
        }
        catch (XPathException xpe)
        {
            System.err.println("XPE: " + xpe);
        }
    }
}
```

After parsing contacts.xml and building the DOM tree, main() instantiates javax.xml.xpath.XPathFactory by calling its XPathFactory newInstance() method. The resulting XPathFactory instance can be used to set features (such as secure processing, to process XML documents securely) by calling its void setFeature(String name, boolean value) method, create a javax.xml.xpath.XPath object by calling its XPath newXPath() method, and more.

XPath declares an XPathExpression compile(String expression) method for compiling the specified expression (an XPath expression) and returning the compiled expression as an instance of a class that implements the javax.xml.xpath.XPathExpression interface. This method throws javax.xml.xpath.XPathExpressionException (a subclass of javax.xml.xpath.XPathException) when the expression cannot be compiled.

XPath also declares several overloaded `evaluate()` methods for immediately evaluating an expression and returning the result. Because it can take time to evaluate an expression, you might choose to compile a complex expression first (to boost performance) when you plan to evaluate this expression many times.

After compiling the expression, `main()` calls `XPathExpression`'s `Object evaluate(Object item, QName returnType)` method to evaluate the expression. The first argument is the context node for the expression, which happens to be a `Document` instance in the example. The second argument specifies the kind of object returned by `evaluate()` and is set to `javax.xml.xpath.XPathConstants.NODESET`, a qualified name for the XPath 1.0 nodeset type, which is implemented via DOM's `NodeList` interface.

> **Note**   The XPath API maps XPath's Boolean, number, string, and nodeset types to Java's `java.lang.Boolean`, `java.lang.Double`, `java.lang.String`, and `NodeList` types, respectively. When calling an `evaluate()` method, you specify XPath types via `XPathConstants` constants (BOOLEAN, NUMBER, STRING, and NODESET), and the method takes care of returning an object of the appropriate type. `XPathConstants` also declares a NODE constant, which doesn't map to a Java type. Instead, it's used to tell `evaluate()` that you only want the resulting nodeset to contain a single node.

After casting `Object` to `NodeList`, `main()` uses this interface's `getLength()` and `item()` methods to traverse the nodelist. For each item in this list, `getNodeValue()` is called to return the node's value, which is subsequently output.

Compile Listing 5-3 as follows:

```
javac XPathSearch.java
```

Run the resulting application as follows:

```
java XPathSearch
```

You should observe the following output:

```
John Doe
Bob Jones
```

Advanced XPath

The XPath API provides three advanced features to overcome limitations with the XPath 1.0 language. These features are namespace contexts, extension functions and function resolvers, and variables and variable resolvers.

Namespace Contexts

When an XML document's elements belong to a namespace (including the default namespace), any XPath expression that queries the document must account for this namespace. For nondefault namespaces, the expression doesn't need to use the same namespace prefix; it only needs to use the same URI. However, when a document specifies the default namespace, the expression must use a prefix even though the document doesn't use a prefix.

To appreciate this situation, suppose Listing 5-1's <contacts> tag was declared as follows to introduce a default namespace: <contacts xmlns="http://www.javajeff.ca/">. Furthermore, suppose that Listing 5-3 included dbf.setNamespaceAware(true); after the line that instantiates DocumentBuilderFactory. If you were to run the revised XPathSearch application against the revised contacts.xml file, you wouldn't see any output.

You can correct this problem by implementing javax.xml.namespace. NamespaceContext to map an arbitrary prefix to the namespace URI, and then registering this namespace context with the XPath instance. Listing 5-4 presents a minimal implementation of the NamespaceContext interface.

Listing 5-4. Minimally Implementing NamespaceContext

```
import java.util.Iterator;

import javax.xml.XMLConstants;

import javax.xml.namespace.NamespaceContext;

public class NSContext implements NamespaceContext
{
    @Override
    public String getNamespaceURI(String prefix)
    {
        if (prefix == null)
            throw new IllegalArgumentException("prefix is null");
        else
        if (prefix.equals("tt"))
            return "http://www.javajeff.ca/";
```

```
        else
            return null;
    }

    @Override
    public String getPrefix(String uri)
    {
        return null;
    }

    @Override
    public Iterator getPreflxes(String uri)
    {
        return null;
    }
}
```

The getNamespaceURI() method is passed a prefix argument that must be mapped to a URI. When this argument is null, a java.lang. IllegalArgumentException object must be thrown (according to the Java documentation). When the argument is the desired prefix value, the namespace URI is returned.

After instantiating the XPath class, you instantiate NSContext and register this object with the XPath object by calling XPath's void setNamespaceContext(NamespaceContext nsContext) method. For example, you specify xp.setNamespaceContext(new NSContext()); after XPath xp = xpf.newXPath(); to register the NSContext object with xp.

All that's left to accomplish is to apply the prefix to the XPath expression, which now becomes //tt:contact[tt:city='Chicago']/tt:name/text() because the contact, city, and name elements are now part of the default namespace, whose URI is mapped to arbitrary prefix tt in the NSContext instance's getNamespaceURI() method.

Compile and run the revised XPathSearch application and you'll see John Doe followed by Bob Jones on separate lines.

Extension Functions and Function Resolvers

The XPath API lets you define functions (via Java methods) that extend XPath's predefined function repertoire by offering new features not already provided. These Java methods cannot have side effects because XPath functions can be evaluated multiple times and in any order. Furthermore, they cannot override predefined functions; a Java method with the same name as a predefined function is never executed.

Suppose you modify Listing 5-1's XML document to include a `birth` element that records a contact's date of birth information in YYYY-MM-DD format. Listing 5-5 shows the resulting XML file.

Listing 5-5. XML-Based Contacts Database with Birth Information

```
<?xml version="1.0"?>
<contacts xmlns="http://www.javajeff.ca/">
    <contact>
        <name>John Doe</name>
        <birth>1953-01-02</birth>
        <city>Chicago</city>
        <city>Denver</city>
    </contact>
    <contact>
        <name>Jane Doe</name>
        <birth>1965-07-12</birth>
        <city>New York</city>
    </contact>
    <contact>
        <name>Sandra Smith</name>
        <birth>1976-11-22</birth>
        <city>Denver</city>
        <city>Miami</city>
    </contact>
    <contact>
        <name>Bob Jones</name>
        <birth>1958-03-14</birth>
        <city>Chicago</city>
    </contact>
</contacts>
```

Now suppose that you want to select contacts based on birth information. For example, you only want to select contacts whose date of birth is greater than 1960-01-01. Because XPath doesn't provide this function for you, you decide to declare a `date()` extension function. Your first step is to declare a `Date` class that implements the `javax.xml.xpath.XPathFunction` interface—see Listing 5-6.

Listing 5-6. An Extension Function for Returning a Date as a Milliseconds Value

```
import java.text.ParsePosition;
import java.text.SimpleDateFormat;

import java.util.List;

import javax.xml.xpath.XPathFunction;
import javax.xml.xpath.XPathFunctionException;
```

```java
import org.w3c.dom.Node;
import org.w3c.dom.NodeList;

public class Date implements XPathFunction
{
    private final static ParsePosition POS = new ParsePosition(0);

    private SimpleDateFormat sdf = new SimpleDateFormat("yyyy-mm-dd");

    @Override
    public Object evaluate(List args) throws XPathFunctionException
    {
        if (args.size() != 1)
            throw new XPathFunctionException("Invalid number of arguments");
        String value;
        Object o = args.get(0);
        if (o instanceof NodeList)
        {
            NodeList list = (NodeList) o;
            value = list.item(0).getTextContent();
        }
        else
        if (o instanceof String)
            value = (String) o;
        else
            throw new XPathFunctionException("Cannot convert argument type");
        POS.setIndex(0);
        return sdf.parse(value, POS).getTime();
    }
}
```

XPathFunction declares a single Object evaluate(List args) method that
XPath calls when it needs to execute the extension function. evaluate()
is passed a java.util.List of objects that describe the arguments that
were passed to the extension function by the XPath evaluator. Furthermore,
this method returns a value of a type appropriate to the extension function
(date()'s long integer return type is compatible with XPath's number type).

The date() extension function is intended to be called with a single
argument, which is either of type nodeset or of type string. This extension
function throws javax.xml.xpath.XPathFunctionException when the
number of arguments (as indicated by the list's size) isn't equal to 1.

When the argument is of type NodeList (a nodeset), the textual content
of the first node in the nodeset is obtained; this content is assumed to
be a date value in YYYY-MM-DD format (for brevity, I'm overlooking error
checking). When the argument is of type String, it's assumed to be a
date value in this format. Any other type of argument results in a thrown
XPathFunctionException object.

Date comparison is simplified by converting the date to a milliseconds value. This task is accomplished with the help of the java.text.SimpleDateFormat and java.text.ParsePosition classes. After resetting the ParsePosition object's index (via setIndex(0)), SimpleDateFormat's Date parse(String text, ParsePosition pos) method is called to parse the string according to the pattern established when SimpleDateFormat was instantiated, and starting from the parse position identified by the ParsePosition index. This index is reset before the parse() method call because parse() updates this object's index.

The parse() method returns a java.util.Date object whose long getTime() method is called to return the number of milliseconds represented by the parsed date.

After implementing the extension function, you need to create a *function resolver*, which is an object whose class implements the javax.xml. xpath.XPathFunctionResolver interface, and which tells the XPath evaluator about the extension function (or functions). Listing 5-7 presents the DateResolver class.

Listing 5-7. A Function Resolver for the date() Extension Function

```
import javax.xml.namespace.QName;

import javax.xml.xpath.XPathFunction;
import javax.xml.xpath.XPathFunctionResolver;

public class DateResolver implements XPathFunctionResolver
{
    private static final QName name = new QName("http://www.javajeff.ca/",
                                                "date", "tt");

    @Override
    public XPathFunction resolveFunction(QName name, int arity)
    {
        if (name.equals(this.name) && arity == 1)
            return new Date();
        return null;
    }
}
```

XPathFunctionResolver declares a single XPathFunction resolveFunction(QName functionName, int arity) method that XPath calls to identify the name of the extension function and obtain an instance of a Java object whose evaluate() method implements the function.

The functionName parameter identifies the function's qualified name because all extension functions must live in a namespace and must be referenced via a prefix (which doesn't have to match the prefix in the document). As a result, you must also bind a namespace to the prefix via a namespace context (as demonstrated previously). The arity parameter identifies the number of arguments that the extension function accepts and is useful when overloading extension functions. If the functionName and arity values are acceptable, the extension function's Java class is instantiated and returned; otherwise, null is returned.

Finally, the function resolver class is instantiated and registered with the XPath object by calling XPath's void setXPathFunctionResolver(XPathFunctionResolver resolver) method.

The following excerpt from Version 3 of this chapter's XPathSearch application (in this book's code archive) demonstrates all of these tasks in order to use date() in XPath expression //tt:contact[tt:date(tt:birth) > tt:date('1960-01-01')]/tt:name/text(), which returns only those contacts whose date of birth is greater than 1960-01-01 (Jane Doe followed by Sandra Smith):

```
DocumentBuilderFactory dbf = DocumentBuilderFactory.newInstance();
dbf.setNamespaceAware(true);
DocumentBuilder db = dbf.newDocumentBuilder();
Document doc = db.parse("contacts.xml");
XPathFactory xpf = XPathFactory.newInstance();
XPath xp = xpf.newXPath();
xp.setNamespaceContext(new NSContext());
xp.setXPathFunctionResolver(new DateResolver());
XPathExpression xpe;
String expr;
expr = "//tt:contact[tt:date(tt:birth) > tt:date('1960-01-01')]" +
       "/tt:name/text()";
xpe = xp.compile(expr);
Object result = xpe.evaluate(doc, XPathConstants.NODESET);
NodeList nl = (NodeList) result;
for (int i = 0; i < nl.getLength(); i++)
   System.out.println(nl.item(i).getNodeValue());
```

Compile and run the revised XPathSearch application and you'll see Jane Doe followed by Sandra Smith on separate lines.

Variables and Variable Resolvers

All of the previously specified XPath expressions have been based on literal text. XPath also lets you specify variables to parameterize these expressions in a similar manner to using variables with SQL prepared statements.

A variable appears in an expression by prefixing its name (which may or may not have a namespace prefix) with a $. For example, /a/b[@c = $d]/text() is an XPath expression that selects all a elements of the root node, and all of a's b elements that have c attributes containing the value identified by variable $d, and returns the text of these b elements. This expression corresponds to Listing 5-8's XML document.

Listing 5-8. A Simple XML Document for Demonstrating an XPath Variable

```
<?xml version="1.0"?>
<a>
   <b c="x">b1</b>
   <b>b2</b>
   <b c="y">b3</b>
   <b>b4</b>
   <b c="x">b5</b>
</a>
```

To specify variables whose values are obtained during expression evaluation, you must register a variable resolver with your XPath object. A *variable resolver* is an instance of a class that implements the javax.xml.xpath.XPathVariableResolver interface in terms of its Object resolveVariable(QName variableName) method, and which tells the evaluator about the variable (or variables).

The variableName parameter contains the qualified name of a variable's name. (Remember that a variable name may be prefixed with a namespace prefix.) This method verifies that the qualified name appropriately names the variable and then returns its value.

After creating the variable resolver, you register it with the XPath object by calling XPath's void setXPathVariableResolver(XPathVariableResolver resolver) method.

The following excerpt from Version 4 of this chapter's XPathSearch application (in this book's code archive) demonstrates all of these tasks in order to specify $d in XPath expression /a/b[@c=$d]/text(), which returns b1 followed by b5. It assumes that Listing 5-8 is stored in a file named example.xml:

```
DocumentBuilderFactory dbf = DocumentBuilderFactory.newInstance();
DocumentBuilder db = dbf.newDocumentBuilder();
Document doc = db.parse("example.xml");
XPathFactory xpf = XPathFactory.newInstance();
XPath xp = xpf.newXPath();
XPathVariableResolver xpvr;
xpvr = new XPathVariableResolver()
        {
            @Override
            public Object resolveVariable(QName varname)
```

```
        {
            if (varname.getLocalPart().equals("d"))
                return "x";
            else
                return null;
        }
    };
xp.setXPathVariableResolver(xpvr);
XPathExpression xpe;
xpe = xp.compile("/a/b[@c = $d]/text()");
Object result = xpe.evaluate(doc, XPathConstants.NODESET);
NodeList nl = (NodeList) result;
for (int i = 0; i < nl.getLength(); i++)
   System.out.println(nl.item(i).getNodeValue());
```

Compile and run the revised XPathSearch application and you'll see b1 followed by b5 on separate lines.

> **Caution**   When you qualify a variable name with a namespace prefix (as in $ns:d), you must also register a namespace context to resolve the prefix.

EXERCISES

The following exercises are designed to test your understanding of Chapter 5's content.

1. Define XPath.
2. Where is XPath commonly used?
3. Identify the seven kinds of nodes that XPath recognizes.
4. True or false: XPath recognizes CDATA sections.
5. Describe what XPath provides for selecting nodes.
6. True or false: In a location path expression, you must prefix an attribute name with the @ symbol.
7. Identify the functions that XPath provides for selecting comment, text, and processing-instruction nodes.
8. What does XPath provide for selecting unknown nodes?
9. How do you perform multiple selections?
10. What is a predicate?
11. Identify the functions that XPath provides for working with nodesets.

12. Identify the three advanced features that XPath provides to overcome limitations with the XPath 1.0 language.

13. True or false: The XPath API maps XPath's number type to `java.lang.Float`.

14. Modify Listing 5-1's contacts document by changing `<name>John Doe</name>` to `<Name>John Doe</Name>`. Because you no longer see John Doe in the output when you run Listing 5-3's `XPathSearch` application (you only see Bob Jones), modify this application's location path expression so that you see John Doe followed by Bob Jones.

Summary

XPath is a nonXML declarative query language for selecting an XML document's infoset items as one or more nodes. It simplifies access to a DOM tree's nodes and is also useful with XSLT where it's typically employed to select those input document elements (via XPath expressions) that are to be copied to an output document.

XPath regards an XML document as a tree of nodes that starts from a root node. This language recognizes seven kinds of nodes: element, attribute, text, namespace, processing instruction, comment, and document. It doesn't recognize CDATA sections, entity references, or document type declarations.

XPath provides location path expressions for selecting nodes. A location path expression locates nodes via a sequence of steps starting from the context node (the root node or some other document node that's the current node). The returned set of nodes, which is known as a nodeset, might be empty, or it might contain one or more nodes.

Location path expressions (which return nodesets) are one kind of XPath expression. XPath also supports general expressions that evaluate to Boolean (such as predicates), number, or string type; for example, `position()` = 2, 6.8, and "Hello". General expressions are often used in XSLT.

The XPath API provides advanced features to overcome limitations with the XPath 1.0 language: namespace contexts (which map arbitrary namespace prefixes to namespace URIs), extension functions and function resolvers (for defining functions that extend XPath's predefined function repertoire), and variables and variable resolvers (for parameterizing XPath expressions).

Chapter 6 introduces you to XSLT for transforming XML documents.

Transforming XML Documents with XSLT

Along with SAX, DOM, StAX, and XPath, Java includes the XSLT API, for transforming XML documents. This chapter introduces you to XSLT.

What Is XSLT?

Extensible Stylesheet Language (XSL) is a family of languages for transforming and formatting XML documents. *XSL Transformation (XSLT)* is the XSL language for transforming XML documents to other formats, such as HTML (for presenting an XML document's content via a web browser).

XSLT accomplishes its work by using XSLT processors and stylesheets. An *XSLT processor* is a software component that applies an *XSLT stylesheet* (an XML-based template consisting of content and transformation instructions) to an input document (without modifying the document), and copies the transformed result to a result tree, which can be output to a file or output stream, or even piped into another XSLT processor for additional transformations. Figure 6-1 illustrates the transformation process.

© Jeff Friesen 2016
J. Friesen, *Java XML and JSON*, DOI 10.1007/978-1-4842-1916-4_6

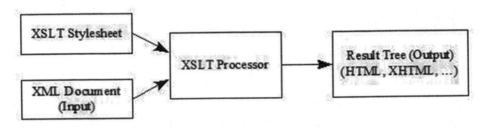

Figure 6-1. An XSLT processor transforms an XML input document into a result tree

The beauty of XSLT is that you don't need to develop custom software applications to perform the transformations. Instead, you simply create an XSLT stylesheet and input it along with the XML document needing to be transformed to an XSLT processor.

Exploring the XSLT API

Java implements XSLT through the types in the javax.xml.transform, javax.xml.transform.dom, javax.xml.transform.sax, javax.xml.transform. stax, and javax.xml.transform.stream packages. The javax.xml. transform package defines the generic APIs for processing transformation instructions and for performing a transformation from a *source* (where the XSLT processor's input originates) to a *result* (where the processor's output is sent). The remaining packages define the APIs for obtaining different kinds of sources and results.

The javax.xml.transform.TransformerFactory class is the starting point for working with XSLT. You instantiate TransformerFactory by calling one of its newInstance() methods. For example, the following code fragment uses TransformerFactory's TransformerFactory newInstance() class method to create the factory:

```
TransformerFactory tf = TransformerFactory.newInstance();
```

Behind the scenes, newInstance() follows an ordered lookup procedure to identify the TransformerFactory implementation class to load. This procedure first examines the javax.xml.transform.TransformerFactory system property, and lastly chooses the Java platform's default TransformerFactory implementation class when no other class is found. If an implementation class isn't available (perhaps the class identified by the javax.xml.transform.TransformerFactory system property doesn't exist) or cannot be instantiated, newInstance() throws an instance of the javax.xml.transform.TransformerFactoryConfigurationError class. Otherwise, it instantiates the class and returns its instance.

After obtaining a TransformerFactory object, you can call various configuration methods to configure the factory. For example, you could call TransformerFactory's void setFeature(String name, boolean value) method to enable a feature (such as secure processing, to transform XML documents securely).

Following the factory's configuration, call one of its newTransformer() methods to create and return instances of the javax.xml.transform.Transformer class. The following code fragment calls Transformer newTransformer() to accomplish this task:

```
Transformer t = tf.newTransformer();
```

The noargument newTransformer() method copies source input to the destination without making any changes. This kind of transformation is known as the *identity transformation*.

To change input, specify a *stylesheet*. Accomplish this task by calling the factory's Transformer newTransformer(Source source) method, where the javax.xml.transform.Source interface describes a source for the stylesheet. The following code fragment accomplishes this task:

```
Transformer t;
t = tf.newTransformer(new StreamSource(new FileReader("recipe.xsl")));
```

This code fragment creates a transformer that obtains a stylesheet from a file named recipe.xsl via a javax.xml.transform.stream.StreamSource object connected to a file reader. It's customary to use the .xsl or .xslt extension to identify XSLT stylesheet files.

The newTransformer() methods throw javax.xml.transform. TransformerConfigurationException when they cannot return a Transformer instance that corresponds to the factory configuration.

After obtaining a Transformer instance, you can call its void setOutputProperty(String name, String value) method to influence a transformation. The javax.xml.transform.OutputKeys class declares constants for frequently used keys. For example, OutputKeys.METHOD is the key for specifying the method for outputting the result tree (as XML, HTML, plain text, or something else).

> **Tip**   To set multiple properties in a single method call, create a java.util. Properties object and pass this object as an argument to Transformer's void setOutputProperties(Properties prop) method. Properties set by setOutputProperty() and setOutputProperties() override the stylesheet's xsl:output instruction settings.

Before you can perform a transformation, you need to obtain instances of classes that implement the Source and javax.xml.transform. Result interfaces. You then pass these instances to Transformer's void transform(Source xmlSource, Result outputTarget) method, which throws an instance of the javax.xml.transform.TransformerException class when a problem arises during the transformation.

The following code fragment shows you how to obtain a source and a result, and perform the transformation:

```
Source source = new DOMSource(doc);
Result result = new StreamResult(System.out);
t.transform(source, result);
```

The first line instantiates the javax.xml.transform.dom.DOMSource class, which acts as a holder for a DOM tree rooted in the org.w3c.dom.Document object specified by doc. The second line instantiates the javax.xml. transform.stream.StreamResult class, which acts as a holder for the standard output stream, to which the transformed data items are sent. The third line reads data from the Source object and outputs transformed data to the Result object.

TRANSFORMER FACTORY FEATURE DETECTION

Although Java's default transformers support the various Source and Result implementation classes that are located in the javax.xml.transform.dom, javax.xml. transform.sax, javax.xml.transform.stax, and javax.xml.transform.stream packages, a nondefault transformer (perhaps specified via the javax.xml.transform. TransformerFactory system property) might be more limited. For this reason, each Source and Result implementation class declares a FEATURE string constant that can be passed to TransformerFactory's boolean getFeature(String name) method. This method returns true when the Source or Result implementation class is supported. For example, tf.getFeature(StreamSource.FEATURE) returns true when stream sources are supported.

The javax.xml.transform.sax.SAXTransformerFactory class provides additional SAX-specific factory methods that can be used only when the TransformerFactory object is also an instance of this class. To help you make the determination, SAXTransformerFactory also declares a FEATURE string constant that you can pass to getFeature(). For example, tf.getFeature(SAXTransformerFactory.FEATURE) returns true when the transformer factory referenced from tf is an instance of SAXTransformerFactory.

Most XML API interface objects and the factories that return them are not thread-safe. This situation also applies to transformers. Although you can reuse the same transformer multiple times on the same thread, you cannot access the transformer from multiple threads.

This problem can be solved for transformers by using instances of classes that implement the `javax.xml.transform.Templates` interface. The Java documentation for the interface has this to say: *Templates must be threadsafe for a given instance over multiple threads running concurrently, and may be used multiple times in a given session.* As well as promoting thread safety, Templates instances can improve performance because they represent compiled XSLT stylesheets.

The following code fragment shows how you might perform a transformation without a `Templates` object:

```
TransformerFactory tf = TransformerFactory.newInstance();
StreamSource ssStyleSheet = new StreamSource(new FileReader("recipe.xsl"));
Transformer t = tf.newTransformer(ssStyleSheet);
t.transform(new DOMSource(doc), new StreamResult(System.out));
```

You cannot access t's transformer from multiple threads. In contrast, the following code fragment shows you how to construct a transformer from a Templates object so that it can be accessed from multiple threads:

```
TransformerFactory tf = TransformerFactory.newInstance();
StreamSource ssStyleSheet = new StreamSource(new FileReader("recipe.xsl"));
Templates te = tf.newTemplates(ssStyleSheet);
Transformer t = te.newTransformer();
t.transform(new DOMSource(doc), new StreamResult(System.out));
```

The differences are the call to `Transformerfactory`'s `Templates` `newTemplates(Source source)` method to create and return objects whose classes implement the `Templates` interface, and the call to this interface's `Transformer newTransformer()` method to obtain the `Transformer` object.

Demonstrating the XSLT API

Listing 3-2 presents a `DOMDemo` application that creates a DOM document tree based on Listing 1-2's movie XML document. Unfortunately, you cannot use the DOM API to assign ISO-8859-1 to the XML declaration's encoding attribute. Also, you cannot use DOM to output this tree to a file or other destination. However, you can overcome these problems with XSLT, as demonstrated in Listing 6-1.

Listing 6-1. Assigning ISO-8859-1 to the XML declaration's encoding Attribute via XSLT

```java
import javax.xml.parsers.DocumentBuilder;
import javax.xml.parsers.DocumentBuilderFactory;
import javax.xml.parsers.FactoryConfigurationError;
import javax.xml.parsers.ParserConfigurationException;

import javax.xml.transform.OutputKeys;
import javax.xml.transform.Result;
import javax.xml.transform.Source;
import javax.xml.transform.Transformer;
import javax.xml.transform.TransformerConfigurationException;
import javax.xml.transform.TransformerException;
import javax.xml.transform.TransformerFactory;
import javax.xml.transform.TransformerFactoryConfigurationError;

import javax.xml.transform.dom.DOMSource;

import javax.xml.transform.stream.StreamResult;

import org.w3c.dom.Document;
import org.w3c.dom.Element;
import org.w3c.dom.Text;

public class XSLTDemo
{
    public static void main(String[] args)
    {
        try
        {
            DocumentBuilderFactory dbf = DocumentBuilderFactory.newInstance();
            DocumentBuilder db = dbf.newDocumentBuilder();
            Document doc = db.newDocument();
            doc.setXmlStandalone(true);
            // Create the root element.
            Element root = doc.createElement("movie");
            doc.appendChild(root);
            // Create name child element and add it to the root.
            Element name = doc.createElement("name");
            root.appendChild(name);
            // Add a text element to the name element.
            Text text =
                doc.createTextNode("Le Fabuleux Destin d'Amélie Poulain");
            name.appendChild(text);
            // Create language child element and add it to the root.
            Element language = doc.createElement("language");
            root.appendChild(language);
            // Add a text element to the language element.
            text = doc.createTextNode("français");
            language.appendChild(text);
```

```
    // Use a transformer to output this tree with ISO-8859-1 encoding
    // to the standard output stream.
    TransformerFactory tf = TransformerFactory.newInstance();
    Transformer t = tf.newTransformer();
    t.setOutputProperty(OutputKeys.METHOD, "xml");
    t.setOutputProperty(OutputKeys.ENCODING, "ISO-8859-1");
    t.setOutputProperty(OutputKeys.INDENT, "yes");
    t.setOutputProperty("{http://xml.apache.org/xslt}indent-amount", "3");
    Source source = new DOMSource(doc);
    Result result = new StreamResult(System.out);
    t.transform(source, result);
}
catch (FactoryConfigurationError fce)
{
    System.err.println("FCE: " + fce);
}
catch (ParserConfigurationException pce)
{
    System.err.println("PCE: " + pce);
}
catch (TransformerConfigurationException tce)
{
    System.err.println("TCE: " + tce);
}
catch (TransformerException te)
{
    System.err.println("TE: " + te);
}
catch (TransformerFactoryConfigurationError tfce)
{
    System.err.println("TFCE: " + tfce);
}
    }
}
```

Listing 6-1 first creates a DOM tree. It then creates a transformer factory and obtains a transformer from this factory. Four properties are then set on the transformer, and a stream source and result are obtained. Finally, the transform() method is called to transform source content to the result.

The four properties set on the transformer influence the transformation. OutputKeys.METHOD specifies that the result tree will be written out as XML, OutputKeys.ENCODING specifies that ISO-8859-1 will be the value of the XML declaration's encoding attribute, and OutputKeys.INDENT specifies that the transformer can output additional whitespace.

The additional whitespace is used to output the XML across multiple lines instead of on a single line. Because it would be nice to indicate the number of spaces for indenting lines of XML, and because this information cannot

be specified via an OutputKeys property, the nonstandard "{http://xml.
apache.org/xslt}indent-amount" property (property keys begin with brace-
delimited URIs) is used to specify an appropriate value (such as 3 spaces).
It's okay to specify this property in this application because Java's default
XSLT implementation is based on Apache's XSLT implementation.

Compile Listing 6-1 as follows:

```
javac XSLTDemo.java
```

Run the resulting application as follows:

```
java XSLTDemo
```

You should observe the following output:

```
<?xml version="1.0" encoding="ISO-8859-1"?><movie>
    <name>Le Fabuleux Destin d'Amélie Poulain</name>
    <language>français</language>
</movie>
```

Although this example shows you how to output a DOM tree and also how
to specify an encoding value for the XML declaration of the resulting XML
document, the example doesn't really demonstrate the power of XSLT
because (apart from setting the encoding attribute value) it performs an
identity transformation. A more interesting example would take advantage of
a stylesheet.

Consider a scenario where you want to convert Listing 1-1's recipe
document to an HTML document for presentation via a web browser.
Listing 6-2 presents a stylesheet that a transformer can use to perform the
conversion.

Listing 6-2. An XSLT Stylesheet for Converting a Recipe Document to an HTML Document

```
<?xml version="1.0"?>
<xsl:stylesheet version="1.0"
                xmlns:xsl="http://www.w3.org/1999/XSL/Transform">
<xsl:template match="/recipe">
<html>
    <head>
        <title>Recipes</title>
    </head>

    <body>
        <h2>
            <xsl:value-of select="normalize-space(title)"/>
        </h2>
```

```
    <h3>Ingredients</h3>

    <ul>
    <xsl:for-each select="ingredients/ingredient">
      <li>
         <xsl:value-of select="normalize-space(text())"/>
         <xsl:if test="@qty"> (<xsl:value-of select="@qty"/>)</xsl:if>
      </li>
    </xsl:for-each>
    </ul>

    <h3>Instructions</h3>

    <xsl:value-of select="normalize-space(instructions)"/>
  </body>
</html>
</xsl:template>
</xsl:stylesheet>
```

Listing 6-2 reveals that a stylesheet is an XML document. Its root element is stylesheet, which identifies the standard namespace for stylesheets. It's conventional to specify xsl as the namespace prefix for referring to XSLT instruction elements, although any prefix could be specified.

A stylesheet is based on template elements that control how an element and its content are converted. A template focuses on a single element that's identified via the match attribute. This attribute's value is an XPath location path expression, which matches all recipe child nodes of the root element node. Regarding Listing 1-1, only the single recipe root element will be matched and selected.

A template element can contain literal text and stylesheet instructions. For example, the value-of instruction in <xsl:value-of select="normalize-space(title)"/> specifies that the value of the title element (which is a child of the recipe context node) is to be retrieved and copied to the output. Because this text is surrounded by space and newline characters, XPath's normalize-string() function is called to remove this whitespace before the title is copied.

XSLT is a powerful declarative language that includes control flow instructions such as for-each and if. In the context of <xsl:for-each select="ingredients/ingredient">, for-each causes all of the ingredient child nodes of the ingredients node to be selected and processed one at a time. For each node, <xsl:value-of select="normalize-space(text())"/> is executed to copy the content of the ingredient node, normalized to remove whitespace. Also, the if instruction in <xsl:if test="@qty"> (<xsl:value-of select="@qty"/>) determines if the ingredient node has a qty attribute, and (if so) copies a space character followed by this attribute's value (surrounded by parentheses) to the output.

> **Note**   There's a lot more to XSLT than can be demonstrated in this short
> example. To learn more about XSLT, I recommend that you check out *Beginning*
> *XSLT 2.0 From Novice to Professional* (www.apress.com/9781590593240),
> an Apress book written by Jeni Tennison. XSLT 2.0 is a superset of XSLT 1.0, and
> Java 8 supports XSLT 1.0.

Listing 6-3 presents the source code to an XSLTDemo application that shows
you how to write the Java code to process Listing 1-1 via Listing 6-2's
stylesheet.

Listing 6-3. Transforming Recipe XML via a Stylesheet

```java
import java.io.FileReader;
import java.io.IOException;

import javax.xml.parsers.DocumentBuilder;
import javax.xml.parsers.DocumentBuilderFactory;
import javax.xml.parsers.FactoryConfigurationError;
import javax.xml.parsers.ParserConfigurationException;

import javax.xml.transform.OutputKeys;
import javax.xml.transform.Result;
import javax.xml.transform.Source;
import javax.xml.transform.Transformer;
import javax.xml.transform.TransformerConfigurationException;
import javax.xml.transform.TransformerException;
import javax.xml.transform.TransformerFactory;
import javax.xml.transform.TransformerFactoryConfigurationError;

import javax.xml.transform.dom.DOMSource;

import javax.xml.transform.stream.StreamResult;
import javax.xml.transform.stream.StreamSource;

import org.w3c.dom.Document;

import org.xml.sax.SAXException;

public class XSLTDemo
{
    public static void main(String[] args)
    {
        try
        {
            DocumentBuilderFactory dbf = DocumentBuilderFactory.newInstance();
            DocumentBuilder db = dbf.newDocumentBuilder();
```

```
          Document doc = db.parse("recipe.xml");
          TransformerFactory tf = TransformerFactory.newInstance();
          StreamSource ssStyleSheet;
          ssStyleSheet = new StreamSource(new FileReader("recipe.xsl"));
          Transformer t = tf.newTransformer(ssStyleSheet);
          t.setOutputProperty(OutputKeys.METHOD, "html");
          t.setOutputProperty(OutputKeys.INDENT, "yes");
          Source source = new DOMSource(doc);
          Result result = new StreamResult(System.out);
          t.transform(source, result);
       }
       catch (IOFxception ioe)
       {
          System.err.println("IOE: " + ioe);
       }
       catch (FactoryConfigurationError fce)
       {
          System.err.println("FCE: " + fce);
       }
       catch (ParserConfigurationException pce)
       {
          System.err.println("PCE: " + pce);
       }
       catch (SAXException saxe)
       {
          System.err.println("SAXE: " + saxe);
       }
       catch (TransformerConfigurationException tce)
       {
          System.err.println("TCE: " + tce);
       }
       catch (TransformerException te)
       {
          System.err.println("TE: " + te);
       }
       catch (TransformerFactoryConfigurationError tfce)
       {
          System.err.println("TFCE: " + tfce);
       }
    }
}
```

Listing 6-3 is similar in structure to Listing 6-1. It reveals that the output method is set to html, and it also reveals that the resulting HTML should be indented. However, the output is only partly indented, as shown here:

```
<html>
<head>
<META http-equiv="Content-Type" content="text/html; charset=UTF-8">
<title>Recipes</title>
</head>
<body>
<h2>Grilled Cheese Sandwich</h2>
<h3>Ingredients</h3>
<ul>
<li>bread slice (2)</li>
<li>cheese slice</li>
<li>margarine pat (2)</li>
</ul>
<h3>Instructions</h3>Place frying pan on element and select medium heat. For
each bread slice, smear one pat of margarine on one side of bread slice.
Place cheese slice between bread slices with margarine-smeared sides away
from the cheese. Place sandwich in frying pan with one margarine-smeared
side in contact with pan. Fry for a couple of minutes and flip. Fry other
side for a minute and serve.</body>
</html>
```

OutputKeys.INDENT and its "yes" value let you output the HTML across multiple lines as opposed to outputting the HTML on a single line. However, the XSLT processor performs no additional indentation, and ignores attempts to specify the number of spaces to indent via code such as t.setO utputProperty("{http://xml.apache.org/xslt}indent-amount", "3");.

Note   An XSLT processor outputs a <META> tag when OutputKeys.METHOD is set to "html".

EXERCISES

The following exercises are designed to test your understanding of Chapter 6's content:

1. Define XSLT.

2. How does XSLT accomplish its work?

3. True or false: Call `TransformerFactory`'s `void transform(Source xmlSource, Result outputTarget)` method to transform a source to a result.

4. Create a `books.xsl` stylesheet file and a `MakeHTML` application with a similar structure to the application that processes Listing 6-2's `recipe.xsl` stylesheet. `MakeHTML` uses `books.xsl` to convert Exercise 1-21's `books.xml` content to HTML. When viewed in a web browser, the HTML should result in a web page that's similar to the page shown in Figure 6-2.

Advanced C++

ISBN: 0201548550
Publication Year: 1992

James O. Coplien

Beginning Groovy and Grails

ISBN: 9781430210450
Publication Year: 2008

Christopher M. Judd
Joseph Faisal Nusairat
James Shingler

Effective Java

ISBN: 0201310058
Publication Year: 2001

Joshua Bloch

Figure 6-2. Exercise 1-21's books.xml content is presented via a web page

Summary

XSL is a family of languages for transforming and formatting XML documents. XSLT is the XSL language for transforming XML documents to other formats, such as HTML (for presenting an XML document's content via a web browser).

XSLT accomplishes its work by using XSLT processors and stylesheets. An XSLT processor applies an XSLT stylesheet to an input document (without modifying the document), and copies the transformed result to a result tree, which can be output to a file or output stream, or even piped into another XSLT processor for additional transformations.

Java implements XSLT through the types in the `javax.xml.transform`, `javax.xml.transform.dom`, `javax.xml.transform.sax`, `javax.xml.transform.stax`, and `javax.xml.transform.stream` packages. The `javax.xml.transform` package defines the generic APIs for processing transformation instructions and for performing a transformation from a source (where the XSLT processor's input originates) to a result (where the processor's output is sent). The remaining packages define the APIs for obtaining different kinds of sources and results.

Chapter 7 introduces you to JSON, a less-verbose alternative to XML.

Introducing JSON

Many applications communicate by exchanging JSON objects instead of XML documents. This chapter introduces JSON, tours its syntax, demonstrates JSON in a JavaScript context, and shows how to validate JSON objects in the context of JSON Schema.

What Is JSON?

JSON (JavaScript Object Notation) is a language-independent data format that expresses JSON objects as human-readable lists of *properties* (name-value pairs). Although derived from a nonstrict subset of JavaScript, code to parse JSON objects into equivalent language-dependent objects is available in many programming languages.

Note   JSON allows the Unicode U+2028 line separator and U+2029 paragraph separator to appear unescaped in quoted strings. Because JavaScript doesn't support this capability, JSON isn't a proper subset of JavaScript.

JSON is commonly used in asynchronous browser/server communication via AJAJ (https://en.wikipedia.org/wiki/AJAJ). JSON is also used with NoSQL database management systems such as MongoDb and CouchDb; with apps from social media web sites such as Twitter, Facebook, LinkedIn, and Flickr; and even with the popular Google Maps API.

© Jeff Friesen 2016

J. Friesen, *Java XML and JSON*, DOI 10.1007/978-1-4842-1916-4_7

> **Note**   Many developers prefer JSON to XML because they see JSON as being less verbose and easier to read. Check out "JSON: The Fat-Free Alternative to XML" (www.json.org/xml.html) for more information.

JSON Syntax Tour

The JSON data format presents a JSON object as a brace-delimited and comma-separated list of properties:

```
{
    property1 ,
    property2 ,
    ...
    propertyN
}
```

A comma is not placed after the final property.

For each property, the name is expressed as a string that's typically quoted (and by a pair of double quotes). The name string is followed by a colon character, which is followed by a value of a specific type ("name": "JSON", for example).

JSON supports the following six types:

- *Number*: A signed decimal number that may contain a fractional part and may use exponential (E) notation. JSON doesn't permit nonnumbers (such as NaN), nor does it make any distinction between integer and floating-point. Furthermore, JSON doesn't recognize the octal and hexadecimal formats. (Although JavaScript uses a double precision floating-point format for all numeric values, other languages implementing JSON may encode numbers differently.)

- *String*: A sequence of zero or more Unicode characters. Strings are delimited with double quotes and support a backslash escaping syntax.

- *Boolean*: Either of the values true or false.

- *Array*: An ordered list of zero or more values, each of which may be of any type. Arrays use square bracket notation with elements being comma-separated.

- *Object*: An unordered collection of properties where the names (also called *keys*) are strings. Because objects are intended to represent associative arrays, it's recommended, although not required, that each key be unique within an object. Objects are delimited with braces and use commas to separate each property. Within each property the colon character separates the key from its value.

- *Null*: An empty value, using the keyword null.

> **Note** JSON Schema (discussed later) recognizes a seventh type: integer. This type doesn't include a fraction or exponent and is a subset of number.

Whitespace is allowed and is ignored around or between syntactic elements (values and punctuation). Four specific characters are considered whitespace for this purpose: space, horizontal tab, line feed, and carriage return. Also, JSON doesn't support comments.

Using this data format, you can specify a JSON object such as the following anonymous object (excerpted from Wikipedia's JSON page at https://en.wikipedia.org/wiki/JSON) for describing a person in terms of first name, last name, and other data items:

```
{
    "firstName": "John",
    "lastName": "Smith",
    "isAlive": true,
    "age": 25,
    "address":
    {
        "streetAddress": "21 2nd Street",
        "city": "New York",
        "state": "NY",
        "postalCode": "10021-3100"
    },
    "phoneNumbers":
    [
        {
            "type": "home",
            "number": "212 555-1234"
        },
```

```
    {
        "type": "office",
        "number": "646 555-4567"
    }
  ],
  "children": [],
  "spouse": null
}
```

In this example, the anonymous object consists of eight properties with the following keys:

- firstName identifies a person's first name and is of type string.

- lastName identifies a person's last name and is of type string.

- isAlive identifies a person's alive status and is of type Boolean.

- age identifies the age of a person and is of type number.

- address identifies a person's location and is of type object. Within this object are four properties (of type string): streetAddress, city, state, and postalCode.

- phoneNumbers identifies a person's phone numbers and is of type array. Within the array are two objects; each object consists of type and number properties (of type string).

- children identifies a person's children (if any) and is of type array.

- spouse identifies a person's partner and is empty.

The previous example shows that objects and arrays can be nested; for example, objects within arrays within objects.

Note   By convention, JSON objects are stored in files with the .json file extension.

Demonstrating JSON with JavaScript

Ideally, I'd demonstrate JSON with Java's standard JSON API. However, Java doesn't officially support JSON.

Note   Oracle previously introduced a Java Enhancement Proposal (JEP) for adding a JSON API to Java 9. Unfortunately, JEP 198: Light-Weight JSON API (http://openjdk.java.net/jeps/198) was dropped.

I'll demonstrate JSON via JavaScript, but in a Java context via Java's Scripting API. (If you're new to Scripting, I'll explain just enough of this API so that you can understand the code.) To get started, Listing 7-1 presents the source code for an application that executes JavaScript code.

Listing 7-1. Executing JavaScript Code with Assistance from Java

```java
import java.io.FileReader;
import java.io.IOException;

import javax.script.ScriptEngine;
import javax.script.ScriptEngineManager;
import javax.script.ScriptException;

public class RunScript
{
   public static void main(String[] args)
   {
      if (args.length != 1)
      {
         System.err.println("usage: java RunScript script");
         return;
      }
      ScriptEngineManager manager = new ScriptEngineManager();
      ScriptEngine engine = manager.getEngineByName("nashorn");
      try
      {
         engine.eval(new FileReader(args[0]));
      }
      catch (ScriptException se)
      {
         System.err.println(se.getMessage());
      }
```

```
      catch (IOException ioe)
      {
         System.err.println(ioe.getMessage());
      }
   }
}
```

Listing 7-1's main() method first verifies that exactly one command-line argument, which names a script file, has been specified. It this isn't the case, it displays usage information and terminates the application.

Assuming that a single command-line argument was specified, the javax.script.ScriptEngineManager class is instantiated. ScriptEngineManager serves as the entry-point into the Scripting API.

Next, the ScriptEngineManager object's ScriptEngine getEngineByName(String shortName) method is called to obtain a script engine corresponding to the desired shortName value. JavaScript supports two script engines: rhino and nashorn. I chose to obtain the more modern nashorn script engine, which is returned as an object whose class implements the javax.script.ScriptEngine interface.

ScriptEngine declares several eval() methods for evaluating a script. main() invokes the Object eval(Reader reader) method to read the script from its java.io.FileReader object argument and (assuming that java.io.IOException isn't thrown) then evaluate the script. This method returns any script return value, which I ignore. Also, this method throws javax.script.ScriptException when an error occurs in the script.

Compile Listing 7-1 as follows:

```
javac RunScript.java
```

Before you can run this application, you need a suitable script file. Listing 7-2 presents a script that declares and accesses a JSON object.

Listing 7-2. Declaring and Accessing a Person Object

```
var person =
{
   "firstName": "John",
   "lastName": "Smith",
   "isAlive": true,
   "age": 25,
   "address":
   {
      "streetAddress": "21 2nd Street",
      "city": "New York",
      "state": "NY",
      "postalCode": "10021-3100"
   },
```

```
     "phoneNumbers":
     [
        {
            "type": "home",
            "number": "212 555-1234"
        },
        {
            "type": "office",
            "number": "646 555-4567"
        }
     ],
     "children": [],
     "spouse": null
};
print(person.firstName);
print(person.lastName);
print(person.address.city);
print(person.phoneNumbers[1].number);
```

Assuming that Listing 7-2 is stored in person.js, run the application as follows:

```
java RunScript person.js
```

You should observe the following output:

```
John
Smith
New York
646 555-4567
```

A JSON object exists as language-independent text. To convert the text to a language-dependent object, you need to parse the text. JavaScript provides a JSON object with a parse() method for this task. Pass the text to be parsed as an argument to parse() and receive the resulting JavaScript-based object as this method's return value. parse() throws SyntaxError when the text doesn't conform to the JSON format.

Listing 7-3 presents a script that demonstrates parse().

Listing 7-3. Parsing a JSON Object

```
var creditCardText =
"{ \"number\": \"1234567890123456\", \"expiry\": \"04/20\", \"type\": " +
"\"visa\" }";
var creditCard = JSON.parse(creditCardText);
print(creditCard.number);
print(creditCard.expiry);
print(creditCard.type);
```

```
var creditCardText2 = "{ 'type': 'visa' }";
var creditCard2 = JSON.parse(creditCardText2);
```

Assuming that Listing 7-3 is stored in `cc.js`, run the application as follows:

```
java RunScript cc.js
```

You should observe the following output:

```
1234567890123456
04/20
visa
SyntaxError: Invalid JSON: <json>:1:2 Expected , or } but found '
{ 'type': 'visa' }
  ^ in <eval> at line number 10
```

The syntax error shows that you cannot delimit a name with single quotes.

This is all I have to say about working with JSON in a JavaScript context. Because this book is Java-focused, subsequent chapters will explore various third-party Java APIs for parsing JSON objects into Java-dependent objects and vice versa.

Validating JSON Objects

It's often necessary for applications to validate JSON objects, to ensure that required properties are present and that additional constraints (such as a price never being less than one dollar) are met. Validation is typically performed in the context of JSON Schema.

JSON Schema is a grammar language for defining the structure, content, and (to some extent) semantics of JSON objects. It lets you specify *metadata* (data about data) about what an object's properties mean and what values are valid for those properties. The result of applying the grammar language is a *schema* (a blueprint) describing the set of JSON objects that are valid according to the schema.

> **Note**   JSON Schema expresses a schema as a JSON object.

JSON Schema is maintained at the JSON Schema web site
(http://json-schema.org). This web site reveals several advantages to
JSON Schema:

- It describes your existing data format.

- If offers clear, human-readable, and machine-readable
  documentation.

- It provides complete structural validation, which
  is useful for automated testing and validating
  client-submitted data.

> **Note**   The JSON Schema web site focuses on draft version 4 of the JSON
> Schema specification. This specification is divided into three parts: JSON
> Schema Core, JSON Schema Validation, and JSON Hyper-Schema.

To understand JSON Schema, consider the following JSON object:

```
{
   "name": "John Doe",
   "age": 35
}
```

This object describes a person in terms of a name and an age. Let's set up
the following constraints: both properties must be present, name must be
of type string and age must be of type number, and age's value must range
from 18 through 64.

The following schema (based on draft version 4 of JSON Schema) provides
the necessary constraints for this object:

```
{
   "$schema": "http://json-schema.org/draft-04/schema#",
   "title": "Person",
   "description": "A person",
   "type": "object",
   "properties":
   {
      "name":
      {
         "description": "A person's name",
         "type": "string"
      },
```

```
   "age":
   {
      "description": "A person's age",
      "type": "number",
      "minimum": 18,
      "maximum": 64
   }
 },
 "required": ["name", "age"]
}
```

Reading from top to bottom, you would interpret this JSON-based schema as follows:

- The $schema keyword states that this schema is written according to the draft version 4 specification.

- The title keyword identifies the JSON object being validated by this schema. In this case, a Person object is being validated.

- The description keyword provides a description of the Person object. As with title, description adds no constraint to the data being validated.

- The type keyword signifies that the containing object is a JSON object (via the object value). Also, it identifies property types (such as string and number).

- The properties keyword introduces an array of the properties that can appear in the JSON object. These properties are identified as name and age. Each property is further described by an object that provides a description keyword to describe the property and a type keyword to identify the type of value that can be assigned to the property. This is a constraint: you must assign a string to name and a number to age. For the age property, minimum and maximum keywords are specified to provide additional constraints: the number assigned to age must range from 18 through 64.

- The required keyword introduces an array that identifies those properties that must be present in the JSON object. In the example, both name and age are required properties.

The JSON Schema web site provides links to various validator implementations for different programming languages (see http://json-schema.org/implementations.html). You can download an implementation and integrate it into your application, subject to license requirements. For this chapter, I chose to use an online tool called JSON Schema Lint (http://jsonschemalint.com/draft4/) to demonstrate validation.

Figure 7-1 shows the previous JSON object and schema in the appropriate windows of the JSON Schema Lint online tool.

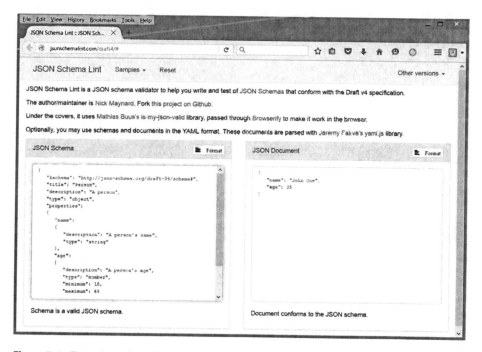

Figure 7-1. The schema is valid and the JSON object conforms to this schema

Let's make some changes to the JSON object so that it no longer conforms to the schema, and see how the JSON Schema Lint tool responds. First, let's assign 65 to age, which exceeds the maximum constraint for the age property. Figure 7-2 shows the result.

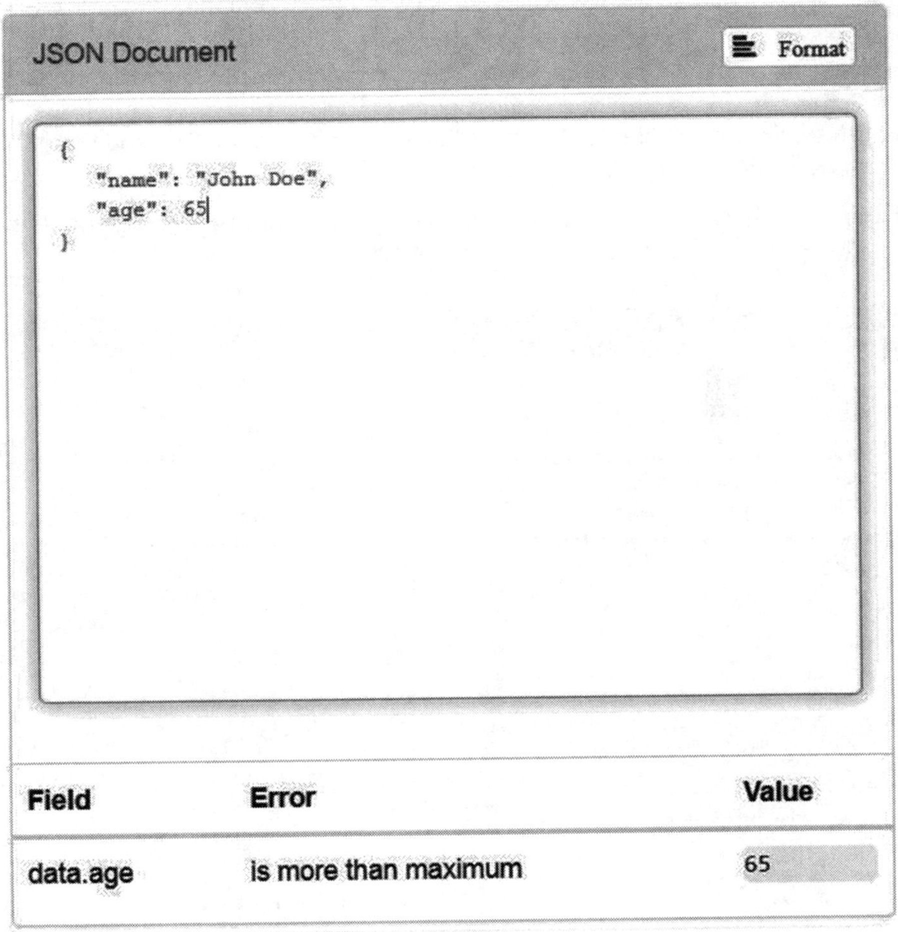

```
JSON Document                                    ☰  Format

{
    "name": "John Doe",
    "age": 65|
}
```

Field	Error	Value
data.age	is more than maximum	65

Figure 7-2. JSON Schema Lint changes its header color to red to signify an error, and also identifies the property and constraint that's been violated

Next, let's restore age's value to 35, but surround it with double quotes, which changes the type from number to string. See Figure 7-3 for the result.

JSON Document   ≣ Format

```
{
    "name": "John Doe",
    "age": "35"
}
```

Field	Error	Value
data.age	is the wrong type	"35"

Figure 7-3. JSON Schema Lint reports that the age property has the wrong type

Finally, let's restore age's value to 35, but eliminate the name property. Figure 7-4 shows JSON Schema Lint's response.

JSON Document	☰ Format

```
{
    "age": 35
}
```

Field	Error	Value

data.name	is required	{
		    "age": 35
		}

Figure 7-4. JSON Schema Lint reports that the name property is required

Note   Check out the "JSON Schema: core definitions and terminology" (http://json-schema.org/latest/json-schema-core.html) and "JSON Schema: interactive and non interactive validation" (http://json-schema.org/latest/json-schema-validation.html) documents to learn more about creating schemas that are based on JSON Schema.

EXERCISES

The following exercises are designed to test your understanding of Chapter 7's content.

1. Define JSON.

2. True or false: JSON is derived from a strict subset of JavaScript.

3. How does the JSON data format present a JSON object?

4. Identify the six types that JSON supports.

5. True or false: JSON doesn't support comments.

6. How would you parse a JSON object into an equivalent JavaScript object?

7. Define JSON Schema.

8. When creating a schema, how do you identify those properties that must be present in those JSON objects that the schema validates?

9. Declare a JSON object for a product in terms of name and price properties. Set the name to "hammer" and the price to 20.

10. Declare a schema for validating the previous JSON object. The schema should constrain name to be a string, price to be a number, price to be at least 1 dollar, and name and price to be present in the object. Use JSON Schema Lint to verify the schema and JSON object.

Summary

JSON is a language-independent data format that expresses JSON objects as human-readable lists of properties. Although derived from JavaScript, code to parse JSON objects into equivalent language-dependent objects is available in many programming languages.

The JSON data format presents a JSON object as a brace-delimited and comma-separated list of properties. For each property, the name is expressed as a doubly-quoted string. The name string is followed by a colon character, which is followed by a value of a specific JSON type.

It's often necessary for applications to validate JSON objects, to ensure that required properties are present and that additional constraints (such as a price never being less than one dollar) are met. JSON Schema is a grammar language that lets you accomplish validation.

Chapter 8 introduces mJson for parsing and creating JSON objects.

Parsing and Creating JSON Objects with mJson

Many third-party APIs are available for parsing and creating JSON objects. This chapter explores one of the simplest of these APIs: mJson.

What Is mJson?

mJson is a small Java-based JSON library for parsing JSON objects into Java objects and vice versa. mJson offers the following features:

- Single universal type (everything is a Json object; there is no type casting)
- Methods for creating Json objects
- Methods for learning about Json objects
- Methods for navigating Json object hierarchies
- Methods for modifying Json objects
- Full support for JSON Schema Draft 4 validation
- Pluggable factory for enhancing Json
- Method chaining for achieving more compact code
- Fast, hand-coded parsing
- Entire library contained in one Java source file

© Jeff Friesen 2016
J. Friesen, *Java XML and JSON*, DOI 10.1007/978-1-4842-1916-4_8

Unlike with other JSON libraries, mJson focuses on manipulating JSON structures in Java without mapping them to strongly-typed Java objects. As a result, mJson reduces verbosity and lets you work with JSON in Java as naturally as in JavaScript.

> **Note**   mJson was created by developer Borislav Lordanov. This library is hosted on GitHub at `http://bolerio.github.io/mjson/`.

Obtaining and Using mJson

mJson is distributed as a single Jar file; `mjson-1.3.jar` is the most recent Jar file at the time of writing. To obtain this Jar file, point your browser to `http://repo1.maven.org/maven2/org/sharegov/mjson/1.3/mjson-1.3.jar`.

`mjson-1.3.jar` contains a `Json` classfile and other classfiles that describe package-private classes nested within the `Json` class. Furthermore, this Jar file reveals that `Json` is located in the `mjson` package.

> **Note**   mJson is licensed according to Apache License Version 2.0 (`www.apache.org/licenses/`).

It's easy to work with `mjson-1.3.jar`. Simply include it in the classpath when compiling source code or running an application, as follows:

```
javac -cp mjson-1.3.jar source file
java -cp mjson-1.3.jar;. main classfile
```

Exploring the Json Class

The `Json` class describes a JSON object or part of a JSON object.
It contains `Schema` and `Factory` interfaces, more than 50 methods, and other members. This section explores most of these methods along with `Schema` and `Factory`.

> **Note**   The API documentation for the `Json` class is located at `http://bolerio.github.io/mjson/apidocs/index.html`.

Creating Json Objects

Json declares several static methods that create and return Json objects. Three of these methods read and parse an external JSON object:

- Json read(String s): Reads a JSON object from the string that was passed to s (of type java.lang.String) and parses this object.

- Json read(URL url): Reads a JSON object from the Uniform Resource Locator (URL) passed to url (of type java.net.URL) and parses this object.

- Json read(CharacterIterator ci): Reads a JSON object from the character iterator passed to ci (of type java.text.CharacterIterator) and parses this object.

Each method returns a Json object that describes the parsed JSON object.

Listing 8-1 presents the source code for an application that demonstrates the read(String) method.

Listing 8-1. Reading and Parsing a String-Based JSON Object

```java
import mjson.Json;

public class mJsonDemo
{
   public static void main(String[] args)
   {
      String jsonStr =
      "{" +
      "\"firstName\": \"John\"," +
      "\"lastName\": \"Smith\"," +
      "\"isAlive\": true," +
      "\"age\": 25," +
      "\"address\":" +
      "{" +
      "\"streetAddress\": \"21 2nd Street\"," +
      "\"city\": \"New York\"," +
      "\"state\": \"NY\"," +
      "\"postalCode\": \"10021-3100\"" +
      "}," +
      "\"phoneNumbers\":" +
      "[" +
      "{" +
      "\"type\": \"home\"," +
      "\"number\": \"212 555-1234\"" +
      "}," +
      "{" +
```

```
         "\"type\": \"office\"," +
         "\"number\": \"646 555-4567\"" +
         "}" +
         "]," +
         "\"children\": []," +
         "\"spouse\": null" +
         "}";
      Json json = Json.read(jsonStr);
      System.out.println(json);
   }
}
```

The `main(String[])` method first declares a Java string-based JSON object
(you could substitute a comma (,) for the colon character (:), but the colon is
clearer); then invokes `Json.read()` to read and parse this object, and return
the object as a `Json` object; and finally outputs a string representation of the
`Json` object (by ultimately calling its `toString()` method to convert the `Json`
object to a Java string).

Compile Listing 8-1 as follows:

```
javac -cp mjson-1.3.jar mJsonDemo.java
```

Run the resulting application as follows:

```
java -cp mjson-1.3.jar;. mJsonDemo
```

You should observe the following output:

```
{"firstName":"John","lastName":"Smith","isAlive":true,"address":{"streetAdd
ress":"21 2nd Street","city":"New York","postalCode":"10021-3100","state":
"NY"},"children":[],"age":25,"phoneNumbers":[{"number":"212 555-1234","type":
"home"},{"number":"646 555-4567","type":"office"}],"spouse":null}
```

The `read()` methods can also parse smaller JSON fragments, such as an
array of different-typed values. See Listing 8-2 for a demonstration.

Listing 8-2. Reading and Parsing a JSON Fragment

```
import mjson.Json;

public class mJsonDemo
{
   public static void main(String[] args)
   {
      Json json = Json.read("[4, 5, {}, true, null, \"ABC\", 6]");
      System.out.println(json);
   }
}
```

When you run this application, you should observe the following output:

```
[4,5,{},true,null,"ABC",6]
```

In addition to the reading and parsing methods, Json provides static methods for creating Json objects:

- Json array(): Returns a Json object representing an empty JSON array.

- Json array(Object... args): Returns a Json object (representing a JSON array) filled with args, a variable number of java.lang.Objects.

- Json make(Object anything): Returns a Json object filled with the contents of anything, which is one of null; a value of type Json, String, java.util. Collection<?>, java.util.Map<?, ?>, java.lang. Boolean, java.lang.Number; or an array of one of these types. Maps, collections, and arrays are recursively copied such that each of their elements is converted to a Json object. A map's keys are normally strings, but any object with a meaningful toString() implementation will work. This method throws java. lang.IllegalArgumentException when the concrete type of the argument passed to anything is unknown.

- Json nil(): Returns a Json object that represents null.

- Json object(): Returns a Json object representing an empty JSON object.

- Json object(Object... args): Returns a Json object (representing a JSON object) filled with args, a variable number of Objects. These objects identify property names and values; the number of objects must be even, with even indexes identifying property names and odd indexes identifying property values. The names are normally of type String, but can be of any other type that has an appropriate toString() method. Each value is first converted to a Json object by calling make(Object).

Listing 8-3 presents the source code for an application that demonstrates most of these additional static methods.

Listing 8-3. Creating a Person JSON Object

```java
import mjson.Json;

public class mJsonDemo
{
   public static void main(String[] args)
   {
      Json jsonAddress =
         Json.object("streetAddress", "21 2nd Street",
                     "city", "New York",
                     "state", "NY",
                     "postalCode", "10021-3100");
      Json jsonPhone1 =
         Json.object("type", "home",
                     "number", "212 555-1234");
      Json jsonPhone2 =
         Json.object("type", "office",
                     "number", "646 555-4567");
      Json jsonPerson =
         Json.object("firstName", "John",
                     "lastName", "Smith",
                     "isAlive", true,
                     "age", 25,
                     "address", jsonAddress,
                     "phoneNumbers", Json.array(jsonPhone1, jsonPhone2),
                     "children", Json.array(),
                     "spouse", Json.nil());
      System.out.println(jsonPerson);
   }
}
```

Listing 8-3 describes an application that creates the same JSON object that's read and parsed in Listing 8-1. Notice that you can pass `Json` objects to `array(Object...)` and `object(Object...)`, which lets you build complete JSON objects from smaller fragments. If you run this application, you'll discover the same output as generated by the application described in Listing 8-1.

Listing 8-4 presents the source code for another application that uses `make(Object)` with Java collections and maps.

Listing 8-4. Making JSON Objects from Java Collections and Maps

```java
import java.util.ArrayList;
import java.util.Arrays;
import java.util.HashMap;
import java.util.List;
import java.util.Map;
```

```java
import mjson.Json;

public class mJsonDemo
{
    public static void main(String[] args)
    {
        List<String> weekdays = Arrays.asList("Sunday", "Monday", "Tuesday",
        "Wednesday", "Thursday", "Friday", "Saturday");
        System.out.println(Json.make(weekdays));

        Map<String, Number> people = new HashMap<>();
        people.put("John", 33);
        people.put("Joan", 27);
        System.out.println(Json.make(people));

        Map<String, String[]> planets = new HashMap<>();
        planets.put("Mercury", null);
        planets.put("Earth", new String[] {"Luna"});
        planets.put("Mars", new String[] {"Phobos", "Deimos"});
        System.out.println(Json.make(planets));
    }
}
```

main(String[]) first creates a list of weekday names and then passes this object to make(Object), whose returned Json object is output. Next, a map of people's names and ages is created and subsequently passed to make(Object). The resulting JSON object is output. Finally, a map of planet names along with arrays of moon names is created. This map is converted into a more complex JSON object, which is output.

If you compile this source code and run the application, you'll discover the following output:

```
["Sunday","Monday","Tuesday","Wednesday","Thursday","Friday","Saturday"]
{"Joan":27,"John":33}
{"Earth":["Luna"],"Mars":["Phobos","Deimos"],"Mercury":null}
```

Learning About Json Objects

Json offers several methods for learning about the JSON entities described by Json objects. For starters, you can call the Object getValue() method to return the JSON value (as a Java object) of the Json object. The returned value will be Java null or have the Java Boolean, String, Number, Map, java.util.List, or an array type. For objects and arrays, this method performs a deep copy of all nested elements.

To identify the JSON type of the JSON value, call one of the following methods:

- boolean isArray(): Returns true for a JSON array value.

- boolean isBoolean(): Returns true for a JSON Boolean value.

- boolean isNull(): Returns true for the JSON null value.

- boolean isNumber(): Returns true for a JSON number value.

- boolean isObject(): Returns true for a JSON object value.

- boolean isPrimitive(): Returns true for a JSON number, string, or Boolean value.

- boolean isString(): Returns true for a JSON string value.

Listing 8-5 presents the source code for an application that demonstrates getValue() and these JSON type-identification methods.

Listing 8-5. Obtaining a Json Object's Value and Identifying Its JSON Type

```
import mjson.Json;

public class mJsonDemo
{
   public static void main(String[] args)
   {
      String jsonStr =
      "{" +
      "\"firstName\": \"John\"," +
      "\"lastName\": \"Smith\"," +
      "\"isAlive\": true," +
      "\"age\": 25," +
      "\"address\":" +
      "{" +
      "\"streetAddress\": \"21 2nd Street\"," +
      "\"city\": \"New York\"," +
      "\"state\": \"NY\"," +
      "\"postalCode\": \"10021-3100\"" +
      "}," +
      "\"phoneNumbers\":" +
      "[" +
      "{" +
      "\"type\": \"home\"," +
      "\"number\": \"212 555-1234\"" +
      "}," +
      "{" +
```

```
        "\"type\": \"office\"," +
        "\"number\": \"646 555-4567\"" +
        "}" +
        "]," +
        "\"children\": []," +
        "\"spouse\": null" +
        "}";
    Json json = Json.read(jsonStr);
    System.out.println("Value = " + json.getValue());
    System.out.println();
    classify(json);
}

static void classify(Json jsonObject)
{
    if (jsonObject.isArray())
        System.out.println("Array");
    else
    if (jsonObject.isBoolean())
        System.out.println("Boolean");
    else
    if (jsonObject.isNull())
        System.out.println("Null");
    else
    if (jsonObject.isNumber())
        System.out.println("Number");
    else
    if (jsonObject.isObject())
        System.out.println("Object");
    else
    if (jsonObject.isString())
        System.out.println("String");
    if (jsonObject.isPrimitive())
        System.out.println("Primitive");
    }
}
```

Compile this source code and run the application, and you'll discover the following output:

```
Value = {firstName=John, lastName=Smith, isAlive=true,
address={streetAddress=21 2nd Street, city=New York, postalCode=10021-3100,
state=NY}, children=[], age=25, phoneNumbers=[{number=212 555-1234,
type=home}, {number=646 555-4567, type=office}], spouse=null}

Object
```

After verifying that a `Json` object represents the expected JSON type, you can call one of `Json`'s "as" methods to obtain the JSON value as a Java value of an equivalent Java type:

- `boolean asBoolean()`: Returns the JSON value as a Java Boolean.

- `byte asByte()`: Returns the JSON value as a Java byte integer.

- `char asChar()`: Returns the first character of the JSON string value as a Java character.

- `double asDouble()`: Returns the JSON value as a Java double precision floating-point value.

- `float asFloat()`: Returns the JSON value as a Java floating-point value.

- `int asInteger()`: Returns the JSON value as a Java integer.

- `List<Json> asJsonList()`: Returns the underlying list representation of a JSON array. The returned list is the actual array representation so any modifications to it are modifications to the `Json` object's list.

- `Map<String, Json> asJsonMap()`: Returns the underlying map of properties of a JSON object. The returned map is the actual object representation so any modifications to it are modifications to the `Json` object's map.

- `List<Object> asList()`: Returns a list of the elements of a `Json` object that describes a JSON array. The returned list is a copy and modifications to it don't affect the `Json` object.

- `long asLong()`: Returns the JSON value as a Java long integer.

- `Map<String, Object> asMap()`: Returns a map of the properties of a `Json` object that describes a JSON object. The returned map is a copy and modifications to it don't affect the `Json` object.

- `short asShort()`: Returns the JSON value as a Java short integer.

- `String asString()`: Returns the JSON value as a Java string.

Listing 8-6 presents the source code for an application that uses `asMap()` to obtain a map of the `Json` object properties describing a JSON object.

Listing 8-6. Iterating Over a Json Object's Properties to Learn About a JSON Object

```java
import java.util.Map;

import mjson.Json;

public class mJsonDemo
{
    public static void main(String[] args)
    {
        String jsonStr =
        "{" +
        "\"firstName\": \"John\"," +
        "\"lastName\": \"Smith\"," +
        "\"isAlive\": true," +
        "\"age\": 25," +
        "\"address\":" +
        "{" +
        "\"streetAddress\": \"21 2nd Street\"," +
        "\"city\": \"New York\"," +
        "\"state\": \"NY\"," +
        "\"postalCode\": \"10021-3100\"" +
        "}," +
        "\"phoneNumbers\":" +
        "[" +
        "{" +
        "\"type\": \"home\"," +
        "\"number\": \"212 555-1234\"" +
        "}," +
        "{" +
        "\"type\": \"office\"," +
        "\"number\": \"646 555-4567\"" +
        "}" +
        "]," +
        "\"children\": []," +
        "\"spouse\": null" +
        "}";
        Json json = Json.read(jsonStr);
        if (json.isObject())
        {
            Map<String, Object> props = json.asMap();
            for (Map.Entry<String, Object> propEntry: props.entrySet())
                System.out.println(propEntry.getKey() + ": " + propEntry.
                getValue());
        }
    }
}
```

main(String[]) declares the same JSON object as presented in Listing 8-1. It then reads and parses this object into a Json object. The isObject() method is called to verify that the Json object represents a JSON object. (It's a good idea to verify first.) Because this should be the case, asMap() is called to return a map of the Json object's properties, which are then iterated over and output.

> **Caution**   If you replace Json json = Json.read(jsonStr); with Json json = Json.make(jsonStr);, you won't see any output because the Json object returned from make() identifies the JSON string type and not the JSON object type.

After studying the source code, compile it and run the application. You'll discover the following output:

```
firstName: John
lastName: Smith
isAlive: true
address: {streetAddress=21 2nd Street, city=New York, postalCode=10021-3100,
state=NY}
children: []
age: 25
phoneNumbers: [{number=212 555-1234, type=home}, {number=646 555-4567,
type=office}]
spouse: null
```

You can access the contents of arrays and objects by calling the following at() methods, which return Json objects that describe array element values or object property values:

- Json at(int index): Returns the value (as a Json object) of the array element at the specified index in this Json object's array. This method applies to JSON arrays only. It throws java.lang.IndexOutOfBoundsException when index is out of bounds for the array.

- Json at(String propName): Returns the value (as a Json object) of the object property whose name is identified by propName in this Json object's map. Returns null when there's no such property. This method applies to JSON objects only.

- Json at(String propName, Json defValue): Returns the value (as a Json object) of the object property whose name is identified by propName in this Json object's map. When there's no such property, it creates a new property whose value is specified by defValue and returns defValue. This method applies to JSON objects only.

- Json at(String propName, Object defValue): Returns the value (as a Json object) of the object property whose name is identified by propName in this Json object's map. When there's no such property, it creates a new property whose value is specified by defValue and returns defValue. This method applies to JSON objects only.

Listing 8-7 presents the source code for an application that uses the first two at() methods to access a JSON object's property values.

Listing 8-7. Obtaining and Outputting a JSON Object's Property Values

```java
import mjson.Json;

public class mJsonDemo
{
   public static void main(String[] args)
   {
      String jsonStr =
      "{" +
      "\"firstName\": \"John\"," +
      "\"lastName\": \"Smith\"," +
      "\"isAlive\": true," +
      "\"age\": 25," +
      "\"address\":" +
      "{" +
      "\"streetAddress\": \"21 2nd Street\"," +
      "\"city\": \"New York\"," +
      "\"state\": \"NY\"," +
      "\"postalCode\": \"10021-3100\"" +
      "}," +
      "\"phoneNumbers\":" +
      "[" +
      "{" +
      "\"type\": \"home\"," +
      "\"number\": \"212 555-1234\"" +
      "}," +
      "{" +
      "\"type\": \"office\"," +
      "\"number\": \"646 555-4567\"" +
      "}" +
      "]," +
```

```
        "\"children\": []," +
        "\"spouse\": null" +
        "}";
        Json json = Json.read(jsonStr);
        System.out.printf("First name = %s%n", json.at("firstName"));
        System.out.printf("Last name = %s%n", json.at("lastName"));
        System.out.printf("Is alive = %s%n", json.at("isAlive"));
        System.out.printf("Age = %d%n", json.at("age").asInteger());
        System.out.println("Address");
        Json jsonAddr = json.at("address");
        System.out.printf("   Street address = %s%n",  jsonAddr.
        at("streetAddress"));
        System.out.printf("   City = %s%n", jsonAddr.at("city"));
        System.out.printf("   State = %s%n", jsonAddr.at("state"));
        System.out.printf("   Postal code = %s%n", jsonAddr.at("postalCode"));
        System.out.println("Phone Numbers");
        Json jsonPhone = json.at("phoneNumbers");
        System.out.printf("   Type = %s%n", jsonPhone.at(0).at("type"));
        System.out.printf("   Number = %s%n", jsonPhone.at(0).at("number"));
        System.out.println();
        System.out.printf("   Type = %s%n", jsonPhone.at(1).at("type"));
        System.out.printf("   Number = %s%n", jsonPhone.at(1).at("number"));
        Json jsonChildren = json.at("children");
        System.out.printf("Children = %s%n", jsonChildren);
        System.out.printf("Spouse = %s%n", json.at("spouse"));
    }
}
```

Expression `json.at("age")` returns a `Json` object describing a JSON number; `asInteger()` returns this value as a 32-bit Java integer.

Compile this source code and run the application. You'll discover the following output:

```
First name = "John"
Last name = "Smith"
Is alive = true
Age = 25
Address
    Street address = "21 2nd Street"
    City = "New York"
    State = "NY"
    Postal code = "10021-3100"
Phone Numbers
    Type = "home"
    Number = "212 555-1234"
```

```
    Type = "office"
    Number = "646 555-4567"
Children = []
Spouse = null
```

You might be wondering how to detect the empty array that's assigned to the children property name. You can accomplish this task by calling asList() to return a List implementation object, and then calling List's size() method on this object, as follows:

```
System.out.printf("Array length = %d%n", jsonChildren.asList().size());
```

This code fragment will report an array length of zero elements.

Finally, Json provides three methods for verifying that property names exist, and that property names or array elements exist with specified values:

- boolean has(String propName): Returns true when this Json object describes a JSON object that has a property identified by propName; otherwise, returns false.

- boolean is(int index, Object value): Returns true when this Json object describes a JSON array that has the specified value at the specified index; otherwise, returns false.

- boolean is(String propName, Object value): Returns true when this Json object describes a JSON object that has a property identified by propName and this property has the value identified by value; otherwise, returns false.

For example, consider Listing 8-7. Expression json.has("firstName") returns true, whereas expression json.has("middleName") returns false.

Navigating Json Object Hierarchies

When one of the previously discussed at() methods returns a Json object describing a JSON object or JSON array, you can navigate into the object or array by chaining another at() method call to the expression. For example, I used this technique in the previous application to access a phone number:

```
System.out.printf("   Number = %s%n", jsonPhone.at(0).at("number"));
```

Here, jsonPhone.at(0) returns a Json object that represents the first array entry in the phoneNumbers JSON array. Because the array entry happens to be a JSON object, calling at("number") on this Json object causes Json to return the value (as a Json object) of the JSON object's number property.

Each Json object that describes a JSON entity belonging to an array or an object holds a reference to its enclosing array- or object-based Json object. You can call Json's Json up() method to return this enclosing Json object, which is demonstrated in Listing 8-8.

Listing 8-8. Accessing Enclosing Json Objects

```java
import mjson.Json;

public class mJsonDemo
{
    public static void main(String[] args)
    {
        String jsonStr =
        "{" +
        "\"propName\": \"propValue\"," +
        "\"propArray\":" +
        "[" +
        "{" +
        "\"element1\": \"value1\"" +
        "}," +
        "{" +
        "\"element2\": \"value2\"" +
        "}" +
        "]" +
        "}";
        Json json = Json.read(jsonStr);
        Json jsonElement1 = json.at("propArray").at(0);
        System.out.println(jsonElement1);
        System.out.println();
        System.out.println(jsonElement1.up());
        System.out.println();
        System.out.println(jsonElement1.up().up());
        System.out.println();
        System.out.println(jsonElement1.up().up().up());
    }
}
```

Compile this source code and run the application, and you'll discover the following output:

```
{"element1":"value1"}

[{"element1":"value1"},{"element2":"value2"}]

{"propArray":[{"element1":"value1"},{"element2":"value2"}],"propName":"prop
Value"}

null
```

The first output line describes the first array element in the array assigned to the `propArray` property. This element is an object consisting of a single `element1` property.

`jsonElement1.up()` returns a `Json` object describing the array that encloses the JSON object that serves as the array's first element. `jsonElement1.up().up()` returns a `Json` object describing the JSON object that encloses the array. Finally, `jsonElement1.up().up().up()` returns a `Json` object describing the `null` value; the JSON object has no parent.

Modifying Json Objects

You'll encounter situations where you'll want to modify existing `Json` objects' JSON values. For example, you might be creating and saving several similar JSON objects and wanting to reuse existing `Json` objects.

`Json` lets you modify `Json` objects that represent JSON arrays and objects. It doesn't let you modify `Json` objects that represent JSON Boolean, number, or string values because they're regarded as immutable.

`Json` declares the following `set()` methods for modifying JSON array elements and JSON object properties:

- `Json set(int index, Object value)`: Sets the value of the JSON array element located at `index` to `value`.

- `Json set(String propName, Json value)`: Sets the value of the JSON object property whose name is specified by `propName` to `value`.

- `Json set(String property, Object value)`: Sets the value of the JSON object property whose name is specified by `propName` to `value`. This method calls `make(Object)` to convert `value` to a `Json` object representing `value` and then invokes `set(String, Json)`.

Listing 8-9 presents the source code for an application that uses the first and third `set()` methods to set object property and array element values.

Listing 8-9. Setting Object Property and Array Element Values

```java
import mjson.Json;

public class mJsonDemo
{
    public static void main(String[] args)
    {
        String jsonStr =
        "{" +
        "\"name\": null," +
        "\"courses\":" +
        "[null]" +
        "}";
        Json json = Json.read(jsonStr);
        System.out.println(json);
        System.out.println();
        json.set("name", "John Doe");
        Json jsonCourses = json.at("courses");
        jsonCourses.set(0, "English");
        System.out.println(json);
    }
}
```

If you compile this source code and run the application, you'll discover the following output:

```
{"courses":[null],"name":null}
```

```
{"courses":["English"],"name":"John Doe"}
```

If you attempt to set a value for a property that doesn't exist, Json adds the property. However, if you attempt to set the value for a nonexistent array element, Json throws IndexOutOfBoundsException. For this reason, you might prefer to call one of the following add() methods instead:

- Json add(Json element): Appends the specified element to the array represented by this Json object.

- Json add(Object anything): Converts anything to a Json object by calling make(Object) and appending the result to the array represented by this Json object.

Listing 8-10 presents the source code for an application that uses the first add() method to append two strings to the empty courses array.

Listing 8-10. Appending Strings to an Empty JSON Array

```java
import mjson.Json;

public class mJsonDemo
{
    public static void main(String[] args)
    {
        String jsonStr =
        "{" +
        "\"name\": null," +
        "\"courses\":" |
        "[]" +
        "}";
        Json json = Json.read(jsonStr);
        System.out.println(json);
        System.out.println();
        json.set("name", "John Doe");
        Json jsonCourses = json.at("courses");
        jsonCourses.add("English");
        jsonCourses.add("French");
        System.out.println(json);
    }
}
```

Compile this source code and run the application. It generates the output shown here:

```
{"courses":[],"name":null}

{"courses":["English","French"],"name":"John Doe"}
```

Json provides a pair of array-oriented remove() methods that take the same arguments as their add() counterparts:

- Json remove(Json element): Removes the specified element from the array represented by this Json object.

- Json remove(Object anything): Converts anything to a Json object by calling make(Object) and removing the result from the array represented by this Json object.

Suppose you append the following lines to Listing 8-10's main(String[]) method:

```java
jsonCourses.remove("English");
System.out.println(json);
```

You should then observe the following additional output:

```
{"courses":["French"],"name":"John Doe"}
```

You can remove an element from an array by index or remove a property from an object by name by calling the following methods:

- Json atDel(int index): Removes the element at the specified index from this Json object's JSON array and returns the element.

- Json atDel(String propName): Removes the property identified by propName from this Json object's JSON object and returns the property value (or null when the property doesn't exist).

- Json delAt(int index): Removes the element at the specified index from this Json object's JSON array.

- Json delAt(String propName): Removes the property identified by propName from this Json object's JSON object.

Listing 8-11 presents the source code for an application that uses the last two delAt() methods to delete a property and an array element.

Listing 8-11. Removing the Last Name and One of the Courses Being Taken

```java
import mjson.Json;

public class mJsonDemo
{
    public static void main(String[] args)
    {
        String jsonStr =
        "{" +
        "\"firstName\": \"John\"," +
        "\"lastName\": \"Doe\"," +
        "\"courses\":" +
        "[\"English\", \"French\", \"Spanish\"]" +
        "}";
        Json json = Json.read(jsonStr);
        System.out.println(json);
        System.out.println();
        json.delAt("lastName");
        System.out.println(json);
        System.out.println();
        json.at("courses").delAt(1);
        System.out.println(json);
    }
}
```

To see the results of the delAt() methods, compile this source code and run the application. Its output is shown here:

```
{"firstName":"John","lastName":"Doe","courses":["English","French","Spanish"]}

{"firstName":"John","courses":["English","French","Spanish"]}

{"firstName":"John","courses":["English","Spanish"]}
```

Json provides an additional method for modifying a JSON object:

- Json with(Json objectorarray): Combines this Json object's JSON object or JSON array with the argument passed to objectorarray. The JSON type of this Json object and the JSON type of objectorarray must match. If objectorarray identifies a JSON object, all of its properties are appended to this Json object's object. If objectorarray identifies a JSON array, all of its elements are appended to this Json object's array.

Listing 8-12 presents the source code for an application that uses with(Json) to append properties to an object and elements to an array.

Listing 8-12. Appending Properties to an Object and Elements to an Array

```java
import mjson.Json;

public class mJsonDemo
{
    public static void main(String[] args)
    {
        String jsonStr =
        "{" +
        "\"firstName\": \"John\"," +
        "\"courses\":" +
        "[\"English\"]" +
        "}";
        Json json = Json.read(jsonStr);
        System.out.println(json);
        System.out.println();
        Json jsono = Json.read("{\"initial\": \"P\", \"lastName\": \"Doe\"}");
        Json jsona = Json.read("[\"French\", \"Spanish\"]");
        json.with(jsono);
        System.out.println(json);
        System.out.println();
        json.at("courses").with(jsona);
        System.out.println(json);
    }
}
```

Compile Listing 8-12 and run the application. Here is the application's output:

```
{"firstName":"John","courses":["English"]}
```

```
{"firstName":"John","courses":["English"],"lastName":"Doe","initial":"P"}
```

```
{"firstName":"John","courses":["English","French","Spanish"],"lastName":"Doe",
"initial":"P"}
```

Validation

Json supports JSON Schema Draft 4 validation via its nested Schema interface and the following static methods:

- Json.Schema schema(Json jsonSchema): Returns a Json. Schema object that validates JSON documents according to the schema described by jsonSchema.

- Json.Schema schema(Json jsonSchema, URI uri): Returns a Json.Schema object that validates JSON documents according to the schema described by jsonSchema and also located at the Uniform Resource Identifier (URI) passed to uri, which is of type java.net.URI.

- Json.Schema schema(URI uri): Returns a Json.Schema object that validates JSON documents according to the schema located at uri.

Validation is performed by calling Schema's Json validate(Json document) method, which attempts to validate a JSON document according to this Schema object. Validation attempts to proceed even when validation errors are detected. The return value is always a Json object whose JSON object contains the Boolean property named ok. When ok is true, there are no other properties. When it's false, the JSON object also contains a property named errors, which is an array of error messages for all detected schema violations.

I've created two sample applications that demonstrate validation. Listing 8-13 is based on example code at the mJson web site.

Listing 8-13. Validating JSON Objects That Include the `id` Property

```java
import mjson.Json;

public class mJsonDemo
{
    public static void main(String[] args)
    {
        // A simple schema that accepts only JSON objects with a
            // mandatory property 'id'.
        Json.Schema schema = Json.schema(Json.object("type", "object",
        "required", Json.array("id")));
        System.out.println(schema.validate(Json.object("id", 666, "name",
        "Britlan")));
        System.out.println(schema.validate(Json.object("ID", 666, "name",
        "Britlan")));
    }
}
```

If you compile this source code and run the application, you'll discover the following output:

```
{"ok":true}
{"ok":false,"errors":["Required property id missing from object {\"name\":\"
Britlan\",\"ID\":666}"]}
```

In Chapter 7, I presented the following JSON object:

```
{
    "name": "John Doe",
    "age": 35
}
```

I also presented the following schema as a JSON object:

```
{
    "$schema": "http://json-schema.org/draft-04/schema#",
    "title": "Person",
    "description": "A person",
    "type": "object",
    "properties":
    {
        "name":
        {
            "description": "A person's name",
            "type": "string"
        },
```

```
    "age":
    {
        "description": "A person's age",
        "type": "number",
        "minimum": 18,
        "maximum": 64
    }
  },
  "required": ["name", "age"]
}
```

Suppose that I copy this schema to a schema.json file and store it on my web site at http://javajeff.ca/schema.json. Listing 8-14 presents the source code for an application that uses Json.Schema schema(URI) to obtain this schema for validating the previous JSON object.

Listing 8-14. Validating JSON Objects via an External Schema

```java
import java.net.URI;
import java.net.URISyntaxException;

import mjson.Json;

public class mJsonDemo
{
    public static void main(String[] args) throws URISyntaxException
    {
        Json.Schema schema =
            Json.schema(new URI("http://javajeff.ca/schema.json"));
        Json json = Json.read("{\"name\": \"John Doe\", \"age\": 35}");
        System.out.println(schema.validate(json));
        json = Json.read("{\"name\": \"John Doe\", \"age\": 65}");
        System.out.println(schema.validate(json));
        json = Json.read("{\"name\": \"John Doe\", \"age\": \"35\"}");
        System.out.println(schema.validate(json));
        json = Json.read("{\"age\": 35}");
        System.out.println(schema.validate(json));
    }
}
```

Compile this source code and run the application. You'll discover the following output:

```
{"ok":true}
{"ok":false,"errors":["Number 65 is above allowed maximum 64.0"]}
{"ok":false,"errors":["Type mistmatch for \"35\", allowed types: [\"number\"]"]}
{"ok":false,"errors":["Required property name missing from object {\"age\":35}"]}
```

Customization via Factories

Json defers the creation of Json objects to a factory, which is an instance of a class that implements the Json.Factory interface's methods:

- Json array()
- Json bool(boolean value)
- Json make(Object anything)
- Json nil()
- Json number(Number value)
- Json object()
- Json string(String value)

The Json.DefaultFactory class provides default implementations of these methods, but you can provide custom implementations when necessary. To avoid implementing all of these methods, you can extend DefaultFactory and override only those methods of interest.

After creating a custom Factory class, you instantiate it and then install the object by calling one of the following static Json methods:

- void setGlobalFactory(Json.Factory factory)
- void attachFactory(Json.Factory factory)

The first method installs the specified factory as a global factory, which is used by all threads that don't have a specific thread-local factory attached to them. The second method attaches the specified factory to the invoking thread only, which lets you use different thread factories in the same classloader. You can remove a thread-local factory and revert to the global factory for a thread by calling the void dettachFactory() method.

One of the customizations mentioned in the mJson documentation is case-insensitive string comparison. You compare two strings for equality by invoking equals() on a string-based Json object with another string-based Json object as an argument:

```
Json json1 = Json.read("\"abc\"");
Json json2 = Json.read("\"abc\"");
Json json3 = Json.read("\"Abc\"");
System.out.println(json1.equals(json2)); // Output: true
System.out.println(json1.equals(json3));
```

Because equals() defaults to being case-sensitive, json1.equals(json3) returns false.

> **Note**   The equals() method that's called is not located in the Json class.
> Instead, it's located in a nested package-private class, such as StringJson.

You can make equals() case-insensitive for string-based Json objects by
first creating the following Factory class:

```
class MyFactory extends Json.DefaultFactory
{
    @Override
    public Json string(String x)
    {
        // Obtain the StringJson instance.
        final Json json = super.string(x);

        class StringIJson extends Json
        {
            private static final long serialVersionUID = 1L;

            String val;

            StringIJson(String val)
            {
                this.val = val;
            }

            @Override
            public byte asByte()
            {
                return json.asByte();
            }

            @Override
            public char asChar()
            {
                return json.asChar();
            }

            @Override
            public double asDouble()
            {
                return json.asDouble();
            }
```

```java
@Override
public float asFloat()
{
    return json.asFloat();
}

@Override
public int asInteger()
{
    return json.asInteger();
}

@Override
public List<Object> asList()
{
    return json.asList();
}

@Override
public long asLong()
{
    return json.asLong();
}

@Override
public short asShort()
{
    return json.asShort();
}

@Override
public String asString()
{
    return json.asString();
}

@Override
public Json dup()
{
    return json.dup();
}

@Override
public boolean equals(Object x)
{
    return x instanceof StringIJson &&
           ((StringIJson) x).val.equalsIgnoreCase(val);
}
```

```
        @Override
        public Object getValue()
        {
            return json.getValue();
        }

        @Override
        public int hashCode()
        {
            return json.hashCode();
        }

        @Override
        public boolean isString()
        {
            return json.isString();
        }

        @Override
        public String toString()
        {
            return json.toString();
        }
    }
    return new StringIJson(x);
  }
}
```

MyFactory overrides the string(String) method, which is responsible for creating Json objects that represent JSON strings. In the Json.java source code (which you can access from the mJson web site), string(String) executes return new StringJson(x, null);.

StringJson is the name of a nested package-private static class. Because it cannot be accessed from outside of the mjson package, MyFactory's overriding string(String) method declares an equivalent StringIJson class (the I is for case-insensitive).

Rather than copy all of the code from StringJson to StringIJson, which is wasteful duplication and won't work anyway because some of the code relies on other package-private types, I chose to use the adapter/wrapper design pattern (https://en.wikipedia.org/wiki/Adapter_pattern).

The idea behind the adapter pattern is to have StringIJson duplicate StringJson methods in terms of their headers, and code the bodies to forward almost all method calls to the StringJson equivalents. This is possible by having MyFactory's string(String) method first invoke DefaultFactory's string(String) method, which returns the StringJson object. It's then a simple matter of forwarding calls to this object.

The exception is the equals() method. StringIJson codifies this method to be nearly identical to its StringJson counterpart. The main difference is the call to String's equalsIgnoreCase() method instead of its equals() method. The result is a case-insensitive equals() method.

Before performing any equality testing, MyFactory needs to be instantiated and registered with Json, which the following method call accomplishes:

```
Json.setGlobalFactory(new MyFactory());
```

This time, json1.equals(json3) returns true.

EXERCISES

The following exercises are designed to test your understanding of Chapter 8's content.

1. Define mJson.

2. Describe the Json class.

3. Identify Json's methods for reading and parsing external JSON objects.

4. True or false: The read() methods can also parse smaller JSON fragments, such as an array of different-typed values.

5. Identify the methods that Json provides for creating JSON objects.

6. What does Json's boolean isPrimitive() method accomplish?

7. How do you return a Json object's JSON array?

8. True or false: Json's Map<String, Json> asJsonMap() method returns a map of the properties of a Json object that describes a JSON object. The returned map is a copy and modifications to it don't affect the Json object.

9. Which Json methods let you access the contents of arrays and objects?

10. What does Json's boolean is(int index, Object value) method accomplish?

11. What does Json do when you attempt to set the value for a nonexistent array element?

12. What is the difference between Json's atDel() and delAt() methods?

13. What does Json's Json with(Json objectorarray) method accomplish?

14. Identify Json's methods for obtaining a Json.Schema object.

15.   How do you validate a JSON document against a schema?

16.   What is the difference between Json's setGlobalFactory() and attachFactory() methods?

17.   Two Json methods that were not discussed in this chapter are Json dup() and String pad(String callback). What do they do?

18.   Write an mJsonDemo application that demonstrates dup() and pad().

Summary

mJson is a small Java-based JSON library for parsing JSON objects into Java objects and vice versa. It consists of a Json class that describes a JSON object or part of a JSON object. Json contains Schema and Factory interfaces, more than 50 methods, and other members.

After obtaining the mJson library, you learned how to use this library to create Json objects, learned about Json objects, navigated Json object hierarchies, modified Json objects, validated JSON documents against a schema, and customized Json by installing nondefault factories.

Chapter 9 introduces Gson for parsing and creating JSON objects.

Parsing and Creating JSON Objects with Gson

Gson is another API for for parsing and creating JSON objects. This chapter explores the latest version of this open source Google product.

What Is Gson?

Gson (also known as *Google Gson*) is a small Java-based library for parsing and creating JSON objects. Google developed Gson for its own projects, but later made Gson publicly available, starting with version 1.0. According to Wikipedia, the latest version (at the time of writing) is 2.6.1.

Gson was developed with the following goals in mind:

- Provide simple `toJson()` and `fromJson()` methods to convert Java objects to JSON objects and vice versa.

- Allow pre-existing unmodifiable objects to be converted to and from JSON.

- Provide extensive support for Java Generics.

- Allow custom representations of objects.

- Support arbitrarily complex objects (with deep inheritance hierarchies and extensive use of generic types).

© Jeff Friesen 2016
J. Friesen, *Java XML and JSON*, DOI 10.1007/978-1-4842-1916-4_9

Gson parses JSON objects by deserializing JSON objects into Java objects. Similarly, it creates JSON objects by serializing Java objects into JSON objects. Gson relies on Java's Reflection API to assist with serialization and deserialization.

Obtaining and Using Gson

Gson is distributed as a single Jar file; gson-2.6.1.jar is the most recent Jar file at the time of writing. To obtain this Jar file, point your browser to http://search.maven.org/#artifactdetails|com.google.code. gson|gson|2.6.1|jar, select gson-2.6.1.jar from the list near the bottom of the page, and download it. Also, you might want to download gson-2.6.1-javadoc.jar, which contains this API's Javadoc.

> **Note**   Gson is licensed according to Apache License Version 2.0 (www.apache.org/licenses/).

It's easy to work with with gson-2.6.1.jar. Simply include it in the classpath when compiling source code or running an application, as follows:

```
javac -cp gson-2.6.1.jar source file
java -cp gson-2.6.1.jar;. main classfile
```

Exploring GSon

Gson consists of more than 30 classes and interfaces distributed among four packages:

- com.google.gson: This package provides access to Gson, the main class for working with Gson.

- com.google.gson.annotations: This package provides annotation types for use with Gson.

- com.google.gson.reflect: This package provides a utility class for obtaining type information from a generic type.

- com.google.gson.stream: This package provides utility classes for reading and writing JSON-encoded values.

In this section, I first introduce you to the Gson class. Then, I focus on Gson deserialization (parsing JSON objects) followed by Gson serialization (creating JSON objects). I close by briefly discussing additional Gson features, such as annotations and type adapters.

Introducing the Gson Class

The Gson class handles the conversion between JSON and Java objects. You can instantiate this class by using the Gson() constructor, or you can obtain a Gson instance by working with the com.google.gson.GsonBuilder class. The following code fragment demonstrates both approaches:

```
Gson gson1 = new Gson();
Gson gson2 = new GsonBuilder()
     .registerTypeAdapter(Id.class, new IdTypeAdapter())
     .serializeNulls()
     .setDateFormat(DateFormat.LONG)
     .setFieldNamingPolicy(FieldNamingPolicy.UPPER_CAMEL_CASE)
     .setPrettyPrinting()
     .setVersion(1.0)
     .create();
```

Call Gson() when you want to work with the default configuration, and use GsonBuilder when you want to override the default configuration. Configuration method calls are chained together, with GsonBuilder's Gson create() method being called last to return the resulting Gson object.

Gson supports the following default configuration (the list isn't complete; check the Gson and GsonBuilder documentation for more information):

- Gson provides default serialization and deserialization for java.lang.Enum, java.util.Map, java.net.URL, java.net.URI, java.util.Locale, java.util.Date, java.math.BigDecimal, and java.math.BigInteger instances. You can change the default representation by registering a *type adapter* (discussed later) via GsonBuilder.registerTypeAdapter(Type, Object).

- The generated JSON text omits all null fields. However, it preserves nulls in arrays because an array is an ordered list. Also, if a field isn't null, but its generated JSON text is empty, the field is kept. You can configure Gson to serialize null values by calling GsonBuilder.serializeNulls().

- The default Date format is the same as java.text.DateFormat.DEFAULT. This format ignores the millisecond portion of the date during serialization. You can change the default format by invoking GsonBuilder.setDateFormat(int) or GsonBuilder.setDateFormat(String).

- The default field-naming policy for the output JSON text is the same as in Java. For example, a Java class field named versionNumber will be output as "versionNumber" in JSON. The same rules are applied for mapping incoming JSON to Java classes. You can change this policy by calling GsonBuilder.setFieldNamingPolicy (FieldNamingPolicy).

- The JSON text that's generated by the toJson() methods is represented compactly: all unneeded whitespace is removed. You can change this behavior by calling GsonBuilder.setPrettyPrinting().

- By default, Gson ignores @Since and @Until annotations. You can enable Gson to use these annotations by calling GsonBuilder.setVersion(double).

- By default, Gson ignores @Expose annotations. You can enable Gson to serialize/deserialize only those fields marked with this annotation by calling GsonBuilder.excludeFieldsWithoutExposeAnnotation().

- By default, Gson excludes transient or static fields from consideration for serialization and deserialization. You can change this behavior by calling GsonBuilder. excludeFieldsWithModifiers(int...).

Once you have a Gson object, you can call various fromJson() and toJson() methods to convert between JSON and Java objects. For example, Listing 9-1 presents a simple application that obtains a Gson object and demonstrates JSON-Java object conversion in terms of JSON primitives.

Listing 9-1. Converting Between JSON and Java Primitives

```
import com.google.gson.Gson;

public class GsonDemo
{
   public static void main(String[] args)
   {
      Gson gson = new Gson();
      String name = gson.fromJson("\"John Doe\"", String.class);
      System.out.println(name);
      gson.toJson(256, System.out);
   }
}
```

Listing 9-1's `main()` method first instantiates Gson, keeping its default configuration. It then invokes Gson's `<T> T fromJson(String json, Class<T> classOfT)` generic method to deserialize the specified `java.lang.String`-based JSON text (in `json`) into an object of the specified class (`classOfT`), which happens to be `String`.

JSON string `"John Doe"` (the double quotes are mandatory), which is expressed as a Java `String` object, is converted (minus the double quotes) to a Java `String` object. A reference to this object is assigned to `name`.

After outputting the returned name, `main()` calls Gson's `void toJson(Object src, Appendable writer)` method to convert autoboxed integer 256 (stored by the compiler in a `java.lang.Integer` object) into a JSON integer and output the result to the standard output stream.

Compile Listing 9-1 as follows:

```
javac -cp gson-2.6.1.jar GsonDemo.java
```

Run the resulting application as follows:

```
java -cp gson-2.6.1.jar;. GsonDemo
```

You should observe the following output:

```
John Doe
256
```

The output isn't impressive, but it's a start. In the next two sections you'll see more useful examples of deserialization and serialization.

Parsing JSON Objects Through Deserialization

Apart from parsing JSON primitives (such as numbers or strings) into their Java equivalents, Gson lets you parse JSON objects into Java objects. For example, suppose you have the following JSON object, which describes a person:

```
{ "name": "John Doe", "age": 45 }
```

Also, suppose you have the following Java class:

```
class Person
{
   String name;
   int age;
}
```

You can use the previous fromJson() method to parse the JSON object into an instance of the Person class, which is demonstrated in Listing 9-2.

Listing 9-2. Parsing a JSON Object into a Java Object

```java
import com.google.gson.Gson;

public class GsonDemo
{
    static class Person
    {
        String name;
        int age;

        Person(String name, int age)
        {
            this.name = name;
            this.age = age;
        }

        @Override
        public String toString()
        {
            return name + ": " + age;
        }
    }

    public static void main(String[] args)
    {
        Gson gson = new Gson();
        String json = "{ name: \"John Doe\", age: 45 }";
        Person person = gson.fromJson(json, Person.class);
        System.out.println(person);
    }
}
```

Listing 9-2 declares a GsonDemo class with a nested Person class that describes a person in terms of a name and an age.

GsonDemo's main() method first instantiates Gson, keeping its default configuration. It then constructs a String-based JSON object representing a person and passes this object along with Person.class to fromJson(String json, Class<T> classOfT). fromJson() parses the name and age stored in the string passed to json, and uses Person.class along with the Reflection API to create a Person object and populate it with the name and age. A reference to the Person object is returned and stored in the person variable, and subsequently passed to System.out.println(). This method ultimately invokes Person's toString() method to return a string representation of the Person object, and then writes this string to the standard output stream.

Compile Listing 9-2 and run the resulting application. You should observe the following output:

```
John Doe: 45
```

Customized JSON Object Parsing

The previous gson.fromJson(json, Person.class) method call relies on Gson's default deserialization mechanism to parse JSON objects. You will often encounter scenarios where you need to parse complex JSON objects into Java objects whose classes don't have the same structure as the JSON objects to be parsed. You can perform this parsing with a custom deserializer, which controls how JSON objects map to Java objects.

The com.google.gson.JsonDeserializer<T> interface describes a custom deserializer. The argument passed to T identifies the type for which the deserializer is being used. For example, you might pass Person to T when needing to parse JSON objects with a somewhat different structure.

JsonDeserializer declares a single method for handling the deserialization (JSON object parsing):

```
T deserialize(JsonElement json,Type typeOfT,
              JsonDeserializationContext context)
```

deserialize() is a callback method that Gson calls during deserialization. This method is called with the following arguments:

- json identifies the JSON element being deserialized.

- typeOfT identifies the type of the Java object in which to deserialize json.

- context identifies a context in which to perform the deserialization. (I'll have more to say about contexts later.)

deserialize() throws com.google.gson.JsonParseException when the JSON element passed to json isn't compatible with the type passed to typeOfT. Because JsonParseException extends java.lang. RuntimeException, you don't have to append a throws clause.

ABOUT JSONELEMENT

The `com.google.gson.JsonElement` class represents a JSON element (such as a number, a Boolean value, or an array). It provides various methods for obtaining an element value, such as double `getAsDouble()`, boolean `getAsBoolean()`, and JsonArray `getAsJsonArray()`.

`JsonElement` is an abstract class that serves as the superclass for the following JSON element classes (in the `com.google.gson` package):

- `JsonArray`: A concrete class that represents JSON's array type. An array is a list of `JsonElements`, each of which can be of a different type. This is an ordered list, meaning that the order in which elements are added is preserved.

- `JsonNull`: A concrete class that represents a JSON null value.

- `JsonObject`: A concrete class that represents JSON's object type. An object consists of name-value pairs, where names are strings and values are any other type of `JsonElement`, which leads to a tree of `JsonElements`. The member elements of this object are maintained in the order they were added.

- `JsonPrimitive`: A concrete class that represents one of JSON's number, string, or Boolean types.

Except for `JsonNull`, each of these subclasses provides various methods for obtaining element values.

After creating a `JsonDeserializer` object, you need to register it with Gson. Accomplish this task by calling the following `GsonBuilder` method:

```
GsonBuilder registerTypeAdapter(Type type, Object typeAdapter)
```

The object passed to `type` identifies the type of the deserializer and the object passed to `typeAdapter` identifies the deserializer. Because `registerTypeAdapter(Type, Object)` returns a `GsonBuilder` object, you can only use this method in a `GsonBuilder` context.

To demonstrate customized JSON object parsing, consider an expanded version of the previous JSON object:

```
{ "first-name": "John", "last-name": "Doe", "age": 45, "address": "Box 1 " }
```

This JSON object differs significantly from the previous JSON object, which consisted of name and age fields:

- The name field has been refactored into first-name and last-name fields. Note that the hyphen (-) isn't a legal character for a Java identifier.

- An address field has been added.

If you modify Listing 9-2 by replacing the object assigned to json with this new object, you shouldn't be surprised by the following output:

```
null: 45
```

The parsing is completely messed up. However, you can fix this problem by introducing the following custom deserializer:

```java
class PersonDeserializer implements JsonDeserializer<Person>
{
   @Override
   public Person deserialize(JsonElement json, Type
   typeOfT,  JsonDeserializationContext context)
   {
      JsonObject jsonObject = json.getAsJsonObject();
      String firstName = jsonObject.get("first-name").getAsString();
      String lastName = jsonObject.get("last-name").getAsString();
      int age = jsonObject.getAsJsonPrimitive("age").getAsInt();
      String address = jsonObject.get("address").getAsString();
      return new Person(firstName + " " + lastName, 45);
   }
}
```

When the custom deserializer is used with the previous JSON object, deserialize() is called only once, and with an object of type JsonObject being passed to json. You could cast this value to a JsonObject, as in JsonObject jsonObject = (JsonObject) json;. Alternatively, you can call JsonElement's JsonObject getAsJsonObject() method to obtain the JsonObject reference, which is what deserialize() first accomplishes.

After obtaining the JsonObject reference, deserialize() calls its JsonElement get(String memberName) method to return a JsonElement for the desired memberName value. The first call passes first-name to get(); you want to obtain the value of this JSON field. Because a JsonPrimitive is returned in place of JsonElement, a call to JsonPrimitive's String getAsString() method is chained to the JsonPrimitive reference, and first-name's value is obtained. This pattern is followed to obtain the values for the last-name and address fields.

For variety, I decided to do something different with the age field. I call JsonObject's JsonPrimitive getAsJsonPrimitive(String memberName) method to return a JsonPrimitive reference corresponding to age. Then, I call JsonPrimitive's int getAsInt() method to return the integer value.

After obtaining all field values, a Person object is created and then returned. Because I'm reusing the Person class shown in Listing 9-2, and because there is no address field in this class, I throw address's value away. You might want to modify Person to include this field.

The following code fragment shows how you would instantiate PersonDeserializer and register it with a GsonBuilder instance, which is also used to obtain a Gson instance in order to call fromJson(), to parse the previous JSON object via the person deserializer:

```
GsonBuilder gsonBuilder = new GsonBuilder();
gsonBuilder.registerTypeAdapter(Person.class, new PersonDeserializer());
Gson gson = gsonBuilder.create();
```

I've combined these code fragments into a working application. Listing 9-3 presents the application's source code.

Listing 9-3. Parsing a JSON Object into a Java Object via a Custom Deserializer

```
import java.lang.reflect.Type;

import com.google.gson.Gson;
import com.google.gson.GsonBuilder;
import com.google.gson.JsonDeserializationContext;
import com.google.gson.JsonDeserializer;
import com.google.gson.JsonElement;
import com.google.gson.JsonObject;
import com.google.gson.JsonParseException;

public class GsonDemo
{
    static class Person
    {
        String name;
        int age;

        Person(String name, int age)
        {
            this.name = name;
            this.age = age;
        }
```

```java
    @Override
    public String toString()
    {
        return name + ": " + age;
    }
}

public static void main(String[] args)
{
    class PersonDeserializer implements JsonDeserializer<Person>
    {
        @Override
        public Person deserialize(JsonElement json, Type typeOfT,
        JsonDeserializationContext context)
        {
            JsonObject jsonObject = json.getAsJsonObject();
            String firstName = jsonObject.get("first-name").getAsString();
            String lastName = jsonObject.get("last-name").getAsString();
            int age = jsonObject.getAsJsonPrimitive("age").getAsInt();
            String address = jsonObject.get("address").getAsString();
            return new Person(firstName + " " + lastName, 45);
        }
    }
    GsonBuilder gsonBuilder = new GsonBuilder();
    gsonBuilder.registerTypeAdapter(Person.class, new PersonDeserializer());
    Gson gson = gsonBuilder.create();
    String json = "{ first-name: \"John\", last-name: \"Doe\", " + "age:
    45, address: \"Box 1\" }";
    Person person = gson.fromJson(json, Person.class);
    System.out.println(person);
}
}
```

Compile Listing 9-3 and run the resulting application. You should observe the following output:

```
John Doe: 45
```

Creating JSON Objects Through Serialization

Gson lets you create JSON objects from Java objects by calling one of Gson's toJson() methods. Listing 9-4 provides a simple demonstration.

Listing 9-4. Creating a JSON Object from a Java Object

```java
import com.google.gson.Gson;

public class GsonDemo
{
   static class Person
   {
      String name;
      int age;

      Person(String name, int age)
      {
         this.name = name;
         this.age = age;
      }
   }

   public static void main(String[] args)
   {
      Person p = new Person("Jane Doe", 59);
      Gson gson = new Gson();
      String json = gson.toJson(p);
      System.out.println(json);
   }
}
```

Listing 9-4's main() method first creates a Person object from the nested Person class. It then creates a Gson object and invokes this object's String toJson(Object src) method to serialize the Person object into its equivalent JSON string representation, which toJson(Object) returns.

Compile Listing 9-4 and run the resulting application. You should observe the following output:

```
{"name":"Jane Doe","age":59}
```

If you prefer to write the JSON object to a file, a string buffer, or some other java.lang.Appendable, you can call void toJson(Object src, Appendable writer) to accomplish this task. This toJson() variant sends its output to the specified writer, as demonstrated in Listing 9-5.

Listing 9-5. Creating a JSON Object from a Java Object and Writing the JSON Object to a File

```java
import java.io.FileWriter;
import java.io.IOException;

import com.google.gson.Gson;

public class GsonDemo
{
   static class Student
   {
      String name;
      int id;
      int[] grades;

      Student(String name, int id, int... grades)
      {
         this.name = name;
         this.id = id;
         this.grades = grades;
      }
   }

   public static void main(String[] args) throws IOException
   {
      Student s = new Student("John Doe", 820787, 89, 78, 97, 65);
      Gson gson = new Gson();
      FileWriter fw = new FileWriter("student.json");
      gson.toJson(s, fw);
      fw.close();
   }
}
```

Listing 9-5's main() method first creates a Student object from the nested Student class. It then creates Gson and java.io.FileWriter objects, and invokes the Gson object's toJson(Object, Appendable) method to serialize the Student object into its equivalent JSON string representation and write the result to student.json. The file writer is then closed so that buffered content can be written to the file (you could specify fw.flush(); instead).

If you run this application, you won't observe any output. However, you should observe a student.json file with the following content:

```json
{"name":"John Doe","id":820787,"grades":[89,78,97,65]}
```

> **Note** void toJson(Object src, Appendable writer) throws the unchecked com.google.gson.JsonIOException when an I/O error arises.

Customized JSON Object Creation

The previous gson.toJson(p) and gson.toJson (s, fw) method calls rely on Gson's default serialization mechanism to create JSON objects. You will often encounter scenarios where you need to create JSON objects from Java objects whose classes don't have the same structure as the JSON objects to be created. You can perform this creation with a custom serializer, which controls how Java objects map to JSON objects.

The com.google.gson.JsonSerializer<T> interface describes a custom serializer. The argument passed to T identifies the type for which the serializer is being used. For example, you might pass Person to T when needing to create JSON objects with a somewhat different structure.

JsonSerializer declares a single method for handling the serialization (JSON object creation):

```
JsonElement serialize(T src, Type typeOfSrc,
                      JsonSerializationContext context)
```

serialize() is a callback method that Gson calls during serialization. This method is called with the following arguments:

- src identifies the Java object that needs to be serialized.

- typeOfSrc identifies the actual type of the Java object, specified by src, to be serialized.

- context identifies a context in which to perform the serialization. (I'll have more to say about contexts later.)

After creating a JsonSerializer object, you need to register it with Gson. Accomplish this task by calling the following GsonBuilder method:

```
GsonBuilder registerTypeAdapter(Type type, Object typeAdapter)
```

The object passed to type identifies the type of the serializer and the object passed to typeAdapter identifies the serializer. Because registerTypeAdapter(Type, Object) returns a GsonBuilder object, you can only use this method in a GsonBuilder context.

To demonstrate customized JSON object creation, consider the Book class that's presented in Listing 9-6.

Listing 9-6. Describing a Book as a Title, List of Authors, and ISBN Numbers

```java
public class Book
{
    private String title;
    private String[] authors;
    private String isbn10;
    private String isbn13;

    public Book(String title, String[] authors, String isbn10, String isbn13)
    {
        this.title = title;
        this.authors = authors;
        this.isbn10 = isbn10;
        this.isbn13 = isbn13;
    }

    public String getTitle()
    {
        return title;
    }

    public String[] getAuthors()
    {
        return authors;
    }

    public String getIsbn10()
    {
        return isbn10;
    }

    public String getIsbn13()
    {
        return isbn13;
    }
}
```

Continuing, suppose that Book objects are to be serialized to JSON objects that have the following format:

```
{
    "title": title
    "lead-author": author0
    "other-authors": [ author1, author2, ... ]
    "isbn-10": isbn10
    "isbn-13": isbn13
}
```

You cannot use default serialization because the Book class doesn't declare
lead-author, other-authors, isbn-10, and isbn-13 fields. In any case,
default serialization creates JSON property names that match a Java class's
field names (and the hyphen character is illegal for Java identifiers). To prove
that you cannot obtain the desired JSON object with default serialization,
suppose you attempt to execute the following code fragment:

```
Book book = new Book("PHP and MySQL Web Development, Second Edition",
new String[] { "Luke Welling", "Laura Thomson" }, "067232525X", "075-2063325254");
Gson gson = new Gson();
System.out.println(gson.toJson(book));
```

This code fragment generates the following output:

```
{"title":"PHP and MySQL Web Development, Second Edition","authors":["Luke
Welling","Laura Thomson"],"isbn10":"067232525X","isbn13":"075-2063325254"}
```

The output doesn't match the expected JSON object. However, you can fix
this problem by introducing the following custom serializer:

```
class BookSerializer implements JsonSerializer<Book>
{
    @Override
    public JsonElement serialize(Book src, Type typeOfSrc,
                                JsonSerializationContext context)
    {
        JsonObject jsonObject = new JsonObject();
        jsonObject.addProperty("title", src.getTitle());
        jsonObject.addProperty("lead-author", src.getAuthors()[0]);
        JsonArray jsonOtherAuthors = new JsonArray();
        for (int i = 1; i < src.getAuthors().length; i++)
        {
            JsonPrimitive jsonAuthor =
                new JsonPrimitive(src.getAuthors()[i]);
            jsonOtherAuthors.add(jsonAuthor);
        }
        jsonObject.add("other-authors", jsonOtherAuthors);
        jsonObject.addProperty("isbn-10", src.getIsbn10());
        jsonObject.addProperty("isbn-13", src.getIsbn13());
        return jsonObject;
    }
}
```

When the custom serializer is used with the previous Java Book object,
serialize() is called only once with the Book object being passed to src.
Because a JSON object is desired as the result of this method, serialize()
first creates a JsonObject instance.

JsonObject declares several addProperty() methods for adding properties to the JSON object that a JsonObject instance represents. serialize() invokes the void addProperty(String property, String value) method to add the title, lead-author, isbn-10, and isbn-13 properties.

The other-authors property is handled differently. First, serialize() creates a JsonArray instance and populates it with all authors except for the first author. Then, it invokes JsonObject's void add(String property, JsonElement value) method to add the JsonArray object to the JsonObject.

When serialization finishes, serialize() returns the created and populated JsonObject.

The following code fragment shows how you instantiate BookSerializer and register it with a GsonBuilder instance, which is also used to obtain a Gson instance in order to call toJson(), to create the desired JSON object via the book serializer:

```
GsonBuilder gsonBuilder = new GsonBuilder();
gsonBuilder.registerTypeAdapter(Book.class, new BookSerializer());
Gson gson = gsonBuilder.create();
```

I've combined these code fragments into a working application. Listing 9-7 presents the application's source code.

Listing 9-7. Creating a JSON Object from a Java Object via a Custom Serializer

```
import java.lang.reflect.Type;

import com.google.gson.Gson;
import com.google.gson.GsonBuilder;
import com.google.gson.JsonArray;
import com.google.gson.JsonElement;
import com.google.gson.JsonObject;
import com.google.gson.JsonPrimitive;
import com.google.gson.JsonSerializationContext;
import com.google.gson.JsonSerializer;

public class GsonDemo
{
   public static void main(String[] args)
   {
      class BookSerializer implements JsonSerializer<Book>
      {
         @Override
         public JsonElement serialize(Book src, Type typeOfSrc,
         JsonSerializationContext context)
```

```
        {
            JsonObject jsonObject = new JsonObject();
            jsonObject.addProperty("title", src.getTitle());
            jsonObject.addProperty("lead-author", src.getAuthors()[0]);
            JsonArray jsonOtherAuthors = new JsonArray();
            for (int i = 1; i < src.getAuthors().length; i++)
            {
                JsonPrimitive jsonAuthor =
                    new JsonPrimitive(src.getAuthors()[i]);
                jsonOtherAuthors.add(jsonAuthor);
            }
            jsonObject.add("other-authors", jsonOtherAuthors);
            jsonObject.addProperty("isbn-10", src.getIsbn10());
            jsonObject.addProperty("isbn-13", src.getIsbn13());
            return jsonObject;
        }
    }
    GsonBuilder gsonBuilder = new GsonBuilder();
    gsonBuilder.registerTypeAdapter(Book.class, new BookSerializer());
    Gson gson = gsonBuilder.setPrettyPrinting().create();
    Book book = new Book("PHP and MySQL Web Development, Second Edition",
new String[] { "Luke Welling", "Laura Thomson" }, "067232525X", "075-
2063325254");
        System.out.println(gson.toJson(book));
    }
}
```

Compile Listing 9-7 and run the resulting application. You should observe the following output, which has been pretty-printed (via the setPrettyPrinting() method call on the GsonBuilder object) to make the output clearer:

```
{
  "title": "PHP and MySQL Web Development, Second Edition",
  "lead-author": "Luke Welling",
  "other-authors": [
    "Laura Thomson"
  ],
  "isbn-10": "067232525X",
  "isbn-13": "075-2063325254"
}
```

Learning More About Gson

Now that you have a fairly good understanding of Gson library basics, you'll probably want to learn about other features that this library offers. In this section, I introduce you to annotations, contexts, Gson's support for generics, and type adapters.

> **Note** My coverage of additional Gson features isn't exhaustive. Check out the "Gson User Guide" (https://github.com/google/gson/blob/master/UserGuide.md) to learn about topics that I haven't covered, such as instance creators.

Annotations

Gson offers several annotation types (in the com.google.gson.annotations package) for simplifying serialization and deserialization:

- Expose: Exposes the annotated field to or hide it from Gson's serialization and/or deserialization mechanisms.

- JsonAdapter: Identifies the type adapter to use with a class or field. (I'll discuss this annotation type later when I focus on type adapters.)

- SerializedName: Indicates that the annotated field or method should be serialized to JSON with the provided name value as its name.

- Since: Identifies the starting version number for serializing a field or type. If a Gson object is created with a version number that is less than the value in the @Since annotation, the annotated field/type will not be serialized.

- Until: Identifies the ending version number for serializing a field or type. If a Gson object is created with a version number that equals or exceeds the value in the @Until annotation, the annotated field/type will not be serialized.

> **Note** According to the Gson documentation, Since and Until are useful for managing the versioning of JSON classes in a web service context.

Exposing and Hiding Fields

By default, Gson will not serialize and deserialize fields that are marked transient (or static). You can call GsonBuilder's GsonBuilder exclude FieldsWithModifiers(int... modifiers) method to change this behavior. Also, Gson lets you selectively determine which non-transient fields to serialize and/or deserialize by annotating these fields with instances of the Expose annotation type.

Expose offers the following elements for determining whether a field can be serialized and whether it can be deserialized:

- serialize: When true, the field marked with this @Expose annotation is serialized to JSON text; otherwise, the field isn't serialized. The default value is true.

- deserialize: When true, the field marked with this @Expose annotation is deserialized from JSON text; otherwise, the field isn't deserialized. The default value is true.

The following code fragment shows how to use Expose and these elements so that a field named someField will be serialized and not deserialized:

```
@Expose(serialize = true, deserialize = false)
int someField;
```

By default, Gson ignores Expose. You must configure Gson to expose/hide fields that are annotated with @Expose by calling the following GsonBuilder method:

```
GsonBuilder excludeFieldsWithoutExposeAnnotation()
```

Create a GsonBuilder object and then call GsonBuilder's excludeFieldsWithoutExposeAnnotation() method followed by its Gson create() method on this object to return a configured Gson object:

```
GsonBuilder gsonb = new GsonBuilder();
gsonb.excludeFieldsWithoutExposeAnnotation();
Gson gson = gsonb.create();
```

Listing 9-8 describes an application that demonstrates the Expose annotation type.

Listing 9-8. Exposing and Hiding Fields to and from Serialization and Deserialization

```java
import com.google.gson.Gson;
import com.google.gson.GsonBuilder;

import com.google.gson.annotations.Expose;

public class GsonDemo
{
    static class SomeClass
    {
        transient int id;
        @Expose(serialize = true, deserialize = true)
        transient String password;
        @Expose(serialize = false, deserialize = false)
        int field1;
        @Expose(serialize = false, deserialize = true)
        int field2;
        @Expose(serialize = true, deserialize = false)
        int field3;
        @Expose(serialize = true, deserialize = true)
        int field4;
        @Expose(serialize = true, descrialize = true)
        static int field5;
        static int field6;
    }

    public static void main(String[] args)
    {
        SomeClass sc = new SomeClass();
        sc.id = 1;
        sc.password = "abc";
        sc.field1 = 2;
        sc.field2 = 3;
        sc.field3 = 4;
        sc.field4 = 5;
        sc.field5 = 6;
        sc.field6 = 7;
        GsonBuilder gsonb = new GsonBuilder();
        gsonb.excludeFieldsWithoutExposeAnnotation();
        Gson gson = gsonb.create();
        String json = gson.toJson(sc);
        System.out.println(json);
        SomeClass sc2 = gson.fromJson(json, SomeClass.class);
        System.out.printf("id = %d%n", sc2.id);
        System.out.printf("password = %s%n", sc2.password);
        System.out.printf("field1 = %d%n", sc2.field1);
        System.out.printf("field2 = %d%n", sc2.field2);
        System.out.printf("field3 = %d%n", sc2.field3);
```

```
      System.out.printf("field4 = %d%n", sc2.field4);
      System.out.printf("field5 = %d%n", sc2.field5);
      System.out.printf("field6 = %d%n", sc2.field6);
   }
}
```

Listing 9-8 demonstrates Expose with transient instance fields along with non-transient instance fields and static fields.

Compile Listing 9-8 and run the resulting application. You should observe the following output:

```
{"field3":4,"field4":5}
id = 0
password = null
field1 = 0
field2 = 0
field3 = 0
field4 = 5
field5 = 6
field6 = 7
```

The first output line shows that only field3 and field4 are serialized. The other fields are not serialized.

The second and third lines show that the transient id and password fields receive default values. transient fields are not serialized/deserialized.

The fourth, fifth, and sixth lines show that default 0 values are assigned to field1, field2, and field3. For field1 and field3, deserialize is assigned false so only default values can be assigned to these fields. Because field2 wasn't serialized, the only value that can be assigned to it is 0.

The seventh line shows that 5 is assigned to field4. This makes sense because the serialize and deserialize elements are assigned true.

Because static fields aren't serialized or deserialized, they keep their initial values, as shown in the eighth and ninth lines (for field5 and field6).

> **Note** Even if Gson serialized static fields, field6 wouldn't be serialized because it isn't annotated with @Expose, and also because of the gsonb. excludeFieldsWithoutExposeAnnotation() method call, which causes Gson to bypass fields not annotated with @Expose.

Changing Field Names

You don't have to use JsonSerializer<T> and JsonDeserializer<T> when you only want to change field and/or method names during serialization and deserialization; for example, changing isbn10 to isbn-10 and isbn13 to isbn-13. You can use SerializedName instead, as shown here:

```
@SerializedName("isbn-10")
String isbn10;
@SerializedName("isbn-13")
String isbn13;
```

The JSON object presents isbn-10 and isbn-13 property names, whereas the Java class presents isbn10 and isbn13 field names.

Listing 9-9 describes an application that demonstrates the SerializedName annotation type.

Listing 9-9. Changing Names

```java
import com.google.gson.Gson;

import com.google.gson.annotations.SerializedName;

public class GsonDemo
{
    static class Book
    {
        String title;
        @SerializedName("isbn-10")
        String isbn10;
        @SerializedName("isbn-13")
        String isbn13;
    }

    public static void main(String[] args)
    {
        Book book = new Book();
        book.title = "PHP and MySQL Web Development, Second Edition";
        book.isbn10 = "067232525X";
        book.isbn13 = "075-2063325254";
        Gson gson = new Gson();
        String json = gson.toJson(book);
        System.out.println(json);
        Book book2 = gson.fromJson(json, Book.class);
        System.out.printf("title = %s%n", book2.title);
        System.out.printf("isbn10 = %s%n", book2.isbn10);
        System.out.printf("isbn13 = %s%n", book2.isbn13);
    }
}
```

Compile Listing 9-9 and run the resulting application. You should observe the following output:

```
{"title":"PHP and MySQL Web Development, Second Edition","isbn-
10":"067232525X","isbn-13":"075-2063325254"}
title = PHP and MySQL Web Development, Second Edition
isbn10 = 067232525X
isbn13 = 075-2063325254
```

Versioning

Since and Until are useful for versioning your classes. Using these annotation types, you can determine which fields and/or types are serialized to JSON objects.

Each @Since and @Until annotation receives a double precision floating-point value as its argument. This value specifies a version number, as demonstrated here:

```
@Since(1.0) private String userID;
@Since(1.0) private String password;
@Until(1.1) private String emailAddress;
```

@Since(1.0) indicates that the field it annotates is to be serialized for all versions greater than or equal to 1.0. Similarly, @Until(1.1) indicates that the field it annotates is to be serialized for all versions less than 1.1.

The version number that's compared to the @Since or @Until version argument is specified by the following GsonBuilder method:

```
GsonBuilder setVersion(double ignoreVersionsAfter)
```

As with Expose, you first create a GsonBuilder object, then call this method with the desired version number on that object, and finally call create() on the GsonBuilder object to return a newly-created Gson object:

```
GsonBuilder gsonb = new GsonBuilder();
gsonb.setVersion(2.0);
Gson gson = gsonb.create();
```

Listing 9-10 describes an application that demonstrates the Since and Until annotation types.

Listing 9-10. Versioning a Class and Its Fields

```java
import com.google.gson.Gson;
import com.google.gson.GsonBuilder;

import com.google.gson.annotations.Since;
import com.google.gson.annotations.Until;

public class GsonDemo
{
    @Since(1.0)
    @Until(2.5)
    static class SomeClass
    {
        @Since(1.1)
        @Until(1.5)
        int field;
    }

    public static void main(String[] args)
    {
        SomeClass sc = new SomeClass();
        sc.field - 1;
        GsonBuilder gsonb = new GsonBuilder();
        gsonb.setVersion(0.9);
        Gson gson = gsonb.create();
        System.out.printf("%s%n%n", gson.toJson(sc));
        gsonb.setVersion(1.0);
        gson = gsonb.create();
        System.out.printf("%s%n%n", gson.toJson(sc));
        gsonb.setVersion(1.1);
        gson = gsonb.create();
        System.out.printf("%s%n%n", gson.toJson(sc));
        gsonb.setVersion(1.5);
        gson = gsonb.create();
        System.out.printf("%s%n%n", gson.toJson(sc));
        gsonb.setVersion(2.5);
        gson = gsonb.create();
        System.out.printf("%s%n", gson.toJson(sc));
    }
}
```

Listing 9-10 presents a nested SomeClass that will be serialized as long as
the version number passed to setVersion() ranges from 1.0 to almost 2.5.
This class presents a field named field that will be serialized as long as the
version number passed to setVersion() ranges from 1.1 to almost 1.5.

Compile Listing 9-10 and run the resulting application. You should observe the following output:

```
null
```

```
{}
```

```
{"field":1}
```

```
{}
```

```
Null
```

Contexts

The serialize() and deserialize() methods that are declared by the JsonSerializer and JsonDeserializer interfaces are called with com.google.gson.JsonSerializationContext and com.google.gson. JsonDeserializationContext objects, respectively, as their final arguments. These objects provide serialize() and deserialize() methods for performing default serialization and default deserialization on specific Java objects. You'll find them handy when working with nested Java objects that don't require special treatment.

Suppose you have the following Date and Employee classes:

```
class Date
{
    int year;
    int month;
    int day;

    Date(int year, int month, int day)
    {
        this.year = year;
        this.month = month;
        this.day = day;
    }
}

class Employee
{
    String name;
    Date hireDate;
}
```

Now, suppose that you decide to create a custom serializer to add emp-name and hire-date properties (instead of name and hireDate properties) to the resulting JSON object. Because you're not changing the names or the order of Date's fields during serialization, you can leverage the *context* passed to JsonSerializer's serialize() method to handle that part of the serialization for you.

The following code fragment presents a serializer that serializes Employee objects and their nested Date objects:

```
class EmployeeSerializer implements JsonSerializer<Employee>
{
   @Override
   public JsonElement serialize(Employee emp, Type typeOfSrc,
                                JsonSerializationContext context)
   {
      JsonObject jo = new JsonObject();
      jo.addProperty("emp-name", emp.name);
      jo.add("hire-date", context.serialize(emp.hireDate));
      return jo;
   }
}
```

serialize() first creates a JsonObject to describe the serialized JSON object. It then adds an emp-name property with the employee name as the value to this JsonObject. Because default serialization can serialize the hireDate field, serialize() calls context.serialize(emp.hireDate) to generate a property value. This value and the hire-date property name are added to the JsonObject, which is returned from the method.

Listing 9-11 presents the source code for an application that demonstrates this serialize() method.

Listing 9-11. Leveraging a Context to Serialize a Date

```
import java.lang.reflect.Type;

import com.google.gson.Gson;
import com.google.gson.GsonBuilder;
import com.google.gson.JsonElement;
import com.google.gson.JsonObject;
import com.google.gson.JsonSerializationContext;
import com.google.gson.JsonSerializer;
```

```java
public class GsonDemo
{
   static class Date
   {
      int year;
      int month;
      int day;

      Date(int year, int month, int day)
      {
         this.year = year;
         this.month = month;
         this.day = day;
      }
   }

   static class Employee
   {
      String name;
      Date hireDate;
   }

   public static void main(String[] args)
   {
      Employee e = new Employee();
      e.name = "John Doe";
      e.hireDate = new Date(1982, 10, 12);
      GsonBuilder gb = new GsonBuilder();
      class EmployeeSerializer implements JsonSerializer<Employee>
      {
         @Override
         public JsonElement serialize(Employee emp, Type typeOfSrc,
         JsonSerializationContext context)
         {
            JsonObject jo = new JsonObject();
            jo.addProperty("emp-name", emp.name);
            jo.add("hire-date", context.serialize(emp.hireDate));
            return jo;
         }
      }
      gb.registerTypeAdapter(Employee.class, new EmployeeSerializer());
      Gson gson = gb.create();
      System.out.printf("%s%n%n", gson.toJson(e));
   }
}
```

Compile Listing 9-11 and run the resulting application. You should observe the following output:

```
{"emp-name":"John Doe","hire-date":{"year":1982,"month":10,"day":12}}
```

Generics Support

When you call String toJson(Object src) or void toJson(Object src, Appendable writer), Gson calls src.getClass() to get src 's java. lang.Class object so that it can reflectively learn about the fields to serialize. Similarly, when you call a deserialization method such as <T> T fromJson(String json, Class<T> classOfT), Gson uses the Class object passed to classOfT to help it reflectively build a result Java object. These operations work properly for objects instantiated from nongeneric types. However, when an object is created from a generic type, problems can occur because the generic type information is lost due to *type erasure*. Consider the following code fragment:

```
List<String> weekdays = Arrays.asList("Sun", "Mon", "Tue", "Wed", "Thu",
"Fri", "Sat");
String json = gson.toJson(weekdays);
System.out.printf("%s%n%n", json);
System.out.printf("%s%n%n",
                  gson.fromJson(json, weekdays.getClass()));
```

Variable weekdays is an object with generic type java.util.List<String>. The toJson() method calls weekdays.getClass() and discovers, instead, List as the type. However, it still successfully serializes weekdays to the following JSON object:

```
["Sun","Mon","Tue","Wed","Thu","Fri","Sat"]
```

Deserialization isn't successful. When gson.fromJson(json, weekdays. getClass()) is called, this method throws an instance of the java.lang. ClassCastException class. Internally, it attempts to cast java.util. ArrayList to java.util.Arrays$ArrayList, which doesn't work.

The solution to this problem is to specify the correct List<String> *parameterized type* (generic type instance) instead of the raw List type that's returned from weekdays.getClass(). You use the com.google.gson. reflect.TypeToken<T> class for this purpose.

TypeToken<T> represents a generic type T and enables the retrieval of type information at runtime, which Gson requires. You instantiate TypeToken using an expression such as the following:

```
Type listType = new TypeToken<List<String>>() {}.getType();
```

This idiom defines an anonymous local inner class whose inherited getType() method returns the fully parameterized type as a java.lang. reflect.Type object. In this code fragment, the following type is returned:

```
java.util.List<java.lang.String>
```

Pass the resulting Type object to the <T> T fromJson(String json, Type typeOfT) method, as follows:

```
gson.fromJson(json, listType)
```

This method call parses and returns the JSON object as a List<String>.

You might want to output the result using an expression such as the following:

```
System.out.printf("%s%n%n", gson.fromJson(json, listType));
```

However, you would receive a thrown ClassCastException stating that you cannot cast ArrayList to java.lang.Object[] instead of observing output. The solution to the problem is to introduce a cast to List, as follows:

```
System.out.printf("%s%n%n", (List) gson.fromJson(json, listType));
```

After making this change, you will observe the following output:

```
[Sun, Mon, Tue, Wed, Thu, Fri, Sat]
```

Listing 9-12 presents the source code for an application that demonstrates this problem along with other generic-oriented serialization/deserialization problems, and how to solve them.

Listing 9-12. Serializing and Deserializing Objects Based on Generic Types

```
import java.lang.reflect.Type;

import java.util.ArrayList;
import java.util.List;
import java.util.Map;
import java.util.HashMap;

import com.google.gson.Gson;

import com.google.gson.reflect.TypeToken;

import java.util.Arrays;
import java.util.List;
```

```java
public class GsonDemo
{
    static
    class Vehicle<T>
    {
        T vehicle;

        T get()
        {
            return vehicle;
        }
        void set(T vehicle)
        {
            this.vehicle = vehicle;
        }

        @Override
        public String toString()
        {
            System.out.printf("Class of vehicle: %s%n", vehicle.getClass());
            return "Vehicle: " + vehicle.toString();
        }
    }

    static
    class Truck
    {
        String make;
        String model;

        Truck(String make, String model)
        {
            this.make = make;
            this.model = model;
        }

        @Override
        public String toString()
        {
            return "Make: " + make + " Model: " + model;
        }
    }

    public static void main(String[] args)
    {
        Gson gson = new Gson();

        // ...
```

```java
System.out.printf("PART 1%n");
System.out.printf("------%n%n");

List<String> weekdays = Arrays.asList("Sun", "Mon", "Tue", "Wed",
"Thu", "Fri", "Sat");
String json = gson.toJson(weekdays);
System.out.printf("%s%n%n", json);
try
{
   System.out.printf("%s%n%n", gson.fromJson(json, weekdays.
   getClass()));
}
catch (ClassCastException cce)
{
   cce.printStackTrace();
   System.out.println();
}
Type listType = new TypeToken<List<String>>() {}.getType(); System.
out.printf("Type = %s%n%n", listType);
try
{
   System.out.printf("%s%n%n", gson.fromJson(json, listType));
}
catch (ClassCastException cce)
{
   cce.printStackTrace();
   System.out.println();
}
System.out.printf("%s%n%n", (List) gson.fromJson(json, listType));

// ...

System.out.printf("PART 2%n");
System.out.printf("------%n%n");

Truck truck = new Truck("Ford", "F150");
Vehicle<Truck> vehicle = new Vehicle<>();
vehicle.set(truck);

json = gson.toJson(vehicle);
System.out.printf("%s%n%n", json);
System.out.printf("%s%n%n", gson.fromJson(json, vehicle.getClass()));

// ...

System.out.printf("PART 3%n");
System.out.printf("------%n%n");
```

```java
        Map<String, String> map = new HashMap<String, String>()
        {
            {
                put("key", "value");
            }
        };
        System.out.printf("Map = %s%n%n", map);
        System.out.printf("%s%n%n", gson.toJson(map));
        System.out.printf("%s%n%n", gson.fromJson(gson.toJson(map),
                                                  map.getClass()));

        // ...

        System.out.printf("PART 4%n");
        System.out.printf("------%n%n");

        Type vehicleType = new TypeToken<Vehicle<Truck>>() {}.getType();
        json = gson.toJson(vehicle, vehicleType);
        System.out.printf("%s%n%n", json);
        System.out.printf("%s%n%n", (Vehicle) gson.fromJson(json,
        vehicleType));

        Type mapType = new TypeToken<Map<String,String>>() {}.getType();
        System.out.printf("%s%n%n", gson.toJson(map, mapType));
        System.out.printf("%s%n%n", (Map) gson.fromJson(gson.toJson(map,
        mapType), mapType));
    }
}
```

Listing 9-12's GsonDemo class is organized into nested Vehicle and Truck
static classes followed by the main() entry-point method. This method is
organized into four sections that demonstrate problems and solutions. Here
is the output, which I'll refer to during my discussion of main():

```
PART 1
------

["Sun","Mon","Tue","Wed","Thu","Fri","Sat"]

java.lang.ClassCastException: Cannot cast java.util.ArrayList to java.util.
Arrays$ArrayList
        at java.lang.Class.cast(Class.java:3369)
        at com.google.gson.Gson.fromJson(Gson.java:766)
        at GsonDemo.main(GsonDemo.java:75)

Type = java.util.List<java.lang.String>
```

```
java.lang.ClassCastException: java.util.ArrayList cannot be cast to [Ljava.
lang.Object;
        at GsonDemo.main(GsonDemo.java:86)

[Sun, Mon, Tue, Wed, Thu, Fri, Sat]

PART 2
------

{"vehicle":{"make":"Ford","model":"F150"}}

Class of vehicle: class com.google.gson.internal.LinkedTreeMap
Vehicle: {make=Ford, model=F150}

PART 3
------

Map = {key=value}

null

null

PART 4
------
{"vehicle":{"make":"Ford","model":"F150"}}

Class of vehicle: class GsonDemo$Truck
Vehicle: Make: Ford Model: F150

{"key":"value"}

{key=value}
```

Part 1 focuses on the previously discussed List<String> example. The output shows successful serialization via toJson(), followed by unsuccessful deserialization via gson.fromJson(json, weekdays.getClass()), followed by the type stored in the first created TypeToken instance, followed by successful deserialization with a cast problem, followed by successful deserialization with no cast problem.

Part 2 focuses on the serialization and deserialization of a Vehicle<Truck> object named vehicle. This generic object is successully serialized via a gson.toJson(vehicle) call. Although you can often pass generic objects to toJson(Object src) successfully, this method occasionally fails, as I will show. A subsequent call to gson.fromJson(json, vehicle.getClass()) attempts to deserialize the output, but there is a problem: you observe

Vehicle: {make=Ford, model=F150} instead of Vehicle: Make: Ford Model: F150. Because Vehicle is specified instead of the full Vehicle<Truck> generic type, the vehicle field in the Vehicle class is assigned com.google. gson.internal.LinkedTreeMap instead of Truck as its type.

Part 3 attempts to serialize and deserialize a map based on an anonymous subclass of java.util.HashMap. The first null value shows that toJson() wasn't successful: toJson()'s internal map.getClass() call returns a GsonDemo$2 reference, which offers no insight into the object to be serialized. The second null value results from passing null to json in fromJson(String json, Class<T> classOfT).

Part 4 shows how to fix the problems in Parts 2 and 3. This section creates TypeToken<Vehicle<Truck>> and TypeToken<Map<String,String>> objects to store the Vehicle<Truck> and Map<String, String> parameterized types. These objects are then passed to the type parameter of the String toJson(Object src, Type typeOfSrc) and <T> T fromJson(String json, Type typeOfT) methods. (Although gson.toJson(vehicle, vehicleType) isn't necessary because serialization works with gson.toJson(vehicle), you should get into the habit of passing a Type object based on a TypeToken instance as a second argument, just to be safe.)

> **Note**   Each of toJson(Object src), <T> T fromJson(String json, Class<T> classOfT), and similar methods work properly when any of the fields of the specified object (src and objects derived from classOfT) are based on generic types. The only stipulation is that the specified object not be generic.

Type Adapters

Previously in this chapter, I showed you how to use JsonSerializer and JsonDeserializer to (respectively) serialize Java objects to JSON strings and vice versa. These interfaces simplify the translation between Java objects and JSON strings, but add an intermediate layer of processing.

The intermediate layer consists of code that converts Java objects and JSON strings to JsonElements. This conversion mitigates the risk of parsing or creating invalid JSON strings, but it does take time to perform, which can impact performance. You can avoid the intermediate layer and create more efficient code by working with the com.google.gson.TypeAdapter<T> class, where T identifies the Java class serialization source and deserialization target.

> **Note**   You should prefer the more efficient TypeAdapter to the less efficient
> JsonSerializer and JsonDeserializer. In fact, Gson uses an internal
> TypeAdapter implementation to handle conversions between Java objects and
> JSON strings.

TypeAdapter is an abstract class that declares several concrete methods along with the following pair of abstract methods:

- T read(JsonReader in): Read a JSON value (array, object, string, number, Boolean, or null) and convert it to a Java object, which is returned. The return value may be null.

- void write(JsonWriter out, T value): Write a JSON value (array, object, string, number, Boolean, or null), which is passed to value.

Each method throws java.io.IOException when an I/O problem occurs.

The read() and write() methods read a sequence of JSON *tokens* and write a sequence of JSON tokens, respectively. For read(), the source of these tokens is an instance of the concrete com.google.gson.stream. JsonReader class. For write(), the destination of these tokens is the concrete com.google.gson.stream.JsonWriter class. Tokens are described by the com.google.gson.stream.JsonToken enum (such as BEGIN_ARRAY for open square bracket). They are read and written by calling JsonReader and JsonWriter methods, such as the following:

- void beginObject(): This JsonReader method consumes the next token from the JSON stream and asserts that it's the beginning of a new object. A companion void endObject() method consumes the next token from the JSON stream and asserts that it's the end of the current object. Either method throws IOException when an I/O problem occurs.

- JsonWriter name(String name): This JsonWriter method encodes the property name, which cannot be null. IOException is thrown when an I/O problem occurs.

After creating a TypeAdapter subclass, you instantiate it and register the instance with Gson by calling the GsonBuilder registerTypeAdapter(Type type, Object typeAdapter) method, which I previously presented. The object that's passed to type represents the class whose objects are serialized or deserialized. The object that's passed to typeAdapter is the type adapter instance.

Listing 9-13 presents the source code for an application that demonstrates a type adapter.

Listing 9-13. Serializing and Deserializing a Country Object via a Type Adapter

```java
import java.io.IOException;

import java.util.ArrayList;
import java.util.List;

import com.google.gson.Gson;
import com.google.gson.GsonBuilder;
import com.google.gson.TypeAdapter;

import com.google.gson.stream.JsonReader;
import com.google.gson.stream.JsonWriter;

public class GsonDemo
{
   static
   class Country
   {
      String name;
      int population;
      String[] cities;

      Country() {}

      Country(String name, int population, String... cities)
      {
         this.name = name;
         this.population = population;
         this.cities = cities;
      }
   }

   public static void main(String[] args)
   {
      class CountryAdapter extends TypeAdapter<Country>
      {
         @Override
         public Country read(JsonReader in) throws IOException
         {
            Country c = new Country();
            List<String> cities = new ArrayList<>();
            in.beginObject();
```

```java
        while (in.hasNext())
          switch (in.nextName())
          {
              case "name":
                 c.name = in.nextString();
                          break;

              case "population":
                 c.population = in.nextInt();
                 break;

              case "cities":
                 in.beginArray();
                 while (in.hasNext())
                    cities.add(in.nextString());
                 in.endArray();
                 c.cities = cities.toArray(new String[0]);
          }
        in.endObject();
        return c;
    }

    @Override
    public void write(JsonWriter out, Country c) throws IOException
    {
       out.beginObject();
       out.name("name").value(c.name);
       out.name("population").value(c.population);
       out.name("cities");
       out.beginArray();
       for (int i = 0; i < c.cities.length; i++)
          out.value(c.cities[i]);
       out.endArray();
       out.endObject();
    }
}
Gson gson = new GsonBuilder().
              registerTypeAdapter(Country.class,
                                  new CountryAdapter()).
              create();

Country c = new Country("England", 53012456 /* 2011 census */,
"London", "Birmingham", "Cambridge");
String json = gson.toJson(c);
System.out.println(json);
c = gson.fromJson(json, c.getClass());
System.out.printf("Name = %s%n", c.name);
```

```
      System.out.printf("Population = %d%n", c.population);
      System.out.print("Cities = ");
      for (String city: c.cities)
         System.out.print(city + " ");
      System.out.println();
   }
}
```

Listing 9-13's GsonDemo class nests a Country class (which describes a country as a name, a population count, and an array of city names) and also presents a main() entry-point method.

The main() method first declares a local CountryAdapter class that extends TypeAdapter<Country>. CountryAdapter overrides the read() and write() methods to handle the serialization and deserialization tasks.

The read() method first creates a new Country object, which will store the values being read from the JSON object being deserialized (and accessed from the JsonReader argument).

After creating a list to store the array of city names that it will be reading, read() calls beginObject() to assert that the next token read from the token stream is the beginning of a JSON object.

At this point, read() enters a while loop. This loop continues while JsonReader's boolean hasNext() method returns true: there is another object element.

Each while loop iteration executes a switch statement that calls JsonReader's String nextName() method to return the next token, which is a property name in the JSON object. It then compares the token to the three possibilities (name, population, or cities) and executes the associated code to retrieve the property value and assign the value to the appropriate field in the previously created Country object.

If the property is name, JsonReader's String nextString() method is called to return the string value of the next token. If the property is population, JsonReader's int nextInt() method is called to return the token's int value.

Processing the cities property is more involved because its value is an array:

1. JsonReader's void beginArray() method is called to signify that a new array has been detected and to consume the open square bracket token.

2. A while loop is entered to repeatedly obtain the next array string value and add it to the previously created cities list.

3. JsonReader's void endArray() method is called to
    signify the end of the current array and to consume
    the close square bracket token.

4. The cities list is converted to a Java array, which is
    assigned to the Country object's cities member.

After the outer while loop ends, read() calls endObject() to assert that
the next token read from the token stream is the end of the current JSON
object, and then returns the Country object.

The write() method is somewhat similar to read(). It calls JsonWriter's
JsonWriter name(String name) method to encode the property name
specified by name to a JSON property name. Also, it calls JsonWriter's
JsonWriter value(long value) and JsonWriter value(String value)
methods to encode value as a JSON number or a JSON string.

The main() method proceeds to create a Gson object from a GsonBuilder
object, which executes registerTypeAdapter(Country.class, new
CountryAdapter()) to instantiate and register CountryAdapter with the Gson
object that will be returned. Country.class indicates that Country objects
will be serialized and deserialized.

Finally, a Country object is created, serialized to a string, and deserialized to
a new Country object.

Compile Listing 9-13 and run the resulting application. You should observe
the following output:

```
{"name":"England","population":53012456,"cities":["London","Birmingham","Ca
mbridge"]}
Name = England
Population = 53012456
Cities = London Birmingham Cambridge
```

Conveniently Associating Type Adapters with Classes and Fields

The JsonAdapter annotation type is used with a TypeAdapter Class object
argument to associate the TypeAdapter instance to use with a class or field.
After doing so, you don't need to register the TypeAdapter with Gson, which
makes for a bit less coding.

Listing 9-14 refactors Listing 9-13 to demonstrate JsonAdapter.

Listing 9-14. Serializing and Deserializing a Country Object Annotated with a Type Adapter

```java
import java.io.IOException;

import java.util.ArrayList;
import java.util.List;

import com.google.gson.Gson;
import com.google.gson.TypeAdapter;

import com.google.gson.annotations.JsonAdapter;

import com.google.gson.stream.JsonReader;
import com.google.gson.stream.JsonWriter;

public class GsonDemo
{
    @JsonAdapter(CountryAdapter.class)
    static
    class Country
    {
        String name;
        int population;
        String[] cities;
        Country() {}

        Country(String name, int population, String... cities)
        {
            this.name = name;
            this.population = population;
            this.cities = cities;
        }
    }

    static
    class CountryAdapter extends TypeAdapter<Country>
    {
        @Override
        public Country read(JsonReader in) throws IOException
        {
            System.out.println("read() called");
            Country c = new Country();
            List<String> cities = new ArrayList<>();
            in.beginObject();
            while (in.hasNext())
                switch (in.nextName())
                {
                    case "name":
                        c.name = in.nextString();
                            break;
```

```
            case "population":
                c.population = in.nextInt();
                break;

            case "cities":
                in.beginArray();
                while (in.hasNext())
                    cities.add(in.nextString());
                in.endArray();
                c.cities = cities.toArray(new String[0]);
        }
        in.endObject();
        return c;
    }

    @Override
    public void write(JsonWriter out, Country c) throws IOException
    {
        System.out.println("write() called");
        out.beginObject();
        out.name("name").value(c.name);
        out.name("population").value(c.population);
        out.name("cities");
        out.beginArray();
        for (int i = 0; i < c.cities.length; i++)
            out.value(c.cities[i]);
        out.endArray();
        out.endObject();
    }
}

public static void main(String[] args)
{
    Gson gson = new Gson();
    Country c = new Country("England", 53012456 /* 2011 census */,
    "London", "Birmingham", "Cambridge");
    String json = gson.toJson(c);
    System.out.println(json);
    c = gson.fromJson(json, c.getClass());
    System.out.printf("Name = %s%n", c.name);
    System.out.printf("Population = %d%n", c.population);
    System.out.print("Cities = ");
    for (String city: c.cities)
        System.out.print(city + " ");
    System.out.println();
}
}
```

In Listing 9-14, I've bolded the two essential differences from Listing 9-13: the Country type adapter class is annotated @JsonAdapter(CountryAdapter.class), and Gson gson = new Gson(); is specified instead of using a GsonBuilder object and its create() method.

Compile Listing 9-14 and run the resulting application. You should observe the following output:

```
write() called
{"name":"England","population":53012456,"cities":["London","Birmingham","Ca
mbridge"]}
read() called
Name = England
Population = 53012456
Cities = London Birmingham Cambridge
```

The read() called and write called() output lines prove that Gson uses the custom type adapter instead of its internal type adapter.

EXERCISES

The following exercises are designed to test your understanding of Chapter 9's content.

1. Define Gson.

2. Identify and describe Gson's packages.

3. What are the two ways to obtain a Gson object?

4. Identify the types for which Gson provides default serialization and deserialization.

5. How would you enable pretty-printing?

6. True or false: By default, Gson excludes transient or static fields from consideration for serialization and deserialization.

7. Once you have a Gson object, what methods can you call to convert between JSON and Java objects?

8. How do you use Gson to customize JSON object parsing?

9. Describe the JsonElement class.

10. Identify the JsonElement subclasses.

11. What GsonBuilder method do you call to register a serializer or deserializer with a Gson object?

12. What method does JsonSerializer provide to serialize a Java object to a JSON object?

13. What annotation types does Gson provide to simplify serialization and deserialization?

14. True or false: To use Expose, it's enough to annotate a field, as in @ Expose(serialize = true, deserialize = false).

15. What do JsonSerializationContext and JsonDeserializationContext provide?

16. True or false: You can call <T> T fromJson(String json, Class<T> classOfT) to deserialize any kind of object.

17. Why should you prefer TypeAdapter to JsonSerializer and JsonDeserializer?

18. Modify Listing 9-8 so that the static field named field5 is also serialized and deserialized.

Summary

Gson is a small Java-based library for parsing and creating JSON objects. Google developed Gson for its own projects, but later made Gson publicly available, starting with version 1.0.

Gson parses JSON objects by deserializing JSON objects into Java objects. Similarly, it creates JSON objects by serializing Java objects into JSON objects. Gson relies on Java's Reflection API to assist with these tasks.

Gson consists of more than 30 classes and interfaces distributed among four packages: com.google.gson (provides access to Gson, the main class), com.google.gson.annotations (provides annotation types for use with Gson), com.google.gson.reflect (provides a utility class for obtaining type information from a generic type), and com.google.gson.stream (provides utility classes for reading and writing JSON-encoded values).

The Gson class handles the conversion between JSON and Java objects. You can instantiate this class by using the Gson() constructor, or you can obtain a Gson instance by working with the GsonBuilder class.

Once you have a Gson object, you can call various fromJson() and toJson() methods to convert between JSON and Java objects. Because these methods rely on Gson's default deserialization and serialization mechanisms, respectively, you can customize deserialization and serialization by working with the JsonDeserializer<T> and JsonSerializer<T> interfaces.

Gson offers additional useful features, including annotations for simplying serialization and deserialization, contexts for automating the serialization of nested objects and arrays, support for generics, and type adapters.

Chapter 10 introduces JsonPath for extracting JSON values.

Extracting JSON Values with JsonPath

XPath is used to extract values from XML documents. JsonPath performs this task for JSON documents. This chapter introduces you to JsonPath.

> **Note** If you're unfamiliar with XPath, I recommend that you read Chapter 5 before reading this chapter. JsonPath was derived from XPath.

What Is JsonPath?

JsonPath is a declarative query language (also known as a path expression syntax) for selecting and extracting a JSON document's property values. For example, you can use JsonPath to locate "John" in {"firstName": "John"} and return this value. JsonPath is based on XPath 1.0.

JsonPath was created by Stefan Goessner (http://goessner.net). Goessner also created JavaScript-based and PHP-based implementations of JsonPath. For complete documentation, check out Goessner's web site (http://goessner.net/articles/JsonPath/index.html).

Swedish software company Jayway (www.jayway.com) subsequently adapted JsonPath to Java. Their Java version of JsonPath is the focus of this chapter. You will find complete documentation on Jayway's implementation of JsonPath at https://github.com/jayway/JsonPath.

© Jeff Friesen 2016
J. Friesen, *Java XML and JSON*, DOI 10.1007/978-1-4842-1916-4_10

Learning the JsonPath Language

JsonPath is a simple language with various features that are similar to their XPath counterparts. This language is used to construct path expressions.

A JsonPath expression begins with the dollar sign ($) character, which refers to the root element of a query. The dollar sign is followed by a sequence of child elements, which are separated via dot (.) notation or via square bracket ([ ]) notation. For example, consider the following JSON object:

```
{
    "firstName": "John",
    "lastName": "Smith",
    "age": 25,
    "address":
    {
        "streetAddress": "21 2nd Street",
        "city": "New York",
        "state": "NY",
        "postalCode": "10021-3100"
    },
    "phoneNumbers":
    [
        {
            "type": "home",
            "number": "212 555-1234"
        },
        {
            "type": "office",
            "number": "646 555-4567"
        }
    ]
}
```

The following dot notation-based JsonPath expression extracts, from the previous anonymous JSON object, the phone number (212 555-1234) that's assigned to the number field in the anonymous JSON object, which is assigned to the first element in the phoneNumbers array:

```
$.phoneNumbers[0].number
```

The $ character represents the anonymous root JSON object. The leftmost dot character separates the object root from the phoneNumbers property name because the value assigned to phoneNumbers is an array. The [0] syntax identifies the first element in the array assigned to phoneNumbers.

The first array element stores an anonymous object consisting of "type": "home" and "number": "212 555-1234" properties. The rightmost dot character accesses this object's number child property name, which is assigned the value 212 555-1234. This value is returned from the expression.

Alternatively, I could specify the following square bracket notation to extract the same phone number:

```
$['phoneNumbers'][0]['number']
```

The Jayway documentation identifies $ as an operator and also identifies several other basic operators. Table 10-1 describes these operators.

Table 10-1. JsonPath Basic Operators

Operator	Description
$	The root element to query. This operator starts all path expressions. It's equivalent to XPath's / symbol.
@	The current node being processed by a filter predicate. It's equivalent to XPath's . symbol.
*	Wildcard. Available anywhere a name or numeric value is required.
..	Deep scan (also known as recursive descent). Available anywhere a name is required. It's equivalent to XPath's // symbol.
.*name*	Dot-notated child. The dot is equivalent to XPath's / symbol.
['*name*' (, '*name*')]	Bracket-notated child or children.
[*number* (, *number*)]	Array index or indexes.
[*start*:*end*]	Array slice operator.
[?(*expression*)]	Filter operator. The *expression* must evaluate to a Boolean value. In other words, it's a *predicate*.

The Jayway documentation also identifies several functions that can be invoked at the tail end of a path—the input to a function is the output of the path expression; the function output is dictated by the function itself. Table 10-2 describes these functions.

Table 10-2. JsonPath Functions

Function	Description
min()	Returns the minimum value (as a double) in an array of numbers.
max()	Returns the maximum value (as a double) in an array of numbers.
avg()	Returns the average value (as a double) of an array of numbers.
stddev()	Returns the standard deviation value (as a double) of an array of numbers.
length()	Returns the length (as an int) of an array.

Finally, the Jayway documentation identifies various operators for *filters*, which use predicates (Boolean expressions) to restrict returned lists of items. Predicates can use the filter operators in Table 10-3 to determine equality, match regular expressions, and test for inclusion.

Table 10-3. JsonPath Filter Operators

Operator	Description
==	Returns true when the left operand equals the right operand. Note that 1 is not equal to '1' (that is, number 1 and string 1 are two different things).
!=	Returns true when the left operand doesn't equal the right operand.
<	Returns true when the left operand is less than the right operand.
<=	Returns true when the left operand is less than or equal to the right operand.
>	Returns true when the left operand is greater than the right operand.
>=	Returns true when the left operand is greater than or equal to the right operand.
=~	Returns true when the left operand matches the regular expression specified by the right operand; for example, [?(@.name =~ /foo.*?/i)].
In	Returns true when the left operand exists in the right operand; for example, [?(@.grade in ['A', 'B'])].
Nin	Returns true when the left operand doesn't exist in the right operand.

This table reveals @.name =~ /foo.*?/i and @.grade in ['A', 'B'] as simple predicates. You can create more complex predicates by using the logical AND operator (&&) and the logical OR operator (||). Also, within a predicate, you must enclose any string literals with single or double quotes.

Obtaining and Using the JsonPath Library

As with Chapter 8's mJson and Chapter 9's Gson, you can obtain JsonPath from the Central Maven Repository (http://search.maven.org/).

> **Note** If you're unfamiliar with Maven, think of it as a build tool for Java projects, although Maven developers think of Maven as more than just a build tool—see http://maven.apache.org/background/philosophy-of-maven.html.

If you're familiar with Maven, add the following XML fragment to the Project Object Model (POM) files for your Maven project(s) that will be dependent on JsonPath, and you will be good to go! (To learn about POM, check out https://maven.apache.org/pom.html#What_is_the_POM.)

```
<dependency>
    <groupId>com.jayway.jsonpath</groupId>
    <artifactId>json-path</artifactId>
    <version>2.2.0</version>
</dependency>
```

This XML fragment reveals 2.2.0 as the version of Jayway JsonPath that I'm using in this chapter.

> **Note** It's common for Maven projects to be dependent on other projects. For example, the mJson project that I discussed in Chapter 8 is dependent on TestNG (https://en.wikipedia.org/wiki/TestNG). I didn't mention or discuss downloading TestNG in that chapter because this library isn't required for normal use. Also, the Gson project that I discussed in Chapter 9 is dependent on JUnit (https://en.wikipedia.org/wiki/JUnit). I didn't mention or discuss downloading JUnit in that chapter because this library isn't required for normal use.

Because I'm not currently using Maven, I downloaded the JsonPath Jar file and all of the Jar files on which JsonPath depends, and then added all of these Jar files to my classpath. The easiest way for me to accomplish the download task was to point my browser to https://github.com/jayway/JsonPath/releases and download json-path-2.2.0-SNAPSHOT-with-dependencies.zip.

After unarchiving the Zip file, I discovered the following subdirectories of the `json-path-2.2.0-SNAPSHOT-with-dependencies` home directory:

- `api`: Contains JsonPath's Javadoc-based API documentation.

- `lib`: Contains Jar files to add to the classpath in order to work with JsonPath—not all Jar files are needed in every situation, but it's best to include all of them in the classpath.

- `lib-optional`: Optional Jar files for configuring JsonPath.

- `source`: A Jar file containing the Java source code for the JsonPath API.

> **Note**   Jayway JsonPath is licensed according to Apache License Version 2.0 (`www.apache.org/licenses/`).

For compiling Java source code that accesses JsonPath, I found that only `json-path-2.2.0-SNAPSHOT.jar` needs to be included in the classpath:

```
javac -cp json-path-2.2.0-SNAPSHOT.jar source file
```

For running applications that access JsonPath, I use the following command line:

```
java -cp accessors-smart-1.1.jar;asm-5.0.3.jar;json-path-2.2.0-SNAPSHOT.jar;
json-smart-2.2.1.jar;slf4j-api-1.7.16.jar;tapestry-json-5.4.0.jar;. main classfile
```

> **Tip**   To facilitate working with these command lines, place them in a pair of batch files on Windows platforms or their counterparts on other platforms.

Exploring the JsonPath Library

The JsonPath library is organized into several packages. You will typically interact with the `com.jayway.jsonpath` package and its types. In this section, I focus exclusively on this package while showing you how to extract values from JSON objects and use predicates to filter items.

Extracting Values from JSON Objects

The com.jayway.jsonpath package provides the JsonPath class as the entry
point into using the JsonPath library. Listing 10-1 introduces this class.

Listing 10-1. A First Taste of JsonPath

```java
import java.util.HashMap;
import java.util.List;

import com.jayway.jsonpath.JsonPath;

public class JsonPathDemo
{
    public static void main(String[] args)
    {
        String json =
        "{" +
        "   \"store\":" +
        "   {" +
        "       \"book\":" +
        "       [" +
        "           {" +
        "               \"category\": \"reference\"," +
        "               \"author\": \"Nigel Rees\"," +
        "               \"title\": \"Sayings of the Century\"," +
        "               \"price\": 8.95" +
        "           }," +
        "           {" +
        "               \"category\": \"fiction\"," +
        "               \"author\": \"Evelyn Waugh\"," +
        "               \"title\": \"Sword of Honour\"," +
        "               \"price\": 12.99" +
        "           }" +
        "       ]," +
        "       \"bicycle\":" +
        "       {" +
        "           \"color\": \"red\"," +
        "           \"price\": 19.95" +
        "       }" +
        "   }" +
        "}";

        JsonPath path = JsonPath.compile("$.store.book[1]");
        HashMap books = path.read(json);
        System.out.println(books);
```

```
        List<Object> authors = JsonPath.read(json, "$.store.book[*].author");
        System.out.println(authors);
        String author = JsonPath.read(json, "$.store.book[1].author");
        System.out.println(author);
    }
}
```

Listing 10-1 provides a JsonPathDemo class whose main() method uses the JsonPath class to extract values from JSON objects. main() first declares a string-based JSON object and assigns its reference to variable json. It then invokes the following static JsonPath method to compile a JsonPath expression (to improve performance) and return the compiled result as a JsonPath object:

```
JsonPath compile(String jsonPath, Predicate... filters)
```

The Predicate varargs list lets you specify an array of filter predicates to respond to filter predicate placeholders (identified as ? characters) in the jsonPath string. I'll demonstrate Predicate and related types later in this chapter.

After compiling the $.store.book[1] JsonPath expression, which identifies the anonymous object in the second element of the array assigned to the book property of the anonymous object assigned to the store property, main() passes this expression to the following JsonPath method:

```
<T> T read(String json)
```

This generic method is called on the previously compiled JsonPath instance. It receives the string-based JSON object (assigned to json) as its argument and applies the JsonPath expression in the compiled JsonPath instance to this argument. The result is the JSON object identified by $.store.book[1].

The read() method is generic because it can return one of several types. In this example, it returns an instance of the java.util.LinkedHashMap class (a subclass of java.util.Hashmap) for storing JSON object property names and their values.

When you intend to reuse JsonPath expressions, it's good to compile them, which improves performance. Because I don't reuse $.store.book[1], I could have used one of JsonPath's static read() methods instead. For example, main() next demonstrates the following read() method:

```
<T> T read(String json, String jsonPath, Predicate... filters)
```

This method creates a new JsonPath object for the jsonPath argument and applies it to the json string. I ignore filters in the example.

The JsonPath expression passed to `jsonPath` is `$.store.book[*].author`. This expression includes the `*` wildcard to match all elements in the book array. It returns the value of the `author` property for each element in this array.

`read()` returns this value as an instance of the `net.minidev.json.JSONArray` class, which is stored in the `json-smart-2.2.1.jar` file that you must include in the classpath. Because `JSONArray` extends `java.util.ArrayList<Object>`, it's legal to cast the returned object to `List<Object>`.

To further demonstrate `read()`, `main()` lastly invokes this method with JsonPath expression `$.store.book[1].author`, which returns the value of the `author` property in the anonymous object stored in the second element of the book array. This time, `read()` returns a `java.lang.String` object.

Note   Regarding the generic `read()` methods, `JsonPath` automatically attempts to cast the result to the type that the method's invoker expects, such as a hashmap for a JSON object, a list of objects for a JSON array, and a string for a JSON string.

Compile Listing 10-1 as follows:

```
javac -cp json-path-2.2.0-SNAPSHOT.jar JsonPathDemo.java
```

Run the resulting application as follows:

```
java -cp accessors-smart-1.1.jar;asm-5.0.3.jar;json-path-2.2.0-SNAPSHOT.
jar;json-smart-2.2.1.jar;slf4j-api-1.7.16.jar;tapestry-json-5.4.0.jar;.
JsonPathDemo
```

You should observe the following output:

```
{category=fiction, author=Evelyn Waugh, title=Sword of Honour, price=12.99}
["Nigel Rees","Evelyn Waugh"]
Evelyn Waugh
```

You'll probably also observe some messages about SLF4J (Simple Logging Façade for Java) not being able to load the `StaticLoggerBinder` class and defaulting to a no-operation logger implementation. You can safely ignore these messages.

Using Predicates to Filter Items

JsonPath supports *filters* for restricting the nodes that are extracted from a JSON document to those that match the criteria specified by predicates (Boolean expressions). You can work with inline predicates, filter predicates, or custom predicates.

Inline Predicates

An *inline predicate* is a string-based predicate. Listing 10-2 presents the source code to an application that demonstrates several inline predicates.

Listing 10-2. Demonstrating Inline Predicates

```java
import java.util.List;

import com.jayway.jsonpath.JsonPath;

public class JsonPathDemo
{
   public static void main(String[] args)
   {
      String json =
      "{" +
      "   \"store\":" +
      "   {" +
      "      \"book\":" +
      "      [" +
      "         {" +
      "            \"category\": \"reference\"," +
      "            \"author\": \"Nigel Rees\"," +
      "            \"title\": \"Sayings of the Century\"," +
      "            \"price\": 8.95" +
      "         }," +
      "         {" +
      "            \"category\": \"fiction\"," +
      "            \"author\": \"Evelyn Waugh\"," +
      "            \"title\": \"Sword of Honour\"," +
      "            \"price\": 12.99" +
      "         }," +
      "         {" +
      "            \"category\": \"fiction\"," +
      "            \"author\": \"J. R. R. Tolkien\"," +
      "            \"title\": \"The Lord of the Rings\"," +
      "            \"isbn\": \"0-395-19395-8\"," +
      "            \"price\": 22.99" +
      "         }" +
```

```
"          ]," +
"          \"bicycle\":" +
"          {" +
"             \"color\": \"red\"," +
"             \"price\": 19.95" +
"          }" +
"       }" +
"}";

String expr = "$.store.book[?(@.isbn)].title";
List<Object> titles = JsonPath.read(json, expr);
System.out.println(titles);
expr = "$.store.book[?(@.category == 'fiction')].title";
titles = JsonPath.read(json, expr);
System.out.println(titles);
expr = "$..book[?(@.author =~ /.*REES/i)].title";
titles = JsonPath.read(json, expr);
System.out.println(titles);
expr = "$..book[?(@.price > 10 && @.price < 20)].title";
titles = JsonPath.read(json, expr);
System.out.println(titles);
expr = "$..book[?(@.author in ['Nigel Rees'])].title";
titles = JsonPath.read(json, expr);
System.out.println(titles);
expr = "$..book[?(@.author nin ['Nigel Rees'])].title";
titles = JsonPath.read(json, expr);
System.out.println(titles);
    }
}
```

Listing 10-2's main() method uses the following JsonPath expressions to narrow the list of returned book title strings:

- $.store.book[?(@.isbn)].title returns the title values for all book elements that contain an isbn property.

- $.store.book[?(@.category == 'fiction')].title returns the title values for all book elements whose category property is assigned the string value fiction.

- $..book[?(@.author =~ /.*REES/i)].title returns the title values for all book elements whose author property value ends with rees (case is insignificant).

- $..book[?(@.price >= 10 && @.price <= 20)].title returns the title values for all book elements whose price property value lies between 10 and 20.

▓ `$..book[?(@.author in ['Nigel Rees'])].title` returns the `title` values for all book elements whose author property value matches `Nigel Rees`.

▓ `$..book[?(@.author nin ['Nigel Rees'])].title` returns the `title` values for all book elements whose author property value doesn't match `Nigel Rees`.

Compile Listing 10-2 and run the resulting application. You should discover the following output:

```
["The Lord of the Rings"]
["Sword of Honour","The Lord of the Rings"]
["Sayings of the Century"]
["Sword of Honour"]
["Sayings of the Century"]
["Sword of Honour","The Lord of the Rings"]
```

Filter Predicates

A *filter predicate* is a predicate expressed as an instance of the abstract `Filter` class, which implements the `Predicate` interface.

To create a filter predicate, you typically chain together invocations of various fluent methods (`https://en.wikipedia.org/wiki/Fluent_interface`) located in the `Criteria` class, which also implements `Predicate`, and pass the result to `Filter`'s `Filter filter(Predicate predicate)` method.

```
Filter filter = Filter.filter(Criteria.where("price").lt(20.00));
```

`Criteria`'s `Criteria where(String key)` static method returns a `Criteria` object that stores the provided key, which is `price` in this example. Its `Criteria lt(Object o)` static method returns a `Criteria` object for the `<` operator that identifies the value that's compared to the value of the key.

To use the filter predicate, first insert a `?` placeholder for the filter predicate into the path:

```
String expr = "$['store']['book'][?].title";
```

> **Note** When multiple filter predicates are provided, they are applied in left-to-right order of the placeholders where the number of placeholders must match the number of provided filter predicates. You can specify multiple predicate placeholders in one filter operation `[?, ?]`; both predicates must match.

Next, because `Filter` implements `Predicate`, you pass the filter predicate to a `read()` method that takes a `Predicate` argument:

```
List<Object> titles = JsonPath.read(json, expr, filter);
```

For each book element, the `read()` method executes the filter predicate when it detects the ? placeholder in the JsonPath expression.

Listing 10-3 presents the source code for an application that demonstrates the previous filter predicate code fragments.

Listing 10-3. Demonstrating Filter Predicates

```java
import java.util.List;

import com.jayway.jsonpath.Criteria;
import com.jayway.jsonpath.Filter;
import com.jayway.jsonpath.JsonPath;

public class JsonPathDemo
{
    public static void main(String[] args)
    {
        String json =
        "{" +
        "    \"store\":" +
        "    {" +
        "        \"book\":" +
        "        [" +
        "            {" +
        "                \"category\": \"reference\"," +
        "                \"author\": \"Nigel Rees\"," +
        "                \"title\": \"Sayings of the Century\"," +
        "                \"price\": 8.95" +
        "            }," +
        "            {" +
        "                \"category\": \"fiction\"," +
        "                \"author\": \"Evelyn Waugh\"," +
        "                \"title\": \"Sword of Honour\"," +
        "                \"price\": 12.99" +
        "            }," +
        "            {" +
        "                \"category\": \"fiction\"," +
        "                \"author\": \"J. R. R. Tolkien\"," +
        "                \"title\": \"The Lord of the Rings\"," +
        "                \"isbn\": \"0-395-19395-8\"," +
        "                \"price\": 22.99" +
        "            }" +
        "        ]," +
```

```
"          \"bicycle\":" +
"          {" +
"              \"color\": \"red\"," +
"              \"price\": 19.95" +
"          }" +
"      }" +
"}";

Filter filter = Filter.filter(Criteria.where("price").lt(20.00));
String expr = "$['store']['book'][?].title";
List<Object> titles = JsonPath.read(json, expr, filter);
System.out.println(titles);
    }
}
```

Compile Listing 10-3 and run the resulting application. You should discover the following output (both books have prices less than 20 dollars):

```
["Sayings of the Century","Sword of Honour"]
```

Custom Predicates

A *custom predicate* is a predicate created from a class that implements the Predicate interface.

To create a custom predicate, instantiate a class that implements Predicate and overrides the following method:

```
boolean apply(Predicate.PredicateContext ctx)
```

PredicateContext is a nested interface whose methods provide information about the context in which apply() is called. For example, Object root() returns a reference to the entire JSON document, and Object item() returns the current item being evaluated by this predicate.

apply() returns the predicate value: true (item is accepted) or false (item is rejected).

The following code fragment creates a custom predicate for returning Book elements containing a price property whose value exceeds 20 dollars:

```
Predicate expensiveBooks =
    new Predicate()
    {
        @Override
        public boolean apply(PredicateContext ctx)
        {
            String value = ctx.item(Map.class).get("price").toString();
```

```
        return Float.valueOf(value) > 20.00;
    }
};
```

PredicateContext's `<T> T item(java.lang.Class<T> class)` generic method maps the JSON object in the Book element to a `java.util.Map`.

To use the custom predicate, first insert a ? placeholder for the custom predicate into the path:

```
String expr = "$.store.book[?]";
```

Next, pass the custom predicate to a `read()` method that takes a Predicate argument:

```
List<Map<String, Object>> titles = JsonPath.read(json, expr,
                                        expensiveBooks);
```

For each book element, `read()` executes the custom predicate associated with the ? and returns a list of maps (one map per accepted item).

Listing 10-4 presents the source code for an application that demonstrates the previous custom predicate code fragments.

Listing 10-4. Demonstrating Custom Predicates

```java
import java.util.List;
import java.util.Map;

import com.jayway.jsonpath.JsonPath;
import com.jayway.jsonpath.Predicate;

public class JsonPathDemo
{
   public static void main(String[] args)
   {
      String json =
      "{" +
      "   \"store\":" +
      "   {" +
      "      \"book\":" +
      "      [" +
      "         {" +
      "            \"category\": \"reference\"," +
      "            \"author\": \"Nigel Rees\"," +
      "            \"title\": \"Sayings of the Century\"," +
      "            \"price\": 8.95" +
      "         }," +
      "         {" +
```

```
"            \"category\": \"fiction\"," +
"            \"author\": \"Evelyn Waugh\"," +
"            \"title\": \"Sword of Honour\"," +
"            \"price\": 12.99" +
"         }," +
"         {" +
"            \"category\": \"fiction\"," +
"            \"author\": \"J. R. R. Tolkien\"," +
"            \"title\": \"The Lord of the Rings\"," +
"            \"isbn\": \"0-395-19395-8\"," +
"            \"price\": 22.99" +
"         }" +
"      ]," +
"      \"bicycle\":" +
"      {" +
"         \"color\": \"red\"," +
"         \"price\": 19.95" +
"      }" +
"   }" +
"}";

Predicate expensiveBooks =
   new Predicate()
   {
      @Override
      public boolean apply(PredicateContext ctx)
      {
         String value = ctx.item(Map.class).get("price").toString();
         return Float.valueOf(value) > 20.00;
      }
   };
String expr = "$.store.book[?]";
List<Map<String, Object>> titles = JsonPath.read(json, expr,
                                                 expensiveBooks);

System.out.println(titles);
   }
}
```

Compile Listing 10-4 and run the resulting application. You should discover the following output (one book has a price greater than 20 dollars):

```
[{"category":"fiction","author":"J. R. R. Tolkien","title":"The Lord of the
Rings","isbn":"0-395-19395-8","price":22.99}]
```

EXERCISES

The following exercises are designed to test your understanding of Chapter 10's content.

1. Define JsonPath.

2. True or false: JsonPath is based on XPath 2.0.

3. Identify the operator that represents the root JSON object.

4. In what notations can you specify JsonPath expressions?

5. What operator represents the current node being processed by a filter predicate?

6. True or false: JsonPath's deep scan operator (..) is equivalent to XPath's / symbol.

7. What does JsonPath's `JsonPath compile(String jsonPath, Predicate... filters)` static method accomplish?

8. What is the return type of the `<T> T read(String json)` generic method that returns JSON object property names and their values?

9. Identify the three predicate categories.

10. Given JSON object `{ "number": [10, 20, 25, 30] }`, write a `JsonPathDemo` application that extracts and outputs the maximum (30), minimum (10), and average (21.25) values.

Summary

JsonPath is a declarative query language (also known as a path expression syntax) for selecting and extracting a JSON document's property values.

JsonPath is a simple language with various features that are similar to their XPath counterparts. This language is used to construct path expressions. Each expression begins with the $ operator, which identifies the root element of the query, and which corresponds to the XPath / symbol.

As with Chapter 8's mJson and Chapter 9's Gson, you can obtain JsonPath from the Central Maven Repository. Alternatively, if you're not using Maven, you can download the JsonPath Jar file and all of the Jar files on which JsonPath depends, and then add all of these Jar files to your classpath.

The JsonPath library is organized into several packages. You will typically interact with the com.jayway.jsonpath package and its types. In this chapter, you focused exclusively on this package while learning how to extract values from JSON objects and use predicates to filter items.

Appendix A presents the answers to each chapter's exercises.

Answers to Exercises

Chapters 1 through 10 close with an "Exercises" section that tests your understanding of the chapter's material. The answers to those exercises are presented in this appendix.

Chapter 1: Introducing XML

1. XML (eXtensible Markup Language) is a metalanguage for defining vocabularies (custom markup languages), which is the key to XML's importance and popularity.

2. The answer is true: XML and HTML are descendants of SGML.

3. XML provides the XML declaration, elements and attributes, character references and CDATA sections, namespaces, and comments and processing instructions language features for use in defining custom markup languages.

4. The XML declaration is special markup that informs an XML parser that the document is XML.

5. The XML declaration's three attributes are version, encoding, and standalone. The version attribute is nonoptional.

© Jeff Friesen 2016
J. Friesen, *Java XML and JSON*, DOI 10.1007/978-1-4842-1916-4

6. The answer is false: an element can consist of the empty-element tag, which is a standalone tag whose name ends with a forward slash (/), such as `<break/>`.

7. Following the XML declaration, an XML document is anchored in a root element.

8. Mixed content is a combination of child elements and content.

9. A character reference is a code that represents a character. The two kinds of character references are numeric character references (such as `&#x03A3;`) and character entity references (such as `&lt;`).

10. A CDATA section is a section of literal HTML or XML markup and content surrounded by the `<![CDATA[` prefix and the `]]>` suffix. You use a CDATA section when you have a large amount of HTML/XML text and don't want to replace each literal `<` (start of tag) and `&` (start of entity) character with its `&lt;` and `&amp;` predefined character entity reference, which is a tedious and possibly error-prone undertaking because you might forget to replace one of these characters.

11. A namespace is a Uniform Resource Identifier-based container that helps differentiate XML vocabularies by providing a unique context for its contained identifiers.

12. A namespace prefix is an alias for a URI.

13. The answer is true: a tag's attributes don't need to be prefixed when those attributes belong to the element.

14. A comment is a character sequence beginning with `<!--` and ending with `-->`. It can appear anywhere in an XML document except before the XML declaration, except within tags, and except within another comment.

15. A processing instruction is an instruction that's made available to the application parsing the document. The instruction begins with `<?` and ends with `?>`.

16. The rules that an XML document must follow to be considered well-formed are as follows: all elements must either have start and end tags or consist of empty-element tags, tags must be nested correctly, all attribute values must be quoted, empty elements must be properly formatted, and you must be careful with case. Furthermore, XML parsers that are aware of namespaces enforce two additional rules: all element and attribute names must not include more than one colon character; and entity names, processing instruction targets, and notation names can't contain colons.

17. For an XML document to be valid, the document must adhere to certain constraints. For example, one constraint might be that a specific element must always follow another specific element.

18. The two common grammar languages are Document Type Definition and XML Schema.

19. The general syntax for declaring an element in a DTD is <!ELEMENT *name content-specifier*>.

20. XML Schema lets you create complex types from simple types.

21. Listing A-1 presents the books.xml document file that was called for in Chapter 1.

Listing A-1. A Document of Books

```xml
<?xml version="1.0"?>
<books>
   <book isbn="0201548550" pubyear="1992">
      <title>
         Advanced C++
      </title>
      394211_1_En
         James O. Coplien
      </author>
      <publisher>
         Addison Wesley
      </publisher>
   </book>
```

```
<book isbn="9781430210450" pubyear="2008">
   <title>
      Beginning Groovy and Grails
   </title>
   394211_1_En
      Christopher M. Judd
   </author>
   394211_1_En
      Joseph Faisal Nusairat
   </author>
   394211_1_En
      James Shingler
   </author>
   <publisher>
      Apress
   </publisher>
</book>
<book isbn="0201310058" pubyear="2001">
   <title>
      Effective Java
   </title>
   394211_1_En
      Joshua Bloch
   </author>
   <publisher>
      Addison Wesley
   </publisher>
</book>
</books>
```

22. Listing A-2 presents the books.xml document file
     with an internal DTD that was called for in Chapter 1.

Listing A-2. A DTD-Enabled Document of Books

```
<?xml version="1.0"?>
<!DOCTYPE books [
   <!ELEMENT books (book+)>
   <!ELEMENT book (title, author+, publisher)>
   <!ELEMENT title (#PCDATA)>
   <!ELEMENT author (#PCDATA)>
   <!ELEMENT publisher (#PCDATA)>
   <!ATTLIST book isbn CDATA #REQUIRED>
   <!ATTLIST book pubyear CDATA #REQUIRED>
]>
```

```xml
<books>
   <book isbn="0201548550" pubyear="1992">
      <title>
         Advanced C++
      </title>
      394211_1_En
         James O. Coplien
      </author>
      <publisher>
         Addison Wesley
      </publisher>
   </book>
   <book isbn="9781430210450" pubyear="2008">
      <title>
         Beginning Groovy and Grails
      </title>
      394211_1_En
         Christopher M. Judd
      </author>
      394211_1_En
         Joseph Faisal Nusairat
      </author>
      394211_1_En
         James Shingler
      </author>
      <publisher>
         Apress
      </publisher>
   </book>
   <book isbn="0201310058" pubyear="2001">
      <title>
         Effective Java
      </title>
      394211_1_En
         Joshua Bloch
      </author>
      <publisher>
         Addison Wesley
      </publisher>
   </book>
</books>
```

Chapter 2: Parsing XML Documents with SAX

1. SAX is an event-based Java API for parsing an XML document sequentially from start to finish. When a SAX-oriented parser encounters an item from the document's infoset, it makes this item available to an application as an event by calling one of the methods in one of the application's handlers, which the application has previously registered with the parser. The application can then consume this event by processing the infoset item in some manner.

2. You obtain a SAX 2-based parser by calling one of the XMLReaderFactory class's createXMLReader() methods, which returns an XMLReader object.

3. The purpose of the XMLReader interface is to describe a SAX parser. This interface makes available several methods for configuring the SAX parser and parsing an XML document's content.

4. You tell a SAX parser to perform validation by invoking XMLReader's setFeature(String name, boolean value) method, passing "http://xml.org/sax/features/validation" to name and true to value.

5. The four kinds of SAX-oriented exceptions that can be thrown when working with SAX are SAXException, SAXNotRecognizedException, SAXNotSupportedException, and SAXParseException.

6. The interface that a handler class implements to respond to content-oriented events is ContentHandler.

7. The three other core interfaces that a handler class is likely to implement are DTDHandler, EntityResolver, and ErrorHandler.

8. Ignorable whitespace is whitespace located between tags where the DTD doesn't allow mixed content.

9. The answer is false: void error(SAXParseException exception) is called only for recoverable errors.

10. The purpose of the DefaultHandler class is to serve as a convenience base class for SAX 2 applications. It provides default implementations for all of the callbacks in the four core SAX 2 handler interfaces: ContentHandler, DTDHandler, EntityResolver, and ErrorHandler.

11. An entity is aliased data. An entity resolver is an object that uses the public identifier to choose a different system identifier. Upon encountering an external entity, the parser calls the custom entity resolver to obtain this identifier.

12. Listing A-3 presents the DumpUserInfo application that was called for in Chapter 2.

Listing A-3. Using SAX to Dump the Apache tomcat-users.xml File's User Information

```java
import java.io.FileReader;
import java.io.IOException;

import org.xml.sax.Attributes;
import org.xml.sax.InputSource;
import org.xml.sax.SAXException;
import org.xml.sax.XMLReader;

import org.xml.sax.helpers.DefaultHandler;
import org.xml.sax.helpers.XMLReaderFactory;

public class DumpUserInfo
{
   public static void main(String[] args)
   {
      try
      {
         XMLReader xmlr = XMLReaderFactory.createXMLReader();
         Handler handler = new Handler();
         xmlr.setContentHandler(handler);
         xmlr.parse(new InputSource(new FileReader("tomcat-users.xml")));
      }
      catch (IOException ioe)
      {
         System.err.println("IOE: " + ioe);
      }
```

```
      catch (SAXException saxe)
      {
         System.err.println("SAXE: " + saxe);
      }
   }
}

class Handler extends DefaultHandler
{
   @Override
   public void startElement(String uri, String localName, String qName,
                            Attributes attributes)
   {
      if (localName.equals("user"))
      {
         for (int i = 0; i < attributes.getLength(); i++)
            System.out.printf("%s = %s%n", attributes.getLocalName(i),
                              attributes.getValue(i));
         System.out.println();
      }
   }
}
```

13. Listing A-4 and Listing A-5 present the SAXSearch and
     Handler classes that were called for in Chapter 2.

Listing A-4. A SAX Driver Class for Searching books.xml for a Specific Publisher's Books

```
import java.io.FileReader;
import java.io.IOException;

import org.xml.sax.InputSource;
import org.xml.sax.SAXException;
import org.xml.sax.XMLReader;

import org.xml.sax.helpers.XMLReaderFactory;

public class SAXSearch
{
   public static void main(String[] args)
   {
      if (args.length != 1)
      {
         System.err.println("usage: java SAXSearch publisher");
         return;
      }
```

```
        try
        {
            XMLReader xmlr = XMLReaderFactory.createXMLReader();
            Handler handler = new Handler(args[0]);
            xmlr.setContentHandler(handler);
            xmlr.setErrorHandler(handler);
            xmlr.setProperty("http://xml.org/sax/properties/lexical-handler",
                                                                    handler);
            xmlr.parse(new InputSource(new FileReader("books.xml")));
        }
        catch (IOException ioe)
        {
            System.err.println("IOE: " + ioe);
        }
        catch (SAXException saxe)
        {
            System.err.println("SAXE: " + saxe);
        }
    }
}
```

Listing A-5. *A SAX Callback Class Whose Methods are Called by the SAX Parser*

```
import org.xml.sax.Attributes;
import org.xml.sax.SAXParseException;

import org.xml.sax.ext.DefaultHandler2;

public class Handler extends DefaultHandler2
{
    private boolean isPublisher, isTitle;

    private String isbn, publisher, pubYear, title, srchText;

    public Handler(String srchText)
    {
        this.srchText = srchText;
    }

    @Override
    public void characters(char[] ch, int start, int length)
    {
        if (isTitle)
        {
            title = new String(ch, start, length).trim();
            isTitle = false;
        }
```

```java
      else
      if (isPublisher)
      {
         publisher = new String(ch, start, length).trim();
         isPublisher = false;
      }
   }

   @Override
   public void endElement(String uri, String localName, String qName)
   {
      if (!localName.equals("book"))
         return;
      if (!srchText.equals(publisher))
         return;
      System.out.println("title = " + title + ", isbn = " + isbn);
   }

   @Override
   public void error(SAXParseException saxpe)
   {
      System.out.println("error() " + saxpe);
   }

   @Override
   public void fatalError(SAXParseException saxpe)
   {
      System.out.println("fatalError() " + saxpe);
   }

   @Override
   public void startElement(String uri, String localName, String qName,
                            Attributes attributes)
   {
      if (localName.equals("title"))
      {
         isTitle = true;
         return;
      }
      else
      if (localName.equals("publisher"))
      {
         isPublisher = true;
         return;
      }
      if (!localName.equals("book"))
         return;
```

```
    for (int i = 0; i < attributes.getLength(); i++)
        if (attributes.getLocalName(i).equals("isbn"))
            isbn = attributes.getValue(i);
        else
        if (attributes.getLocalName(i).equals("pubyear"))
            pubYear = attributes.getValue(i);
    }

    @Override
    public void warning(SAXParseException saxpe)
    {
        System.out.println("warning() " + saxpe);
    }
}
```

14. When you use Listing 2-1's SAXDemo application to validate Exercise 1-22's books.xml content against its DTD, you should observe no validation errors.

Chapter 3: Parsing and Creating XML Documents with DOM

1. DOM is a Java API for parsing an XML document into an in-memory tree of nodes and for creating an XML document from a tree of nodes. After a DOM parser has created a document tree, an application uses the DOM API to navigate over and extract infoset items from the tree's nodes.

2. The answer is false: Java 8 supports DOM Levels 1, 2, and 3.

3. The 12 types of DOM nodes are attribute node, CDATA section node, comment node, document node, document fragment node, document type node, element node, entity node, entity reference node, notation node, processing instruction node, and text node.

4. You obtain a document builder by first instantiating DocumentBuilderFactory via one of its newInstance() methods and then invoking newDocumentBuilder() on the returned DocumentBuilderFactory object to obtain a DocumentBuilder object.

5. You use a document builder to parse an XML document by invoking one of `DocumentBuilder`'s `parse()` methods.

6. The answer is true: `Document` and all other `org.w3c.dom` interfaces that describe different kinds of nodes are subinterfaces of the `Node` interface.

7. You use a document builder to create a new XML document by invoking `DocumentBuilder`'s `Document newDocument()` method and by invoking `Document`'s various "create" methods.

8. You determine if a node has children by calling `Node`'s boolean `hasChildNodes()` method, which returns `true` when a node has child nodes.

9. The answer is false: when creating a new XML document, you cannot use the DOM API to specify the XML declaration's `encoding` attribute.

10. Listing A-6 presents the `DumpUserInfo` application that was called for in Chapter 3.

Listing A-6. Using DOM to Dump the Apache `tomcat-users.xml` File's User Information

```java
import java.io.IOException;

import javax.xml.parsers.DocumentBuilder;
import javax.xml.parsers.DocumentBuilderFactory;
import javax.xml.parsers.FactoryConfigurationError;
import javax.xml.parsers.ParserConfigurationException;

import org.w3c.dom.Attr;
import org.w3c.dom.Document;
import org.w3c.dom.Element;
import org.w3c.dom.NamedNodeMap;
import org.w3c.dom.Node;
import org.w3c.dom.NodeList;

import org.xml.sax.SAXException;

public class DumpUserInfo
{
    public static void main(String[] args)
    {
```

```java
      try
      {
         DocumentBuilderFactory dbf = DocumentBuilderFactory.newInstance();
         DocumentBuilder db = dbf.newDocumentBuilder();
         Document doc = db.parse("tomcat-users.xml");
         NodeList nl = doc.getChildNodes();
         for (int i = 0; i < nl.getLength(); i++)
         {
            Node node = nl.item(i);
            if (node.getNodeType() == Node.ELEMENT_NODE)
               dump((Element) node);
         }
      }
      catch (IOException ioe)
      {
         System.err.println("IOE: " + ioe);
      }
      catch (SAXException saxe)
      {
         System.err.println("SAXE: " + saxe);
      }
      catch (FactoryConfigurationError fce)
      {
         System.err.println("FCE: " + fce);
      }
      catch (ParserConfigurationException pce)
      {
         System.err.println("PCE: " + pce);
      }
   }

   static void dump(Element e)
   {
      if (e.getNodeName().equals("user"))
      {
         NamedNodeMap nnm = e.getAttributes();
         if (nnm != null)
            for (int i = 0; i < nnm.getLength(); i++)
            {
               Node node = nnm.item(i);
               Attr attr = e.getAttributeNode(node.getNodeName());
               System.out.printf("%s = %s%n", attr.getName(),
                                 attr.getValue());
            }
         System.out.println();
      }
```

```
      NodeList nl = e.getChildNodes();
      for (int i = 0; i < nl.getLength(); i++)
      {
         Node node = nl.item(i);
         if (node instanceof Element)
            dump((Element) node);
      }
   }
}
```

11.   Listing A-7 presents the DOMSearch application that
      was called for in Chapter 3.

Listing A-7. Using DOM to Search books.xml for a Specific Publisher's Books

```java
import java.io.IOException;

import java.util.ArrayList;
import java.util.List;

import javax.xml.parsers.DocumentBuilder;
import javax.xml.parsers.DocumentBuilderFactory;
import javax.xml.parsers.FactoryConfigurationError;
import javax.xml.parsers.ParserConfigurationException;

import org.w3c.dom.Document;
import org.w3c.dom.Element;
import org.w3c.dom.NamedNodeMap;
import org.w3c.dom.Node;
import org.w3c.dom.NodeList;

import org.xml.sax.SAXException;

public class DOMSearch
{
   public static void main(String[] args)
   {
      if (args.length != 1)
      {
         System.err.println("usage: java DOMSearch publisher");
         return;
      }

      try
      {
         DocumentBuilderFactory dbf = DocumentBuilderFactory.newInstance();
         DocumentBuilder db = dbf.newDocumentBuilder();
         Document doc = db.parse("books.xml");
```

```
   class BookItem
   {
      String title;
      String isbn;
   }
   List<BookItem> bookItems = new ArrayList<BookItem>();
   NodeList books = doc.getElementsByTagName("book");
   for (int i = 0; i < books.getLength(); i++)
   {
      Element book = (Element) books.item(i);
      NodeList children = book.getChildNodes();
      String title = "";
      for (int j = 0; j < children.getLength(); j++)
      {
         Node child = children.item(j);
         if (child.getNodeType() == Node.ELEMENT_NODE)
         {
            if (child.getNodeName().equals("title"))
               title = child.getFirstChild().getNodeValue().trim();
            else
            if (child.getNodeName().equals("publisher"))
            {
               // Compare publisher name argument (args[0]) with text
               // of publisher's child text node. The trim() method
               // call removes whitespace that would interfere with
               // the comparison.
               if (args[0].equals(child.getFirstChild().
                                  getNodeValue().trim()))
               {
                  BookItem bookItem = new BookItem();
                  bookItem.title = title;
                  NamedNodeMap nnm = book.getAttributes();
                  Node isbn = nnm.getNamedItem("isbn");
                  bookItem.isbn = isbn.getNodeValue();
                  bookItems.add(bookItem);
                  break;
               }
            }
         }
      }
   }
   for (BookItem bookItem: bookItems)
      System.out.println("title = " + bookItem.title + ", isbn = " +
      bookItem.isbn);
}
catch (IOException ioe)
{
   System.err.println("IOE: " + ioe);
}
```

```
      catch (SAXException saxe)
      {
          System.err.println("SAXE: " + saxe);
      }
      catch (FactoryConfigurationError fce)
      {
          System.err.println("FCE: " + fce);
      }
      catch (ParserConfigurationException pce)
      {
          System.err.println("PCE: " + pce);
      }
   }
}
```

12. Listing A-8 presents the DOMValidate application that
     was called for in Chapter 3.

Listing A-8. Using DOM to Validate XML Content

```
import java.io.IOException;

import javax.xml.parsers.DocumentBuilder;
import javax.xml.parsers.DocumentBuilderFactory;
import javax.xml.parsers.FactoryConfigurationError;
import javax.xml.parsers.ParserConfigurationException;

import org.w3c.dom.Attr;
import org.w3c.dom.Document;
import org.w3c.dom.Element;
import org.w3c.dom.NamedNodeMap;
import org.w3c.dom.Node;
import org.w3c.dom.NodeList;

import org.xml.sax.SAXException;

public class DOMValidate
{
   public static void main(String[] args)
   {
      if (args.length != 1)
      {
          System.err.println("usage: java DOMValidate xmlfile");
          return;
      }
```

```java
    try
    {
        DocumentBuilderFactory dbf = DocumentBuilderFactory.newInstance();
        dbf.setNamespaceAware(true);
        dbf.setValidating(true);
        DocumentBuilder db = dbf.newDocumentBuilder();
        Document doc = db.parse(args[0]);
        System.out.printf("Version = %s%n", doc.getXmlVersion());
        System.out.printf("Encoding = %s%n", doc.getXmlEncoding());
        System.out.printf("Standalone = %b%n%n", doc.getXmlStandalone());
        if (doc.hasChildNodes())
        {
            NodeList nl = doc.getChildNodes();
            for (int i = 0; i < nl.getLength(); i++)
            {
                Node node = nl.item(i);
                if (node.getNodeType() == Node.ELEMENT_NODE)
                    dump((Element) node);
            }
        }
    }
    catch (IOException ioe)
    {
        System.err.println("IOE: " + ioe);
    }
    catch (SAXException saxe)
    {
        System.err.println("SAXE: " + saxe);
    }
    catch (FactoryConfigurationError fce)
    {
        System.err.println("FCE: " + fce);
    }
    catch (ParserConfigurationException pce)
    {
        System.err.println("PCE: " + pce);
    }
}

static void dump(Element e)
{
    System.out.printf("Element: %s, %s, %s, %s%n", e.getNodeName(),
    e.getLocalName(), e.getPrefix(), e.getNamespaceURI());
    NamedNodeMap nnm = e.getAttributes();
    if (nnm != null)
        for (int i = 0; i < nnm.getLength(); i++)
        {
            Node node = nnm.item(i);
            Attr attr = e.getAttributeNode(node.getNodeName());
```

```
            System.out.printf("  Attribute %s = %s%n", attr.getName(), attr.
            getValue());
         }
      NodeList nl = e.getChildNodes();
      for (int i = 0; i < nl.getLength(); i++)
      {
         Node node = nl.item(i);
         if (node instanceof Element)
            dump((Element) node);
      }
   }
}
```

Chapter 4: Parsing and Creating XML Documents with StAX

1. StAX is a Java API for parsing an XML document sequentially from start to finish, and also for creating XML documents.

2. The javax.xml.stream, javax.xml.stream.events, and javax.xml.stream.util packages make up the StAX API.

3. The answer is false: an event-based reader extracts the next infoset item from an input stream by obtaining an event.

4. You obtain a document reader by calling one of the various "create" methods that are declared in the XMLInputFactory class. You obtain a document writer by calling one of the various "create" methods that are declared in the XMLOutputFactory class.

5. When you call XMLOutputFactory's void setProperty(String name, Object value) method with XMLOutputFactory.IS_REPAIRING_NAMESPACES as the property name and true as the value, the document writer takes care of all namespace bindings and declarations, with minimal help from the application. The output is always well formed with respect to namespaces.

6. Listing A-9 presents the ParseXMLDoc application that was called for in Chapter 4.

Listing A-9. A StAX Stream-Based Parser for Parsing an XML Document

```java
import java.io.FileReader;
import java.io.IOException;

import javax.xml.stream.XMLEventReader;
import javax.xml.stream.XMLInputFactory;
import javax.xml.stream.XMLStreamException;
import javax.xml.stream.XMLStreamReader;

public class ParseXMLDoc
{
   public static void main(String[] args)
   {
      if (args.length != 1)
      {
         System.err.println("usage: java ParseXMLDoc pathname");
         return;
      }
      XMLInputFactory xmlif = XMLInputFactory.newFactory();
      XMLStreamReader xmlsr = null;
      try (FileReader fr = new FileReader(args[0]))
      {
         xmlsr = xmlif.createXMLStreamReader(fr);
         int item = xmlsr.getEventType();
         if (item != XMLStreamReader.START_DOCUMENT)
         {
            System.err.println("START_DOCUMENT expected");
            return;
         }
         while ((item = xmlsr.next()) != XMLStreamReader.END_DOCUMENT)
            switch (item)
            {
               case XMLStreamReader.ATTRIBUTE:
                  System.out.println("ATTRIBUTE");
                  break;
               case XMLStreamReader.CDATA:
                  System.out.println("CDATA");
                  break;
               case XMLStreamReader.CHARACTERS:
                  System.out.println("CHARACTERS");
                  break;
               case XMLStreamReader.COMMENT:
                  System.out.println("COMMENT");
                  break;
               case XMLStreamReader.DTD:
                  System.out.println("DTD");
                  break;
```

```
            case XMLStreamReader.END_ELEMENT:
               System.out.println("END_ELEMENT");
               break;
            case XMLStreamReader.ENTITY_DECLARATION:
               System.out.println("ENTITY_DECLARATION");
               break;
            case XMLStreamReader.ENTITY_REFERENCE:
               System.out.println("ENTITY_REFERENCE");
               break;
            case XMLStreamReader.NAMESPACE:
               System.out.println("NAMESPACE");
               break;
            case XMLStreamReader.NOTATION_DECLARATION:
               System.out.println("NOTATION_DECLARATION");
               break;
            case XMLStreamReader.PROCESSING_INSTRUCTION:
               System.out.println("PROCESSING_INSTRUCTION");
               break;
            case XMLStreamReader.SPACE:
               System.out.println("SPACE");
               break;
            case XMLStreamReader.START_ELEMENT:
               System.out.println("START_ELEMENT");
               System.out.println("Name = " + xmlsr.getName());
               System.out.println("Local name = " +
                                  xmlsr.getLocalName());
            int nAttrs = xmlsr.getAttributeCount();
            for (int i = 0; i < nAttrs; i++)
               System.out.println("Attribute [" +
                                  xmlsr.getAttributeLocalName(i) +
                                  ", " +
                                  xmlsr.getAttributeValue(i) + "]");
         }
      }
      catch (IOException ioe)
      {
         ioe.printStackTrace();
      }
      catch (XMLStreamException xmlse)
      {
         xmlse.printStackTrace();
      }
      finally
      {
         if (xmlsr != null)
            try
            {
               xmlsr.close();
            }
```

```
        catch (XMLStreamException xmlse)
        {
        }
    }
  }
}
```

Chapter 5: Selecting Nodes with XPath

1. XPath is a nonXML declarative query language (defined by the W3C) for selecting an XML document's infoset items as one or more nodes.

2. XPath is commonly used to simplify access to a DOM tree's nodes and in the context of XSLT to select those input document elements (via XPath expressions) that are to be copied to an output document.

3. The seven kinds of nodes that XPath recognizes are element, attribute, text, namespace, processing instruction, comment, and document.

4. The answer is false: XPath doesn't recognize CDATA sections.

5. XPath provides location path expressions for selecting nodes. A location path expression locates nodes via a sequence of steps starting from the context node, which is the root node or some other document node that is the current node. The returned set of nodes might be empty, or it might contain one or more nodes.

6. The answer is true: in a location path expression, you must prefix an attribute name with the @ symbol.

7. The functions that XPath provides for selecting comment, text, and processing-instruction nodes are comment(), text(), and processing-instruction(), respectively.

8. XPath provides wildcards for selecting unknown nodes. The * wildcard matches any element node regardless of the node's type. It doesn't match attributes, text nodes, comments, or processing-instruction nodes. When you place a namespace prefix before the *, only elements belonging to that namespace are matched. The node() wildcard is a function that matches all nodes. Finally, the @* wildcard matches all attribute nodes.

9. You perform multiple selections by using the vertical bar (|). For example, author/*|publisher/* selects the children of author and the children of publisher.

10. A predicate is a square bracket-delimited Boolean expression that's tested against each selected node. If the expression evaluates to true, that node is included in the set of nodes returned by the XPath expression; otherwise, the node isn't included in the set.

11. The functions that XPath provides for working with nodesets are last(), position(), id(), local-name(), namespace-uri(), and name().

12. The three advanced features that XPath provides to overcome limitations with the XPath 1.0 language are namespace contexts, extension functions and function resolvers, and variables and variable resolvers.

13. The answer is false: the XPath API maps XPath's number type to java.lang.Double.

14. Listing A-10 and Listing A-11 present the contacts.xml document file and XPathSearch application that were called for in Chapter 5.

Listing A-10. A Contacts Document with a Titlecased Name Element

```
<?xml version="1.0"?>
<contacts>
   <contact>
      <Name>John Doe</Name>
      <city>Chicago</city>
      <city>Denver</city>
   </contact>
   <contact>
```

```
         <name>Jane Doe</name>
         <city>New York</city>
      </contact>
      <contact>
         <name>Sandra Smith</name>
         <city>Denver</city>
         <city>Miami</city>
      </contact>
      <contact>
         <name>Bob Jones</name>
         <city>Chicago</city>
      </contact>
</contacts>
```

Listing A-11. Searching for name or Name Elements via a Multiple Selection

```java
import java.io.IOException;

import javax.xml.parsers.DocumentBuilder;
import javax.xml.parsers.DocumentBuilderFactory;
import javax.xml.parsers.FactoryConfigurationError;
import javax.xml.parsers.ParserConfigurationException;

import javax.xml.xpath.XPath;
import javax.xml.xpath.XPathConstants;
import javax.xml.xpath.XPathException;
import javax.xml.xpath.XPathExpression;
import javax.xml.xpath.XPathFactory;

import org.w3c.dom.Document;
import org.w3c.dom.NodeList;

import org.xml.sax.SAXException;

public class XPathSearch
{
   public static void main(String[] args)
   {
      try
      {
         DocumentBuilderFactory dbf = DocumentBuilderFactory.newInstance();
         DocumentBuilder db = dbf.newDocumentBuilder();
         Document doc = db.parse("contacts.xml");
         XPathFactory xpf = XPathFactory.newInstance();
         XPath xp = xpf.newXPath();
         XPathExpression xpe;
         xpe = xp.compile("//contact[city = 'Chicago']/name/text()|" +
                          "//contact[city = 'Chicago']/Name/text()");
```

```
      Object result = xpe.evaluate(doc, XPathConstants.NODESET);
      NodeList nl = (NodeList) result;
      for (int i = 0; i < nl.getLength(); i++)
         System.out.println(nl.item(i).getNodeValue());
   }
   catch (IOException ioe)
   {
      System.err.println("IOE: " + ioe);
   }
   catch (SAXException saxe)
   {
      System.err.println("SAXE: " + saxe);
   }
   catch (FactoryConfigurationError fce)
   {
      System.err.println("FCE: " + fce);
   }
   catch (ParserConfigurationException pce)
   {
      System.err.println("PCE: " + pce);
   }
   catch (XPathException xpe)
   {
      System.err.println("XPE: " + xpe);
   }
  }
}
```

Chapter 6: Transforming XML Documents with XSLT

1. XSLT is a family of languages for transforming and formatting XML documents.

2. XSLT accomplishes its work by using XSLT processors and stylesheets. An XSLT processor is a software component that applies an XSLT stylesheet (an XML-based template consisting of content and transformation instructions) to an input document (without modifying the document), and copies the transformed result to a result tree, which can be output to a file or output stream, or even piped into another XSLT processor for additional transformations.

3. The answer is false: call Transformer's
   void transform(Source xmlSource, Result
   outputTarget) method to transform a source to a
   result.

4. Listing A-12 and Listing A-13 present the books.xsl
   document stylesheet file and MakeHTML application
   that were called for in Chapter 6.

Listing A-12. A Stylesheet for Converting books.xml Content to HTML

```
<?xml version="1.0"?>
<xsl:stylesheet version="1.0"
                xmlns:xsl="http://www.w3.org/1999/XSL/Transform">
<xsl:template match="/books">
<html>
<head>
<title>Books</title>
</head>
<body>
<xsl:for-each select="book">
<h2>
<xsl:value-of select="normalize-space(title/text())"/>
</h2>
ISBN: <xsl:value-of select="@isbn"/><br/>
Publication Year: <xsl:value-of select="@pubyear"/><br/>
<br/><xsl:text>
</xsl:text>
<xsl:for-each select="author">
<xsl:value-of select="normalize-space(text())"/><br/><xsl:text>
</xsl:text>
</xsl:for-each>
</xsl:for-each>
</body>
</html>
</xsl:template>
</xsl:stylesheet>
```

Listing A-13. Converting Books XML to HTML via a Stylesheet

```
import java.io.FileReader;
import java.io.IOException;

import javax.xml.parsers.DocumentBuilder;
import javax.xml.parsers.DocumentBuilderFactory;
import javax.xml.parsers.FactoryConfigurationError;
import javax.xml.parsers.ParserConfigurationException;
```

```java
import javax.xml.transform.OutputKeys;
import javax.xml.transform.Result;
import javax.xml.transform.Source;
import javax.xml.transform.Transformer;
import javax.xml.transform.TransformerConfigurationException;
import javax.xml.transform.TransformerException;
import javax.xml.transform.TransformerFactory;
import javax.xml.transform.TransformerFactoryConfigurationError;

import javax.xml.transform.dom.DOMSource;

import javax.xml.transform.stream.StreamResult;
import javax.xml.transform.stream.StreamSource;

import org.w3c.dom.Document;

import org.xml.sax.SAXException;

public class MakeHTML
{
    public static void main(String[] args)
    {
        try
        {
            DocumentBuilderFactory dbf = DocumentBuilderFactory.newInstance();
            DocumentBuilder db = dbf.newDocumentBuilder();
            Document doc = db.parse("books.xml");
            TransformerFactory tf = TransformerFactory.newInstance();
            StreamSource ssStyleSheet;
            ssStyleSheet = new StreamSource(new FileReader("books.xsl"));
            Transformer t = tf.newTransformer(ssStyleSheet);
            t.setOutputProperty(OutputKeys.METHOD, "html");
            t.setOutputProperty(OutputKeys.INDENT, "yes");
            Source source = new DOMSource(doc);
            Result result = new StreamResult(System.out);
            t.transform(source, result);
        }
        catch (IOException ioe)
        {
            System.err.println("IOE: " + ioe);
        }
        catch (FactoryConfigurationError fce)
        {
            System.err.println("FCE: " + fce);
        }
        catch (ParserConfigurationException pce)
        {
            System.err.println("PCE: " + pce);
        }
```

```
   catch (SAXException saxe)
   {
      System.err.println("SAXE: " + saxe);
   }
   catch (TransformerConfigurationException tce)
   {
      System.err.println("TCE: " + tce);
   }
   catch (TransformerException te)
   {
      System.err.println("TE: " + te);
   }
   catch (TransformerFactoryConfigurationError tfce)
   {
      System.err.println("TFCE: " + tfce);
   }
   }
}
```

Chapter 7: Introducing JSON

1. JSON (JavaScript Object Notation) is a language-independent data format that expresses JSON objects as human-readable lists of properties.

2. The answer is false: JSON is derived from a nonstrict subset of JavaScript.

3. The JSON data format presents a JSON object as a brace-delimited and comma-separated list of properties.

4. The six types that JSON supports are number, string, Boolean, array, object, and null.

5. The answer is true: JSON doesn't support comments.

6. You would parse a JSON object into an equivalent JavaScript object by calling the JSON object's parse() method with the text to be parsed as this method's argument.

7. JSON Schema is a grammar language for defining the structure, content, and (to some extent) semantics of JSON objects.

8. When creating a schema, you identify those properties that must be present in those JSON objects that the schema validates by placing their names in the array that's assigned to the schema's `required` property name.

9. Listing A-14 presents the JSON object that was called for in Chapter 7.

Listing A-14. A Product in Terms of Name and Price

```
{
   "name": "hammer",
   "price": 20
}
```

10. Listing A-15 presents the schema that was called for in Chapter 7.

Listing A-15. A Schema for Validating Product Objects

```
{
   "$schema": "http://json-schema.org/draft-04/schema#",
   "title": "Product",
   "description": "A product",
   "type": "object",
   "properties":
   {
      "name":
      {
         "description": "A product name",
         "type": "string"
      },
      "price":
      {
         "description": "A product price",
         "type": "number",
         "minimum": 1
      }
   },
   "required": ["name", "price"]
}
```

Chapter 8: Parsing and Creating JSON Objects with mJson

1. mJson is a small Java-based JSON library for parsing JSON objects into Java objects and vice versa.

2. The Json class describes a JSON object or part of a JSON object. It contains Schema and Factory interfaces, more than 50 methods, and other members.

3. Json's methods for reading and parsing external JSON objects are Json read(String s), Json read(URL url), and Json read(CharacterIterator ci).

4. The answer is true: the read() methods can also parse smaller JSON fragments, such as an array of different-typed values.

5. The methods that Json provides for creating JSON objects are Json array(), Json array(Object... args), Json make(Object anything), Json nil(), Json object(), and Json object(Object... args).

6. Json's boolean isPrimitive() method returns true when the invoking Json object describes a JSON number, string, or Boolean value.

7. You return a Json object's JSON array by calling List<Json> asJsonList() to return a list of Json objects (one per array element) or by calling List<Object> asList() to return a list of Java objects (each object describes one of the elements).

8. The answer is false: Json's Map<String, Object> asMap() method returns a map of the properties of a Json object that describes a JSON object. The returned map is a copy and modifications to it don't affect the Json object.

9. Json's Json at(int index), Json at(String propName), Json at(String propName, Json defValue), and Json at(String propName, Object defValue) methods let you access the contents of arrays and objects.

10. `Json`'s `boolean is(int index, Object value)` method returns `true` when this `Json` object describes a JSON array that has the specified value at the specified `index`; otherwise, it returns `false`.

11. When you attempt to set the value for a nonexistent array element, `Json` throws `IndexOutOfBoundsException`.

12. The difference between `Json`'s `atDel()` and `delAt()` methods is as follows: the `atDel()` methods return the removed array element or object property, whereas the `delAt()` methods do not return the removed array element or object property.

13. `Json`'s `Json with(Json objectorarray)` method combines this `Json` object's JSON object or JSON array with the argument passed to `objectorarray`. The JSON type of this `Json` object and the JSON type of `objectorarray` must match. If `objectorarray` identifies a JSON object, all of its properties are appended to this `Json` object's object. If `objectorarray` identifies a JSON array, all of its elements are appended to this `Json` object's array.

14. `Json`'s methods for obtaining a `Json.Schema` object are `Json.Schema schema(Json jsonSchema)`, `Json.Schema schema(Json jsonSchema, URI uri)`, and `Json.Schema schema(URI uri)`.

15. You validate a JSON document against a schema by calling `Json.Schema`'s `Json validate(Json document)` method with the JSON document passed as a `Json` argument to this method.

16. The difference between `Json`'s `setGlobalFactory()` and `attachFactory()` methods is that `setGlobalFactory()` installs the specified factory as a global factory, which is used by all threads that don't have a specific thread-local factory attached to them, whereas `attachFactory()` attaches the specified factory to the invoking thread only.

17. The Json dup() method returns a clone (a duplicate)
     of this Json entity. The String pad(String callback)
     method wraps a function named callback around
     the JSON object described by the current Json
     object. This is done for the reason explained in
     Wikipedia's "JSONP" entry (https://en.wikipedia.
     org/wiki/JSONP).

18. Listing A-16 presents the mJsonDemo application that
     was called for in Chapter 8.

Listing A-16. Demonstrating Json's dup() and pad() Methods

```java
import mjson.Json;

public class mJsonDemo
{
   public static void main(String[] args)
   {
      Json json1 = Json.read("{\"name\": \"John Doe\"}");
      Json json2 = json1.dup();
      System.out.println(json1);
      System.out.println();
      System.out.println(json2);
      System.out.println();
      System.out.printf("json1 == json2: %b%n", json1 == json2);
      System.out.printf("json1.equals(json2): %b%n", json1.equals(json2));
      System.out.println();
      System.out.println(json1.pad("func"));

      /*
         The following output is generated:

         {"name":"John Doe"}

         {"name":"John Doe"}

         json1 == json2: false
         json1.equals(json2): true

         func({"name":"John Doe"});
      */
   }
}
```

Chapter 9: Parsing and Creating JSON Objects with Gson

1. Gson is a small Java-based library for parsing and creating JSON objects. Google developed Gson for its own projects, but later made Gson publicly available, starting with version 1.0.

2. Gson's packages are com.google.gson (provides access to Gson, the main class for working with Gson), com.google.gson.annotations (provides annotation types for use with Gson), com.google.gson.reflect (provides a utility class for obtaining type information from a generic type), and com.google.gson.stream (provides utility classes for reading and writing JSON-encoded values).

3. The two ways to obtain a Gson object are to call the Gson() constructor or to invoke the create() method on a GsonBuilder object.

4. The types for which Gson provides default serialization and deserialization are java.lang.Enum, java.util.Map, java.net.URL, java.net.URI, java.util.Locale, java.util.Date, java.math.BigDecimal, and java.math.BigInteger.

5. You enable pretty-printing by calling GsonBuilder's setPrettyPrinting() method.

6. The answer is true: by default, Gson excludes transient or static fields from consideration for serialization and deserialization.

7. Once you have a Gson object, you can call various fromJson() and toJson() methods to convert between JSON and Java objects.

8. You use Gson to customize JSON object parsing by implementing the JsonDeserializer<T> interface, instantiating an object from the implementation, and registering with Gson the deserializer object along with the class object of the Java class whose objects are to be serialized/deserialized.

9. The `JsonElement` class represents a JSON element (such as a number, a Boolean value, or an array). It provides various methods for obtaining an element value, such as `double getAsDouble()`, `boolean getAsBoolean()`, and `JsonArray getAsJsonArray()`.

10. The `JsonElement` subclasses are `JsonArray`, `JsonNull`, `JsonObject`, and `JsonPrimitive`.

11. You call GsonBuilder's `GsonBuilder registerTypeAdapter(Type type, Object typeAdapter)` method to register a serializer or deserializer with a Gson object.

12. `JsonSerializer` provides the `JsonElement serialize(T src, Type typeOfSrc, JsonSerializationContext context)` method to serialize a Java object to a JSON object.

13. Gson provides the `Expose`, `JsonAdapter`, `SerializedName`, `Since`, and `Until` annotation types to simplify serialization and deserialization.

14. The answer is false: to use `Expose`, it's not enough to annotate a field, as in `@Expose(serialize = true, deserialize = false)`. You also have to call GsonBuilder's `GsonBuilder excludeFieldsWithoutExposeAnnotation()` method.

15. `JsonSerializationContext` and `JsonDeserializationContext` provide access to methods for performing default serialization and default deserialization, which is handy when dealing with nested arrays and objects that don't require special treatment.

16. The answer is false: you can call `<T> T fromJson(String json, Class<T> classOfT)` to deserialize nongeneric objects (that is, objects created from nongeneric classes) only.

17. You should prefer TypeAdapter to JsonSerializer
     and JsonDeserializer because TypeAdapter
     is more efficient. Unlike JsonSerializer and
     JsonDeserializer, which are associated with an
     intermediate layer of code that converts Java and
     JSON objects to JsonElements, TypeAdapter doesn't
     perform this conversion.

18. Listing A-17 presents the GsonDemo application that
     was called for in Chapter 9.

Listing A-17. Serializing and Deserializing Properly Exposed static Fields

```java
import java.lang.reflect.Modifier;

import com.google.gson.Gson;
import com.google.gson.GsonBuilder;

import com.google.gson.annotations.Expose;

public class GsonDemo
{
   static class SomeClass
   {
      transient int id;
      @Expose(serialize = true, deserialize = true)
      transient String password;
      @Expose(serialize = false, deserialize = false)
      int field1;
      @Expose(serialize = false, deserialize = true)
      int field2;
      @Expose(serialize = true, deserialize = false)
      int field3;
      @Expose(serialize = true, deserialize = true)
      int field4;
      @Expose(serialize = true, deserialize = true)
      static int field5;
      static int field6;
   }
   public static void main(String[] args)
   {
      SomeClass sc = new SomeClass();
      sc.id = 1;
      sc.password = "abc";
      sc.field1 = 2;
      sc.field2 = 3;
      sc.field3 = 4;
```

```
        sc.field4 = 5;
        sc.field5 = 6;
        sc.field6 = 7;
        GsonBuilder gsonb = new GsonBuilder();
        gsonb.excludeFieldsWithoutExposeAnnotation();
        gsonb.excludeFieldsWithModifiers(Modifier.TRANSIENT);
        Gson gson = gsonb.create();
        String json = gson.toJson(sc);
        System.out.println(json);
        SomeClass sc2 = gson.fromJson(json, SomeClass.class);
        System.out.printf("id = %d%n", sc2.id);
        System.out.printf("password = %s%n", sc2.password);
        System.out.printf("field1 = %d%n", sc2.field1);
        System.out.printf("field2 = %d%n", sc2.field2);
        System.out.printf("field3 = %d%n", sc2.field3);
        System.out.printf("field4 = %d%n", sc2.field4);
        System.out.printf("field5 = %d%n", sc2.field5);
        System.out.printf("field6 = %d%n", sc2.field6);
    }
}
```

The gsonb.excludeFieldsWithModifiers(Modifier.TRANSIENT); expression prevents only transient fields from being serialized and deserialized: static fields will be serialized and deserialized by default. Of course, static fields that are not annotated with @Expose have no chance to be serialized and deserialized because of gsonb.excludeFieldsWithoutExposeAnnotation();.

When you run this application, you should discover the following output:

```
{"field3":4,"field4":5,"field5":6}
id = 0
password = null
field1 = 0
field2 = 0
field3 = 0
field4 = 5
field5 = 6
field6 = 7
```

The first line shows that the static field named field5 was serialized.

Chapter 10: Extracting JSON Property Values with JsonPath

1. JsonPath is a declarative query language (also known as a path expression syntax) for selecting and extracting a JSON document's property values.

2. The answer is false: JsonPath is based on XPath 1.0.

3. The operator that represents the root JSON object is $.

4. You can specify JsonPath expressions in dot notation and square bracket notation.

5. The @ operator represents the current node being processed by a filter predicate.

6. The answer is false: JsonPath's deep scan operator (..) is equivalent to XPath's // symbol.

7. JsonPath's JsonPath compile(String jsonPath, Predicate... filters) static method compiles the JsonPath expression stored in the jsonPath-referenced string to a JsonPath object (to improve performance when JsonPath expressions are reused). The array of predicates is applied to ? placeholders appearing in the string.

8. The return type of the <T> T read(String json) generic method that returns JSON object property names and their values is LinkedHashMap.

9. The three predicate categories are inline predicates, filter predicates, and custom predicates.

10. Listing A-18 presents the JsonPathDemo application that was called for in Chapter 10.

Listing A-18. Extracting and Outputting Maximum, Minimum, and Average Numeric Values

```java
import com.jayway.jsonpath.JsonPath;

public class JsonPathDemo
{
    public static void main(String[] args)
    {
        String json =
        "{" +
        "   \"numbers\": [10, 20, 25, 30]" +
        "}";

        String expr = "$.numbers.max()";
        double d = JsonPath.read(json, expr);
        System.out.printf("Max value = %f%n", d);
        expr = "$.numbers.min()";
        d = JsonPath.read(json, expr);
        System.out.printf("Min value = %f%n", d);
        expr = "$.numbers.avg()";
        d = JsonPath.read(json, expr);
        System.out.printf("Average value = %f%n", d);
    }
}
```

Index

© Jeff Friesen 2016
J. FRIESEN, *Java XML and JSON*, DOI 10.1007/978-1-4842-1916-4

Get the eBook for only $5!

Why limit yourself?

Now you can take the weightless companion with you wherever you go and access your content on your PC, phone, tablet, or reader.

Since you've purchased this print book, we're happy to offer you the eBook in all 3 formats for just $5.

Convenient and fully searchable, the PDF version enables you to easily find and copy code—or perform examples by quickly toggling between instructions and applications. The MOBI format is ideal for your Kindle, while the ePUB can be utilized on a variety of mobile devices.

To learn more, go to www.apress.com/companion or contact support@apress.com.

CPSIA information can be obtained
at www.ICGtesting.com
Printed in the USA
FFOW01n1251060617
36449FF